Biology

Adapted Reading and Study Workbook B

PEARSON

Prentice Hall

Upper Saddle River, New Jersey
Boston, Massachusetts

Copyright © by Pearson Education, Inc., publishing as Pearson Prentice Hall, Boston, Massachusetts 02116. All rights reserved. Printed in the United States of America. This publication is protected by copyright, and permission should be obtained from the publisher prior to any prohibited reproduction, storage in a retrieval system, or transmission in any form or by any means, electronic, mechanical, photocopying, recording, or likewise. The publisher hereby grants permission to reproduce these pages, in part or in whole, for classroom use only, the number not to exceed the number of students in each class. Notice of copyright must appear on all copies. For information regarding permission(s), write to: Rights and Permissions Department, One Lake Street, Upper Saddle River, New Jersey 07458.

Pearson Prentice Hall™ is a trademark of Pearson Education, Inc.
Pearson® is a registered trademark of Pearson plc.
Prentice Hall® is a registered trademark of Pearson Education, Inc.

ISBN 0-13-201355-X

2 3 4 5 6 7 8 9 10   10 09 08 07

How to Use the *Adapted Reading and Study Workbook B*

Did you know that learning to study more effectively can make a real difference in your performance at school? Students who master study skills are more confident and have more fun learning. This book, the *Adapted Reading and Study Workbook* for Prentice Hall *Biology,* is designed to help you acquire the skills that will allow you to study biology more effectively. Your active participation in class and use of this book can go a long way toward helping you achieve success in biology.

The *Adapted Reading and Study Workbook* can be used to
• preview a chapter,
• learn key vocabulary terms,
• master difficult concepts, and
• review for chapter and unit tests.

The *Adapted Reading and Study Workbook* concentrates on the Key Concepts presented in each chapter of the textbook. Each chapter in the *Adapted Reading and Study Workbook* begins with a chapter summary. This review material stresses the Key Concepts and facts you should focus on in that particular chapter. As you read the chapter summary, try to relate the material you have read in the chapter to the material stressed in the summary. If parts of the summary are not clear to you, go back to that part of the section in the textbook and read it again.

An alternate way of using the chapter summary is to read it before you read the chapter in the textbook. In that way, you will be alerted to the important facts contained in the chapter. Used in this manner, the summary can be a prereading guide to the chapter material.

Following the chapter summary, you will find specific workbook activities designed to help you read and understand the textbook. Completing these worksheets will help you master the Key Concepts and Vocabulary in each section.

The final part of each chapter consists of Vocabulary Reviews. The Vocabulary Reviews take a variety of formats including crossword puzzles, multiple-choice questions, and matching exercises.

© Pearson Education, Inc., publishing as Pearson Prentice Hall.

Contents

© Pearson Education, Inc., publishing as Pearson Prentice Hall.

© Pearson Education, Inc., publishing as Pearson Prentice Hall.

© Pearson Education, Inc., publishing as Pearson Prentice Hall.

© Pearson Education, Inc., publishing as Pearson Prentice Hall.

© Pearson Education, Inc., publishing as Pearson Prentice Hall.

© Pearson Education, Inc., publishing as Pearson Prentice Hall.

© Pearson Education, Inc., publishing as Pearson Prentice Hall.

© Pearson Education, Inc., publishing as Pearson Prentice Hall.

Chapter 34 Animal Behavior

Chapter 35 Nervous System

Chapter 36 Skeletal, Muscular, and Integumentary Systems

Chapter 37 Circulatory and Respiratory Systems

© Pearson Education, Inc., publishing as Pearson Prentice Hall.

© Pearson Education, Inc., publishing as Pearson Prentice Hall.

Chapter 1   The Science of Biology

Summary

1–1 What Is Science?

The goal of science is to investigate and understand the natural world, to explain events in the natural world, and to use those explanations to make useful predictions.

Science is different from other human works:
- Science deals only with the natural world.
- Scientists collect and organize information in a careful, orderly way. They look for patterns and connections among events.
- Scientists propose explanations that can be tested by looking carefully at evidence.

So **science** is defined as an organized way of using evidence to learn about the natural world. Work in science usually follows a path that includes these steps:

1. *Make **observations** using the senses.* The information gathered is called **data.** Scientists use data to make inferences. An **inference** is a logical explanation based on knowledge or experience.

2. *Suggest one or more hypotheses.* A **hypothesis** is a likely explanation for a set of observations. Scientists form hypotheses using knowledge, inference, and informed imagination.

3. *Test the hypothesis.* Some hypotheses are tested by doing controlled experiments. Others are tested by gathering more data.

4. *Draw valid conclusions from the data.* To be valid, a conclusion must be based on logical analysis of reliable data.

1–2 How Scientists Work

A scientific investigation has several steps. These include:
- asking a question
- forming a hypothesis
- setting up a controlled experiment
- recording and analyzing results
- drawing a conclusion

© Pearson Education, Inc., publishing as Pearson Prentice Hall.

Whenever possible, a hypothesis should be tested by an experiment in which only one variable is changed at a time. All other variables should be kept unchanged, or controlled. This type of experiment is called a **controlled experiment**.
- The variable that is changed is called the **manipulated variable.**
- A variable that changes in response to the manipulated variable is called the **responding variable.**

A key idea in science is that experimental results can be repeated. As evidence from many studies builds up, a hypothesis may be so well supported that scientists regard it as a theory. **In science, the word** *theory* **applies to a well-tested explanation that unifies a broad range of observations.** Scientists use theories to predict what will happen in new situations.

1–3 Studying Life

Although all living things may look different, they all have certain things in common. **All living things share the following characteristics:**

1. **Living things are made up of cells.** A **cell** is living matter enclosed in a barrier. The barrier separates the cell from its surroundings. A cell is the smallest unit of an organism that can be thought of as alive.

2. **Living things reproduce and produce new offspring.** In **sexual reproduction,** two cells from different parents join to form the first cell of the new organism. In **asexual reproduction,** a unicellular organism divides and forms two new organisms.

3. **Living things are based on a universal genetic code.** The directions for inheritance are carried by a molecule called DNA.

4. **Living things grow and develop.** All living things grow. Many multicellular organisms go through a process called development in which cells divide and change in shape and structure.

5. **Living things obtain and use materials and energy.** Living things use energy and materials to stay alive, grow, develop, and reproduce. **Metabolism** is all the chemical reactions by which an organism builds up or breaks down materials as it carries out its life processes.

6. **Living things respond to their environment.** A **stimulus** is a signal to which an organism responds. Organisms detect and respond to stimuli from their environment.

7. **Living things maintain a stable internal environment.** The process by which they do this is called **homeostasis.**

8. **Taken as a group, living things change over time.** Evolution is change over time in living things.

© Pearson Education, Inc., publishing as Pearson Prentice Hall.

The study of biology is tied together by themes, or big ideas. These big ideas include: science as a way of knowing; matter and energy; interdependence in nature; cellular basis of life; information and heredity; unity and diversity of life; evolution; structure and function; homeostasis; and science, technology, and society. As you read your textbook, you will see these "big ideas" again and again.

Scientists study life at different levels. These levels include molecules, cells, organisms, populations of a single kind of organism, communities of different organisms in an area, and the biosphere. At all these levels, smaller living systems are found within larger systems.

1–4 Tools and Procedures

Most scientists use the metric system when collecting data and performing experiments. The **metric system** is a decimal system of measurement. Its units are based on standards and are scaled on multiples of 10.

A **microscope** is a device that forms a magnified image of structures too small to see with the unaided eye. Light microscopes and **electron microscopes** are two kinds of microscopes.

- **Light microscopes produce magnified images by focusing visible light rays.** A **compound light microscope** uses two lenses to form an image as they allow light to pass through the specimen. Most school microscopes are compound light microscopes.
- **Electron microscopes produce magnified images by focusing beams of electrons.** These microscopes produce more detailed images than light microscopes. There are two types of electron microscopes—scanning electron microscopes (SEMs) and transmission electron microscopes (TEMs). Scanning electron microscopes scan a narrow beam of electrons back and forth across the surface of an object. SEMs produce images of the surfaces of objects. Transmission electron microscopes shine a beam of electrons through a thin specimen. TEMs can be used to see structures inside cells.

Safety rules are important in the biology laboratory. The most important safety rule is simple: Always follow your teacher's instructions and the textbook directions exactly. It's also important to thoroughly wash your hands after every scientific activity.

Name_____ Class_____ Date_____

Metric Measuring Tools

Circle the laboratory equipment that can be used to take metric measurements.

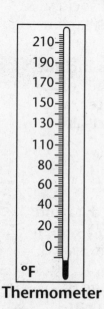

Thermometer

Thermometer

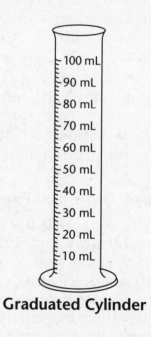

Graduated Cylinder

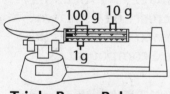

Triple-Beam Balance

Bunsen Burner

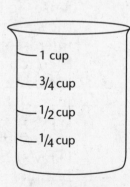

Measuring Cup

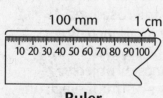

Ruler

Ruler

Use the diagrams to answer the questions.

1. Why is it important to use the metric system when conducting

scientific investigations? _____

_____

_____

© Pearson Education, Inc., publishing as Pearson Prentice Hall.

Variables

In a controlled experiment, only one variable is changed. This is called the manipulated variable. The variable that changes in response to the manipulated variable is called the responding variable. The variables that are kept constant are called controlled variables.

Identify the manipulated variable, the responding variable, and two of the controlled variables in the experiment shown.

Types of Variables	
Manipulated Variable	
Responding Variable	
Controlled Variables	

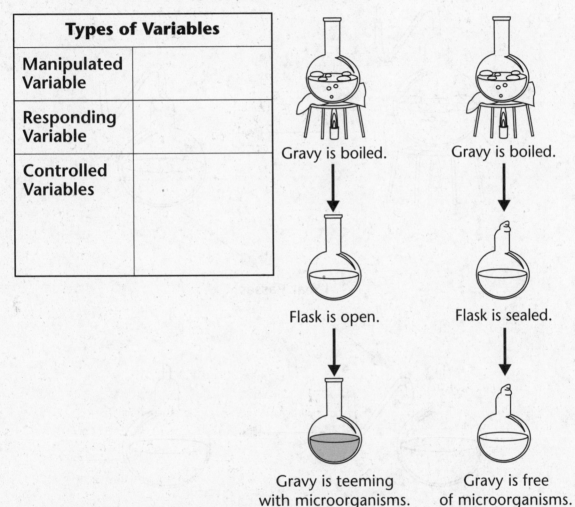

Gravy is boiled.   Gravy is boiled.

Flask is open.   Flask is sealed.

Gravy is teeming with microorganisms.   Gravy is free of microorganisms.

Use the diagram and table to answer the question.

1. Suppose the scientist had put one type of gravy in the flask he left open and another in the flask he sealed. Would this be a well-designed controlled experiment? Explain.

_____

_____

© Pearson Education, Inc., publishing as Pearson Prentice Hall.

Pasteur's Test of Spontaneous Generation

The theory of spontaneous generation stated that life could arise from nonliving matter. Louis Pasteur did an experiment that disproved this theory. He put boiled broth in a flask that allowed air but not microorganisms to reach the broth. A year later, he broke the neck of the flask.

Color the broth in the flask in which microorganisms grew.

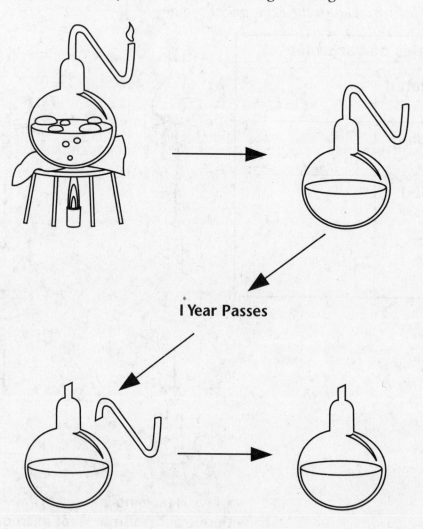

I Year Passes

Use the diagram to answer the questions.

1. Would the results of this experiment have changed if Pasteur had let the unbroken flask sit for three years instead of one? Why or why not?

_____

_____

© Pearson Education, Inc., publishing as Pearson Prentice Hall.

Living and Nonliving Things

Look at the drawings. Label each thing as living or nonliving in the spaces provided.

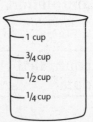

_____

_____

_____

_____

_____

_____

_____

_____

Answer the question below.

1. What characteristics do the living things share?

_____

_____

_____

© Pearson Education, Inc., publishing as Pearson Prentice Hall.

Chapter 1   The Science of Biology

Vocabulary Review

Completion   *Use the words below to fill in the blanks with terms from the chapter.*

controlled experiment	homeostasis	manipulated
data	hypothesis	

1. The process by which an organism keeps internal conditions fairly constant is _____.

2. A(An) _____ is a procedure that changes only one variable at a time and keeps the others constant.

3. The information you gather from observations makes up your

   _____.

4. A(An) _____ is a proposed and testable scientific explanation for a set of observations.

5. In a controlled experiment, the variable that is changed is

   called the _____ variable.

Completion   *Use the words below to fill in the blanks with terms from the chapter.*

cell	metabolism
electron	theory

6. The smallest functional unit of life is the _____.

7. The chemical reactions by which an organism builds up or breaks down the materials needed for life is

   _____.

8. A well-supported hypothesis is called a(an)

   _____.

9. A(An) _____ microscope produces images by focusing beams of electrons.

© Pearson Education, Inc., publishing as Pearson Prentice Hall.

Chapter 2 The Chemistry of Life

Summary

2–1 The Nature of Matter

The **atom** is the basic unit of matter. **The particles that make up atoms are protons, neutrons, and electrons.**

- Protons and neutrons form the **nucleus,** or center of the atom. Protons are positively (+) charged. Neutrons have no charge. Protons and neutrons have about the same mass.
- **Electrons** are negatively (−) charged particles.

Atoms have equal numbers of electrons and protons. For this reason, atoms do not have a charge.

A chemical **element** is a pure substance made up of only one type of atom. An element's atomic number is the number of protons in one atom of an element. Atoms of the same element can have different numbers of neutrons. These are called **isotopes.** All the isotopes of an element have the same number of protons and electrons. **Because they have the same number of electrons, all isotopes of an element have the same chemical properties.**

A chemical **compound** is a substance formed by the joining of two or more elements in definite proportions. Chemical bonds hold the atoms in compounds together. **The main types of chemical bonds are ionic bonds and covalent bonds.**

- An **ionic bond** forms when one or more electrons are transferred from one atom to another.
- A **covalent bond** forms when electrons are shared between atoms.

Atoms joined together by covalent bonds form molecules. A **molecule** is the smallest unit of most compounds.

2–2 Properties of Water

Water molecules (H_2O) are neutral. Yet, the oxygen end of a water molecule has a slight positive charge. The hydrogen end has a slight negative charge. **A molecule in which there is an uneven distribution of charges between atoms is called a polar molecule.** A water molecule is polar.

Polar molecules can attract one another. A hydrogen bond forms from the attraction between the hydrogen atom on one water molecule and the oxygen atom on another. **Cohesion** is an attraction between molecules of the same substance. **Adhesion** is an attraction between molecules of different substances.

© Pearson Education, Inc., publishing as Pearson Prentice Hall.

A **mixture** is formed by two or more elements or compounds that are physically mixed together but not chemically joined. Salt and pepper stirred together are a mixture. Two types of mixtures that can be made with water are solutions and suspensions.

- In a **solution,** all the components are evenly spread out. The substance dissolved in a solution is the **solute.** The substance in which the solute dissolves is the **solvent.** For example, in a salt-water solution, the salt is the solute and the water is the solvent.

- Mixtures of water and undissolved materials are **suspensions.** For example, if you mix sand and water, the water will become cloudy. However, once you stop mixing, the sand particles will filter out and settle to the bottom. This is an example of a suspension.

A water molecule (H_2O) can form a hydrogen ion (H^+) and a hydroxide ion (OH^-). Chemists often measure the concentration of hydrogen ions. The **pH scale** indicates the concentration of H^+ ions in a solution. The pH scale ranges from 0 to 14.

- Pure water has a pH of 7.
- An **acid** forms H^+ ions in solution. **Acidic solutions have higher concentrations of H^+ ions than pure water. They have pH values below 7.**
- A **base** forms OH^- ions in solution. **Basic, or alkaline, solutions have lower concentrations of H^+ ions than pure water. They have pH values above 7.**

2–3 Carbon Compounds

Organic chemistry is the study of compounds with bonds between carbon atoms. Carbon compounds also are known as organic compounds. Many molecules in living things are very large. Very large molecules are called macromolecules. Macromolecules form through polymerization. In this process, smaller units, called **monomers,** join to form macromolecules, called **polymers.**

Four groups of organic compounds found in living things are carbohydrates, lipids, nucleic acids, and proteins.

Carbohydrates (starches and sugars) are compounds of carbon, hydrogen, and oxygen. **Living things use carbohydrates as their main energy source. Plants and some animals also use carbohydrates for structural purposes.** Simple sugars are called **monosaccharides.** When two or more monosaccharides join, they are called **polysaccharides.**

© Pearson Education, Inc., publishing as Pearson Prentice Hall.

Lipids (fats, oils, and waxes) are made mostly of carbon and hydrogen. Lipid molecules are made up of compounds of fatty acids and glycerol.

In the body, lipids are used to:
- **store energy**
- **form parts of membranes**
- **form waterproof coverings**

Nucleic acids contain hydrogen, oxygen, nitrogen, carbon, and phosphorus. **Nucleic acids store and transmit hereditary, or genetic, information.** There are two kinds of nucleic acids: DNA and RNA.

Proteins are made of nitrogen, carbon, hydrogen, and oxygen. Proteins are polymers of **amino acids.**

Proteins are used to:
- **control the rate of reactions**
- **regulate cell processes**
- **help form bones and muscles**
- **carry substances into or out of cells**
- **help fight disease**

2–4 Chemical Reactions and Enzymes

Everything that happens in an organism is based on chemical reactions. A **chemical reaction** is a process that changes one set of chemicals into another set of chemicals. The elements or compounds that enter into the reaction are the **reactants.** The elements or compounds produced by the reaction are known as products. **Chemical reactions always involve breaking the bonds in reactants and forming new bonds in products.**

Some chemical reactions release energy; others absorb energy. **Chemical reactions that release energy often occur spontaneously. Chemical reactions that absorb energy require a source of energy.** Every chemical reaction needs energy to get started. The energy that starts a chemical reaction is called **activation energy.**

Some chemical reactions that make life possible are too slow. A **catalyst** is a substance that speeds up the rate of a chemical reaction. Catalysts work by lowering a reaction's activation energy.

Enzymes are proteins that act as biological catalysts. **Enzymes speed up chemical reactions that take place in cells.** In an enzyme-catalyzed reaction, the reactants are known as substrates. Substrates bind to a site on the enzyme called an active site. The fit of substrates binding to an active site is so specific that they are often compared to a lock and key. Substrates remain bound to the enzyme until the reaction is done. Once the reaction is over, the products are released.

© Pearson Education, Inc., publishing as Pearson Prentice Hall.

Protons, Neutrons, and Electrons

The diagram shows a model of an atom. It shows the nucleus, protons, neutrons, and electrons. The diagram is not to scale.

Label a proton, *a* neutron, *an* electron, *and the* nucleus. *Then, color the protons green, the neutrons purple, and the electrons orange.*

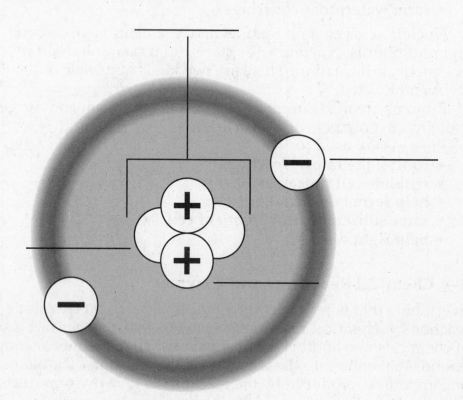

Helium Atom

Use the diagram to answer the questions.

1. What are the negatively charged electrons attracted to?

   _____

   _____

2. Which of the following describes the charge of a neutron? Circle the correct answer.

   positive   negative   no charge

© Pearson Education, Inc., publishing as Pearson Prentice Hall.

Isotopes

Isotopes are atoms of an element that have the same number of protons but a different number of neutrons. The number of protons plus the number of neutrons in an isotope is called its mass number. Carbon-12, for example, has 6 protons and 6 neutrons so its mass number is 12.

Draw the correct number of protons and neutrons for each isotope. Indicate protons with a plus sign (+). Write the number of protons and neutrons in each isotope.

Isotopes of Carbon		
Nonradioactive carbon-12	**Nonradioactive carbon-13**	**Radioactive carbon-14**
6 electrons	6 electrons	6 electrons
6 protons	_____ protons	_____ protons
6 neutrons	_____ neutrons	_____ neutrons

Use the diagram to answer the questions.

1. Name one difference between carbon-12 and carbon-14.

_____

_____

2. Name one way in which carbon-12 and carbon-14 are alike.

_____

_____

© Pearson Education, Inc., publishing as Pearson Prentice Hall.

Ionic Bonds

In an ionic bond, one atom transfers one or more electrons to another atom. The atom that loses the electron(s) becomes a positively charged ion. The atom that gains the electron(s) becomes a negatively charged ion.

Count the electrons in each atom or ion. Write this number in the space provided. Then, determine the charge of the atom or ion.

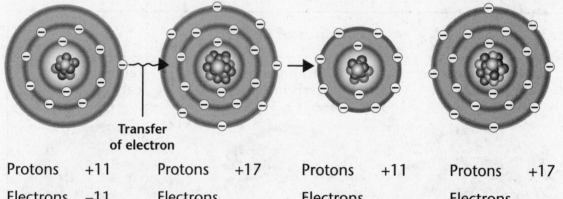

Sodium atom (Na)	Chlorine atom (Cl)	Sodium ion (Na⁺)	Chloride ion (Cl⁻)

Transfer
of electron

Protons	+11	Protons	+17	Protons	+11	Protons	+17
Electrons	−11	Electrons		Electrons		Electrons	
Charge	0	Charge		Charge		Charge	

Use the diagram to answer the questions. Circle the correct answer.

1. Which of these is negatively charged?

   sodium atom   chloride ion

2. Which of these is positively charged?

   sodium ion   chlorine atom

3. The diagram above shows the formation of sodium chloride. What kind of substance is sodium chloride?

   a compound   an element

Covalent Bonds

In a covalent bond, two atoms share electrons. The electrons move in the orbitals of both atoms. In a single covalent bond, they share two electrons. One oxygen atom can form single covalent bonds with two hydrogen atoms to make water.

Color the electrons in the oxygen atom orange. Use purple to fill in the electrons in both hydrogen atoms.

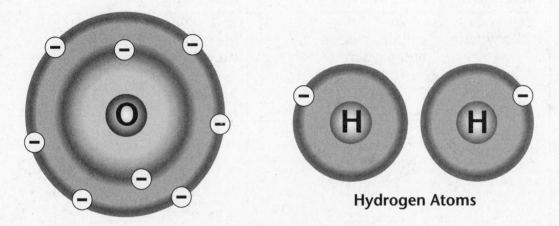

Hydrogen Atoms

In the water molecule circle the shared electrons.

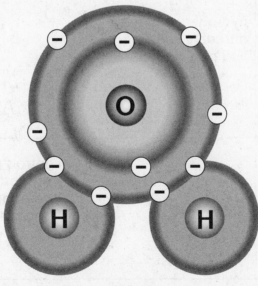

Water

Use the illustrations to answer the question.

1. What is the name of the structure formed when atoms are joined by covalent bonds?

_____

© Pearson Education, Inc., publishing as Pearson Prentice Hall.

Types of Molecules

Living things need organic compounds called carbohydrates, lipids, nucleic acids, and proteins.

Fill in the missing cells in the table. Identify the function of the molecule or the main components (types of atoms) that make up the molecule. The first row has been done for you.

Type of Molecule	Components of Molecule	Function of Molecule
carbohydrate	carbon, hydrogen, and oxygen	main source of energy; structural purposes
lipid	mostly carbon and hydrogen	
nucleic acid	hydrogen, oxygen, nitrogen, carbon, and phosphorus	
protein		controls rate of reactions; transports substances into or out of cell; fights disease

Use the table to answer the question.

1. Which of the types of molecules in the table contain carbon?

_____

_____

© Pearson Education, Inc., publishing as Pearson Prentice Hall.

Energy in Reactions

The graphs below show the amount of energy present during two chemical reactions. The top graph has been labeled to show the reactants, products, and activation energy. Recall that activation energy is the energy needed to start a chemical reaction.

Label the reactants *and* products *on the bottom graph. Then, draw an arrow to show the activation energy.*

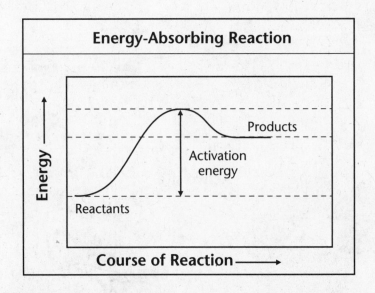

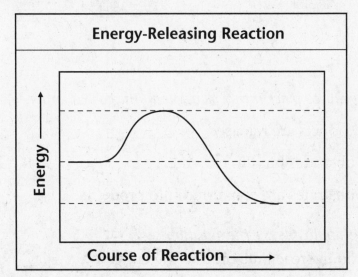

Use the graphs to answer the question. Circle the correct answer.

1. Which type of reaction often occurs spontaneously?

energy-absorbing   energy-releasing

© Pearson Education, Inc., publishing as Pearson Prentice Hall.

Enzymes

Many chemical reactions in cells take place on enzymes. The reactants bind to the enzyme until the reaction is complete. These reactants are called substrates. When the reaction is complete, the products are released.

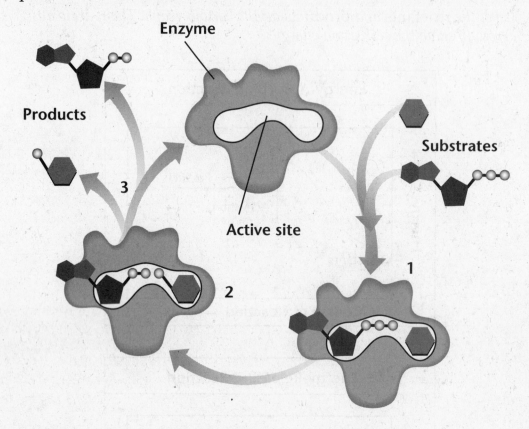

Use the diagram to place the steps below in the correct order.

_____ Products are released.

_____ Substrates bind to enzyme.

_____ Substrates are converted into products.

Use the diagram to answer the questions.

1. Where do the reactants bind to the enzyme?

_____

2. What is the function of enzymes in living things? Circle the correct answer.

catalyze chemical reactions   inhibit chemical reactions

© Pearson Education, Inc., publishing as Pearson Prentice Hall.

Chapter 2   The Chemistry of Life

Vocabulary Review

Matching   *In the space provided, write the letter of the definition that best matches each term.*

_____ **1.** protein

_____ **2.** acid

_____ **3.** catalyst

_____ **4.** carbohydrate

_____ **5.** element

a. type of molecule that serves as a living thing's main source of energy

b. a pure substance made up of only one kind of atom

c. a compound that forms H⁺ ions in solution

d. substance that speeds up a chemical reaction

e. large molecule made up of amino acids

Matching   *In the space provided, write the letter of the definition that best matches each term.*

_____ **6.** solvent

_____ **7.** molecule

_____ **8.** atom

_____ **9.** chemical reaction

_____ **10.** solution

a. basic unit of matter

b. atoms joined by covalent bonds

c. the substance in which a solute dissolves

d. mixture in which all substances are evenly distributed

e. process that changes one set of chemicals into another set of chemicals

© Pearson Education, Inc., publishing as Pearson Prentice Hall.

Chapter 3   The Biosphere

Summary

3–1 What Is Ecology?

Ecology is the scientific study of the interactions of organisms and their environment. All these organisms live and interact in the biosphere. The **biosphere** is the part of Earth where life exists. **To understand relationships within the biosphere, ecologists study events and organisms that range in complexity from a single individual to the entire biosphere.** Ecologists study many levels of organization.

- individual organisms
- **species**—a group of similar organisms that breed and produce fertile offspring
- **population**—a group of individuals of the same species that live in the same area
- **community**—a collection of different populations that live together in an area
- **ecosystem**—all of the organisms living in a specific place, together with their physical environment
- **biome**—a group of ecosystems with the same climate and similar dominant communities
- **biosphere**—the part of the planet (land, water, and air) where all life exists

Scientists conduct ecological research using three basic approaches: observing, experimenting, and modeling. All of these approaches rely on the application of scientific methods to guide ecological inquiry. Observing is often the first step in asking ecological questions. Observations can also be used when designing experiments and making models. Experiments can be used to test hypotheses. They may be done in a laboratory or in the field. Modeling helps scientists understand complex processes.

3–2 Energy Flow

Organisms use energy from the environment for life processes. Living things get energy in different ways. **Sunlight is the main energy source for life on Earth.**

Organisms that use the energy in sunlight or chemicals to make food are called **autotrophs.** Autotrophs, also called **producers,** make food in two ways.

- Some autotrophs use light energy to make food. This process is called **photosynthesis.** In photosynthesis, carbon dioxide and water are changed to carbohydrates and oxygen. Plants, some algae, and certain bacteria carry out photosynthesis.

© Pearson Education, Inc., publishing as Pearson Prentice Hall.

- **Some types of organisms rely on the energy stored in organic chemical compounds.** The process in which autotrophs use chemical energy to make carbohydrates is called chemosynthesis. Only certain types of bacteria carry out chemosynthesis.

Many organisms rely on other organisms for energy and food. These organisms are called **heterotrophs.** Heterotrophs also are called **consumers.** There are many types of heterotrophs.
- **Herbivores,** such as cows, get energy by eating only plants.
- **Carnivores,** such as snakes, get energy by eating only animals.
- **Omnivores,** such as humans, get energy by eating both plants and animals.
- **Detritivores,** such as earthworms, feed on the remains (dead matter) or wastes of other organisms.
- **Decomposers,** such as fungi, break down organic matter.

Energy flows through an ecosystem in one direction. It flows from the sun (or inorganic compounds) to autotrophs and then to heterotrophs. A **food chain** shows how living things transfer energy by eating and being eaten. For example, a food chain might consist of grass (producer), an antelope (herbivore), and a coyote (carnivore). A **food web** links together all of the food chains in an ecosystem. For example, rabbits may also feed on the grass in the food chain above. These rabbits may be eaten by the coyotes. The feeding relationships of the grass, rabbits, antelopes, and coyotes make up a food web.

Each step in a food chain or food web is called a **trophic level.** Producers are at the first trophic level. Consumers make up higher trophic levels. Each consumer depends on the trophic level below it for energy.

Ecological pyramids are diagrams that show the relative amounts of energy or matter at each trophic level. **Only about 10 percent of the energy available at one trophic level is passed on to organisms at the next trophic level.** Three types of ecological pyramids are
- Energy pyramids. Energy pyramids show how much energy is available at each trophic level.
- Biomass pyramids. Biomass pyramids show the **biomass,** or total amount of living tissue, at each trophic level.
- Pyramid of numbers. A pyramid of numbers shows the relative number of individual organisms at each trophic level.

© Pearson Education, Inc., publishing as Pearson Prentice Hall.

3–3 Cycles of Matter

Energy and matter move through the biosphere very differently. **Unlike the one-way flow of energy, matter is recycled within and between ecosystems.** Matter, including water and nutrients, moves through organisms and parts of the biosphere through **biogeochemical cycles.**

The Water Cycle. All living things need water to survive. Water cycles between the ocean, atmosphere, land, and living things. Many processes are part of the water cycle. For example, during **evaporation** liquid water changes to a gas. **Transpiration** is the evaporation of water from the leaves of plants. Water changes from a gas to a liquid through the process of condensation. Water vapor in the atmosphere condenses into tiny droplets that form clouds. When the droplets get large enough, they fall to Earth's surface as precipitation.

Nutrients are chemical substances that organisms need to survive. **Every living organism needs nutrients to build tissues and carry out essential life functions. Like water, nutrients are passed between organisms and the environment through biogeochemical cycles.**

The Carbon Cycle. Carbon is a key part of living tissue. Photosynthesis and cellular respiration are parts of the carbon cycle. Human activities such as burning fossil fuels are also parts of the carbon cycle.

The Nitrogen Cycle. Organisms need nitrogen to build proteins. Different forms of nitrogen cycle through the biosphere.
* Nitrogen gas is the most abundant form of nitrogen on Earth. However, only certain kinds of bacteria can use this form directly.
* These bacteria change nitrogen gas into ammonia in a process called **nitrogen fixation.** Other bacteria in the soil convert ammonia into nitrates and nitrites.
* When organisms die, decomposers return nitrogen to the soil. Other bacteria change nitrogen compounds called nitrates back into nitrogen gas. This process is called **denitrification.**

The Phosphorus Cycle. Most phosphorus is stored in rocks and ocean sediments. This phosphorus is slowly released into water and soil and then used by organisms. Phosphorus is a key part of DNA and RNA.

Primary productivity is the rate at which producers form organic matter in an ecosystem. Nutrient availability affects primary productivity. A nutrient that is scarce or cycles slowly through an ecosystem is a **limiting nutrient.** A limiting nutrient can affect ecosystem health.

© Pearson Education, Inc., publishing as Pearson Prentice Hall.

Levels of Organization

Use the words to label each level of organization on the diagram.

biome	community	individual
biosphere	ecosystem	population

Use the diagram to answer the questions.

1. Which level of organization contains all of the organisms of one species that live in a certain area?

_____

2. What is the highest level of organization studied by ecologists?

_____

© Pearson Education, Inc., publishing as Pearson Prentice Hall.

Energy Flow in Food Chains

A food chain is a series of steps in which organisms transfer energy by eating and being eaten. Producers make their own food and are the first step in a food chain. Consumers rely on other organisms for energy and food.

Draw arrows between the organisms to show how energy moves through this food chain. One arrow has been drawn as an example.

- The squid eats the small fish.
- The zooplankton eat the algae.
- The shark eats the squid.
- The small fish eat the zooplankton.

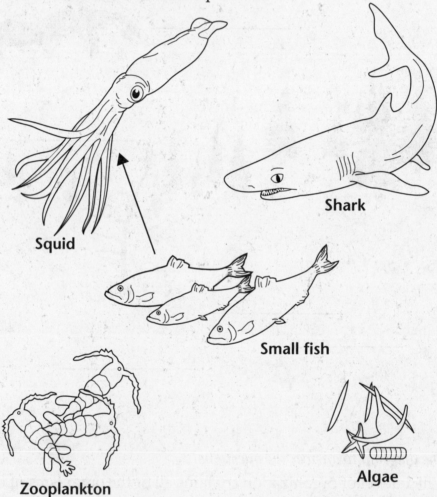

Squid

Shark

Small fish

Zooplankton

Algae

Use the food chain to answer the questions.

1. List the producer(s). _____

2. List the consumer(s). _____

_____

© Pearson Education, Inc., publishing as Pearson Prentice Hall.

Trophic Levels

A food web is a complex network of feeding relationships. Each step in a food web is called a trophic level. Producers are the first trophic level.

Color the organisms in each trophic level. Follow the prompts below.
- Color the producer(s) green.
- Color the first-level consumer(s) brown.
- Color the second-level consumer(s) blue.
- Color the third-level consumer(s) purple.

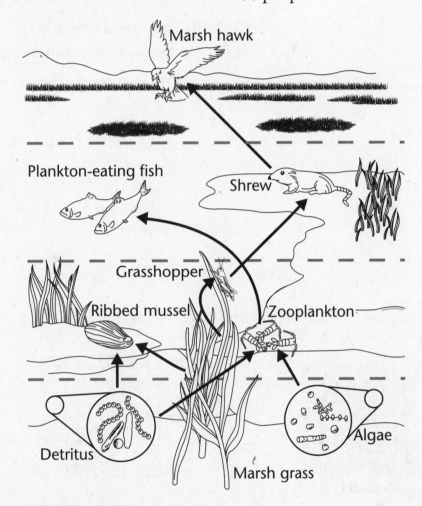

Marsh hawk

Plankton-eating fish

Shrew

Grasshopper

Ribbed mussel

Zooplankton

Detritus

Algae

Marsh grass

Use the diagram above to answer the question.

1. Write one food chain that includes the marsh grass.

_____

_____

_____

© Pearson Education, Inc., publishing as Pearson Prentice Hall.

Energy Pyramids

In an ecosystem, only 10 percent of the energy available at one trophic level is transferred to the next level above it. This relationship can be shown in an energy pyramid. You can also show the change in energy by using grids of 100 boxes.

Color the "Producers" section of the pyramid green. Color the "First-level consumers" section brown. Color the "Second-level consumers" section blue. Color the "Third-level consumers" section purple.

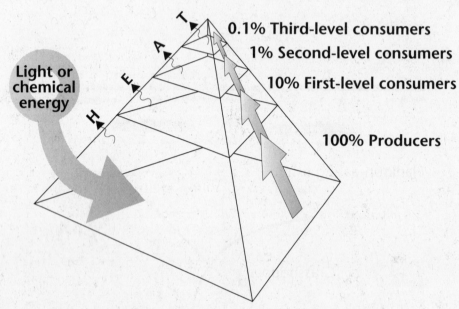

Light or chemical energy

0.1% Third-level consumers
1% Second-level consumers
10% First-level consumers

100% Producers

Label each grid with the trophic level it represents. The first one has been done for you.

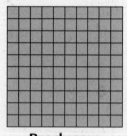

Producers

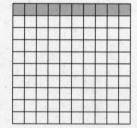

_____

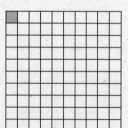

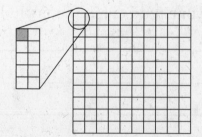

_____   _____

© Pearson Education, Inc., publishing as Pearson Prentice Hall.

The Water Cycle

The water cycle is the movement of water between the ocean, the atmosphere, land, and living things.

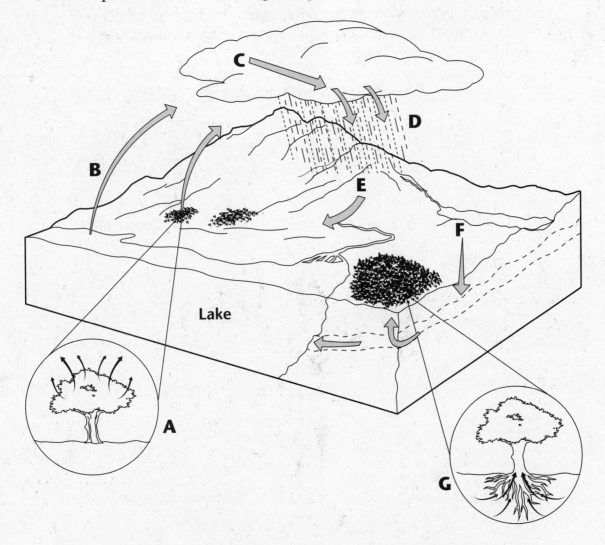

The processes involved in the water cycle are labeled with letters A–G in the diagram. Use the words below to identify each process and write it on the lines provided.

condensation	root uptake	seepage
evaporation	runoff	transpiration
precipitation		

A _____   E _____

B _____   F _____

C _____   G _____

D _____

© Pearson Education, Inc., publishing as Pearson Prentice Hall.

The Carbon Cycle

The carbon cycle describes how carbon moves between the atmosphere, the ocean, land, and living things.

Color the arrows that show carbon moving into the atmosphere blue.
Color the arrows that show carbon moving out of the atmosphere yellow.

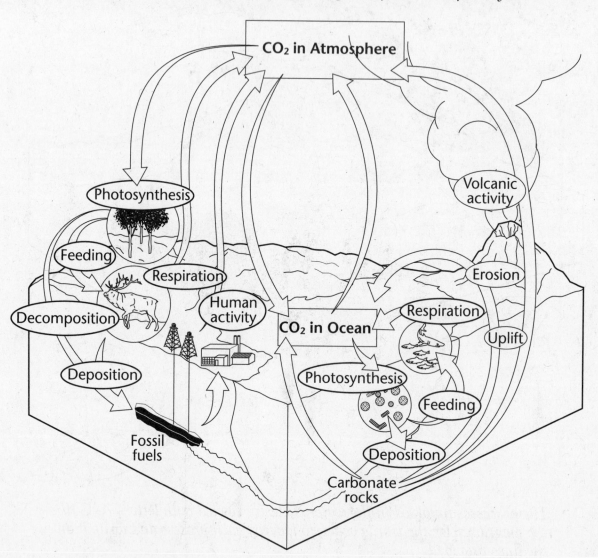

Use the diagram to answer the questions. Circle the correct answer.

1. Which process releases carbon into the atmosphere?

photosynthesis   respiration

2. Which process removes carbon from the land?

human activity   deposition

© Pearson Education, Inc., publishing as Pearson Prentice Hall.

Name_____ Class_____ Date _____

The Nitrogen Cycle

Nitrogen cycles through the biosphere in several forms. Nitrogen gas is a major component of the atmosphere, but only certain types of bacteria can use it directly. These bacteria convert the nitrogen into forms that producers can use.

Color the arrows that show nitrogen moving in a form that plants cannot use blue. Color the arrows that show nitrogen moving in a form that is useful to producers red.

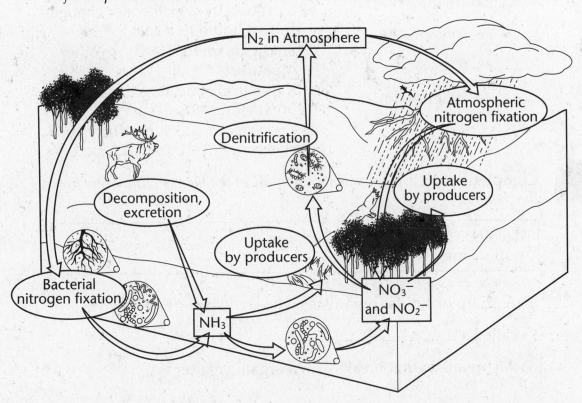

Use the diagram to answer the question.

1. By which process do certain bacteria convert nitrogen gas into ammonia (NH_3)?

_____

_____

2. Look at the diagram. Which forms of nitrogen are useful to producers?

_____

_____

© Pearson Education, Inc., publishing as Pearson Prentice Hall.

Chapter 3 The Biosphere

Vocabulary Review

Matching   *In the space provided, write the letter of the definition that best matches each term.*

_____ **1.** nutrient

_____ **2.** chemosynthesis

_____ **3.** consumer

_____ **4.** ecosystem

_____ **5.** evaporation

a. all the organisms in one area and their physical environment

b. a process by which water changes from a liquid to a gas

c. an organism that feeds on other organisms

d. a chemical substance that an organism needs to survive

e. a process in which producers use chemical energy to make food

Completion   *Use the words below to fill in the blanks with terms from the chapter.*

decomposer	photosynthesis
population	species

6. A group of similar organisms whose offspring can breed is

called a _____.

7. An organism that breaks down organic matter is a

_____.

8. The process in which producers use light energy to make food

is _____.

9. A group of organisms of the same species that live in an area is

a _____.

© Pearson Education, Inc., publishing as Pearson Prentice Hall.

Chapter 4   Ecosystems and Communities

Summary

4–1 The Role of Climate

In the atmosphere, temperature, precipitation, and other environmental factors combine to produce weather and climate. **Weather** is the day-to-day condition of Earth's atmosphere at a certain time and place. **Climate** is the average yearly condition of temperature and precipitation in a region. Climate affects ecosystems. Several factors decide climate.

- **Carbon dioxide and other atmospheric gases trap heat energy and maintain Earth's temperature range.** These gases function like the glass windows of a greenhouse. Therefore, the trapping of heat by gases in the atmosphere is called the **greenhouse effect.** This greenhouse effect helps temperatures on Earth stay within a range that supports life.
- **Latitude also affects climate. Earth has three main climate zones: polar, temperate, and tropical.**
  - **Polar zones** are cold areas where the sun's rays strike Earth at a very long angle.
  - **Temperate zones** sit between the polar zones and the tropics. The climate in these zones ranges from hot to cold, depending on the season.
  - The **tropical zone,** or tropics, is near the equator. The climate here is almost always warm.
- Unequal heating of Earth's surface also causes winds and ocean currents. Winds and currents move heat through the biosphere.

4–2 What Shapes an Ecosystem?

Organisms in ecosystems are affected by both biotic and abiotic factors. **Biotic factors** are all of the living things with which organisms interact. **Abiotic factors** are nonliving, physical things. They include temperature and soil type. **Together, biotic and abiotic factors determine the survival and growth of an organism and the productivity of the ecosystem in which an organism lives.**

A **habitat** is the area where an organism lives. A habitat has both biotic and abiotic factors. A **niche** includes all of the abiotic and biotic things in an organism's habitat and the way the organism uses those things. For example, a niche includes what an organism eats and how it gets its food.

© Pearson Education, Inc., publishing as Pearson Prentice Hall.

Community interactions, such as competition, predation, and symbiosis, can powerfully affect an ecosystem.

- Competition occurs when living things try to use the same **resources.** Competition often results in one organism dying out.
- **Predation** occurs when one organism (the predator) captures and eats another (the prey).
- **Symbiosis** occurs when two species live close together in one of three ways.
  1. **Mutualism:** Both species benefit from the relationship.
  2. **Commensalism:** One species benefits. The other is neither helped nor harmed.
  3. **Parasitism:** One species benefits by living in or on the other. The other species is harmed.

Ecosystems are constantly changing in response to natural and human disturbances. As an ecosystem changes, older inhabitants gradually die out and new organisms move in, causing further changes in the community. **Ecological succession** is the series of predictable changes that occur in a community over time.

- **Primary succession** takes place on bare rock surfaces where no soil exists. **Pioneer species** are the first species to live in these areas.
- **Secondary succession** occurs when a disturbance changes a community without removing the soil.

4–3 Biomes

A **biome** is a group of land communities that covers a large area and has a certain soil type and climate. Within a biome, there may be microclimates. A **microclimate** is a small area where the climate differs from that of the surrounding area. A species may live over a large or small area, depending on its ability to survive and reproduce under tough conditions.

There are ten major biomes: tropical rain forest, tropical dry forest, tropical savanna, desert, temperate grassland, temperate woodland and shrubland, temperate forest, northwestern coniferous forest, boreal forest (or taiga), and tundra.

Each biome has its own set of abiotic factors and a typical collection of organisms. Some areas, such as mountains and polar ice caps, do not fall neatly into the major biomes.

© Pearson Education, Inc., publishing as Pearson Prentice Hall.

4–4 Aquatic Ecosystems

Unlike land biomes, which are grouped geographically, aquatic ecosystems are grouped by the abiotic factors that affect them. **Aquatic ecosystems are described mainly by the depth, flow, temperature, and chemistry of their water.**

In many aquatic ecosystems, tiny free-floating swimming organisms can be found. These organisms are called **plankton.** Two types of plankton are phytoplankton and zooplankton. **Phytoplankton** are unicellular algae that use nutrients in water to make food. They form the base of many aquatic food webs. **Zooplankton** are animals that feed on phytoplankton.

There are three main groups of aquatic ecosystems.

1. **Freshwater ecosystems can be divided into several types.**
   - **Flowing-water ecosystems** (rivers and streams) flow over land.
   - **Standing-water ecosystems** include lakes and ponds.
   - **Freshwater wetlands** include bogs, marshes, and swamps. In wetlands, water covers the soil or is present at or near the surface for at least part of the year.
2. **Estuaries** are wetlands formed where rivers meet the sea. They contain a mixture of fresh and salt water. Most food made in estuaries enters food webs as tiny pieces of organic matter, called **detritus.**
   - **Salt marshes** are temperate estuaries. Salt-tolerant grasses and seagrasses are the dominant plant life in salt marshes.
   - **Mangrove swamps** are tropical estuaries. The dominant plant life in mangrove swamps includes several species of salt-tolerant trees, called mangroves, and seagrasses.
3. **Marine ecosystems** exist in the ocean. The ocean is divided into zones based on how much light penetrates the water.
   - The **photic zone** is the well-lit upper layer of water. Photosynthesis can take place here.
   - The **aphotic zone** is the permanently dark lower layer of water. Producers here use chemosynthesis to make food.

The ocean is also divided into three zones based on depth and distance from shore: the intertidal zone, the coastal ocean, and the open ocean.
   - Organisms in the intertidal zone are exposed to regular and extreme changes in their surroundings.
   - The coastal zone is relatively shallow, lies entirely within the photic zone, and is often rich in plankton and other organisms. Coral reefs grow in tropical coastal oceans.
   - The open ocean is the largest zone, covering more than 90 percent of the surface area of the world's oceans. These areas typically have low levels of nutrients and support only small producers.

© Pearson Education, Inc., publishing as Pearson Prentice Hall.

Earth's Climate Zones

Label Earth's main climate zones as temperate, tropical, or polar. You will use some terms more than once.

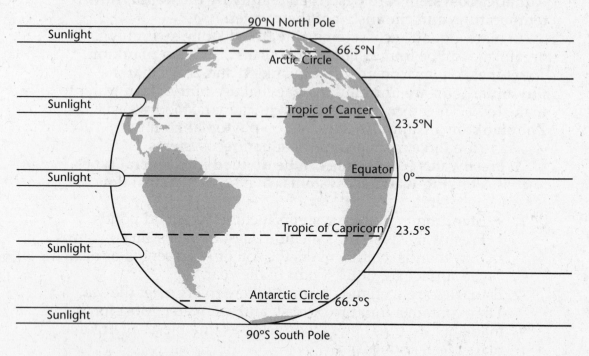

Use the map to answer the questions.

1. Which climate zone receives the most direct sunlight year-round?

   _____

   _____

2. Why are the polar zones colder than the other zones?

   _____

   _____

   _____

© Pearson Education, Inc., publishing as Pearson Prentice Hall.

Biotic and Abiotic Factors in an Ecosystem

In an ecosystem, biotic factors are biological influences on organisms. Abiotic factors are nonliving (or physical) influences on organisms.

Circle each abiotic factor. Draw an X over each biotic factor.

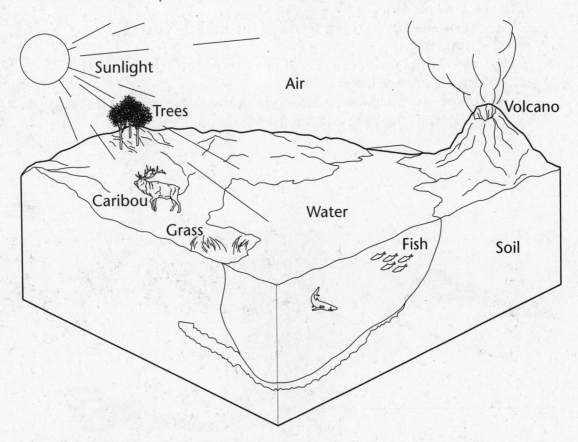

Use the illustration to answer the questions.

1. Are factors related to climate, such as rainfall and temperature, biotic, or abiotic factors?

_____

_____

2. Which factors make up an organism's niche? Circle the best answer.

abiotic factors only   both biotic and abiotic factors

© Pearson Education, Inc., publishing as Pearson Prentice Hall.

The Niche

A niche is the range of physical and biological conditions in which an organism lives and the way that the organism uses those conditions.

The prompts describe the niches of three bird species. Use the prompts to help you label the birds in the diagram.

- Bay-Breasted Warbler: feeds in the middle part of a spruce tree
- Cape May Warbler: feeds at the tips of branches near the top of a spruce tree
- Yellow-Rumped Warbler: feeds in the lower part of a spruce tree and at the bases of the middle branches

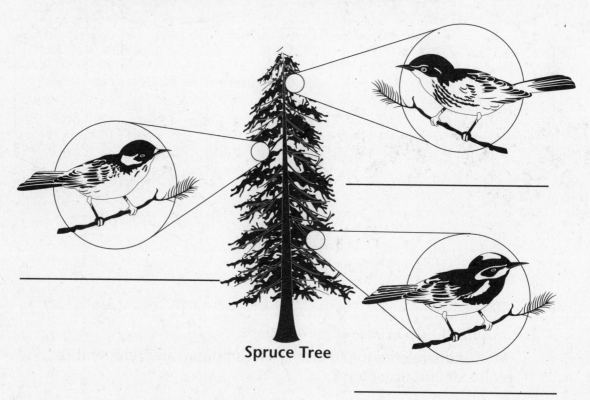

Spruce Tree

Use the illustration to answer the question.

1. Why can all three species of warbler live in the same spruce tree?

_____

_____

_____

2. Do all three species of warbler share the same niche?

_____

© Pearson Education, Inc., publishing as Pearson Prentice Hall.

Symbiosis

Symbiosis is a close relationship between two species. A symbiotic relationship can help both species, help one species while harming the other, or help one species while the other is unaffected.

Write how the deer, flower, and whale are affected by the symbiotic relationship shown. Write benefits, harmed, *or* unaffected.

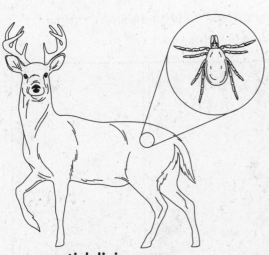

**a tick living on
the body of a deer**

a bee and a flower

Flower: _____

Deer: _____

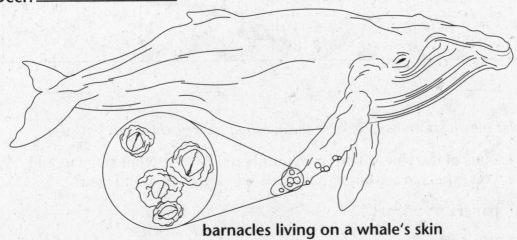

barnacles living on a whale's skin

Whale: _____

Use the illustrations to answer the question.

1. What, if anything, does the bee get from its relationship with the flower?

_____

_____

© Pearson Education, Inc., publishing as Pearson Prentice Hall.

Ecological Succession

The first panel below shows an area covered with rock and ash from a volcanic eruption. When organisms begin to colonize an area such as this, they appear in a predictable order. This is called ecological succession. The first species to colonize this area are called pioneer species.

The panels following the first panel show different stages of succession. Number these panels in the order that they occur.

1

Use the illustrations to answer the questions. Circle the correct answer.

1. Look at the panels you have numbered 2–4. At what stage would you expect to see large mammals moving back to the area?

   panel 2   panel 4

2. What type of succession is shown in the illustrations above?

   primary succession   secondary succession

3. Suppose a fire disturbed the community shown in the panel you numbered 4. What type of succession will likely follow this fire?

   primary succession   secondary succession

© Pearson Education, Inc., publishing as Pearson Prentice Hall.

Earth's Biomes

A biome is a group of ecosystems that have certain climate, soil conditions, and particular plants and animals.

Use the words below to identify each biome in the table. The first one has been done for you.

| desert | tropical rain forest |
| temperate grassland | tundra |

Biome	Climate and Soil	Sample Plants and Animals
tropical dry forest	warm year-round with wet and dry seasons; rich soil	tall deciduous trees, succulents; large mammals such as tigers and elephants, birds, insects, and reptiles
	hot and wet year-round; nutrient-poor soil	broad-leaved evergreen trees, vines; wide range of mammals, birds, insects, reptiles, and fish
	cold, dark winters and short, soggy summers; permafrost	ground-hugging plants; birds and mammals that can tolerate the harsh conditions
	warm to hot summers, cold winters; fertile soil	grasses and herbs; predator and herbivore mammals, birds, reptiles, and insects
	low precipitation with variable temperatures	plants with short growth cycles, cacti; mammals, birds, insects, and reptiles adapted to extreme conditions

Use the table to answer the question.

1. Which biome is characterized by a layer of permanently frozen subsoil?

_____

© Pearson Education, Inc., publishing as Pearson Prentice Hall.

Biome Climate Comparison

The graphs below show temperature and precipitation for Belem, Brazil, and Barrow, Alaska. The line graphs show the average temperature for each month. The bar graphs show the average precipitation in each month.

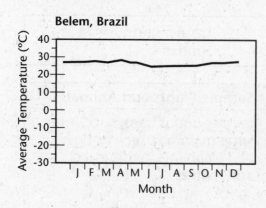

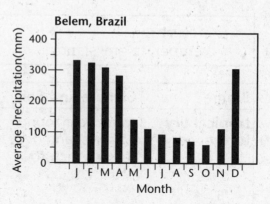

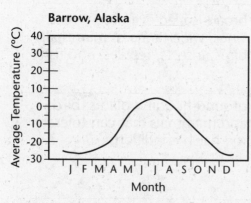

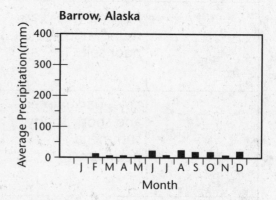

Use the graphs to answer the questions.

1. What is the driest month in Belem, Brazil?

_____

2. Is Belem in a warm climate or a cool one?

_____

3. Which city is cooler in September?

_____

4. In which biome is Barrow most likely located? Circle the best answer.

temperate forest   tundra   tropical rain forest

© Pearson Education, Inc., publishing as Pearson Prentice Hall.

Marine Ecosystems

*Color the photic zone in the diagram yellow. Then, use the words below
to label the marine zones that are based on depth and distance from shore.*

benthic zone	intertidal zone	open ocean
coastal ocean	ocean trench	

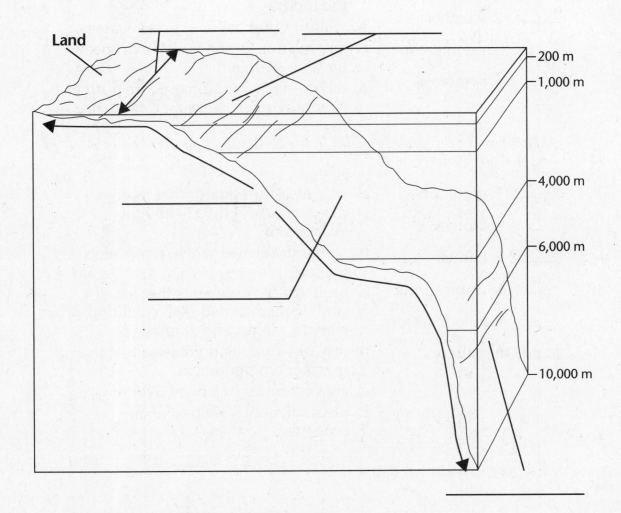

Use the diagram to answer the questions.

1. What is the aphotic zone?

_____

_____

2. Where do algae and other photosynthetic producers grow?
Circle the correct answer.

aphotic zone   photic zone

© Pearson Education, Inc., publishing as Pearson Prentice Hall.

Chapter 4   Ecosystems and Communities

Vocabulary Review

Matching   *In the space provided, write the letter of the definition that best matches each term.*

____ **1.** photic zone

____ **2.** weather

____ **3.** permafrost

____ **4.** symbiosis

a. layer of permanently frozen subsoil in the tundra

b. well-lit upper layer of ocean water

c. any relationship in which two species live closely together

d. day-to-day condition of Earth's atmosphere at a particular time and place

Matching   *In the space provided, write the letter of the definition that best matches each term.*

____ **5.** plankton

____ **6.** biome

____ **7.** habitat

____ **8.** tropical zone

____ **9.** abiotic factor

____ **10.** estuary

a. area near the equator that receives direct or nearly direct sunlight year-round

b. wetlands formed where rivers meet the sea

c. group of environments that have similar characteristic soil conditions, climate, plants, and animals

d. tiny free-floating organisms that live in water environments

e. area where an organism lives

f. physical, nonliving part of an ecosystem

© Pearson Education, Inc., publishing as Pearson Prentice Hall.

Chapter 5   Populations

Summary

5–1 How Populations Grow

Three important characteristics of a population are geographic distribution, density, and growth rate.

- Geographic distribution, or range, is the area in which a population lives.
- **Population density** is the number of individuals per unit area. An example is the number of people per square kilometer.
- Growth rate is how quickly a population increases or decreases in size.

Three factors can affect population size: the number of births, the number of deaths, and the number of individuals that enter or leave the population. Populations increase through births and immigration. **Immigration** is the movement of individuals into an area. Populations get smaller through deaths and emigration. **Emigration** is the movement of individuals out of an area.

Exponential growth occurs when members of a population reproduce at a constant rate. This growth pattern is shown by a J-shaped curve. As the population grows, the number of reproducing members keeps rising. Thus the population grows faster and faster. **Under ideal conditions with unlimited resources, a population will grow exponentially.** In nature, exponential growth does not go on for long. Resources are used up in time. This causes population growth to slow or stop. Predators and disease also slow exponential growth.

As resources become less available, the growth of a population slows or stops. This is called **logistic growth**. Logistic growth is shown by an S-shaped curve. Logistic growth occurs when a population's growth slows or stops following a period of exponential growth. For example, if food resources start to run out or space becomes limited, a population that was growing exponentially may start to exhibit logistic growth. The population size when growth stops is called carrying capacity. **Carrying capacity** is the number of individuals of a specific species a given environment can support.

© Pearson Education, Inc., publishing as Pearson Prentice Hall.

5–2 Limits to Growth

A **limiting factor** is anything that slows population growth. There are two kinds of limiting factors.

- **Density-dependent limiting factors** rely on population size. **They include competition, predation, parasitism, and disease.** Competition occurs when organisms are using the same ecological resource at the same time. Predation occurs when one organism captures and feeds on another organism. The organism that gets eaten is the prey. The organism that eats the prey is the predator. Predator-prey relationships can affect the size of both the predator population and the prey population. For example, a decrease in the prey population will be followed, sooner or later, by a decrease in the predator population.
- **Density-independent limiting factors** do not rely on population size. **They include natural disasters and human activities such as damming rivers.** When such factors occur, many species show a rapid drop in population size.

5–3 Human Population Growth

The size of the human population tends to increase with time. For most of human existence, the population grew slowly. About 500 years ago the population began growing faster. Agriculture and later industry made food more available. Improved sanitation and medicine reduced death rates. However, birthrates stayed high in most places. This led to exponential growth. Today, the human population continues to grow exponentially.

Demography is the scientific study of human populations. Demographers try to predict how human populations will change over time. **Birthrates, death rates, and the age structure of a population help predict why some countries have high growth rates while other countries grow more slowly.**

Over the past century, population growth in the United States, Japan, and much of Europe slowed greatly. Demographers call this shift a **demographic transition.** The transition began as death rates fell, causing a brief rise in population growth. Then birthrates fell, slowing population growth. Most people live in countries that still have high population growth.

Demographers use **age-structure diagrams** to help predict population growth. An age-structure diagram is a bar graph. It shows how many people of each gender are in each age group in the population. To predict how world population will change, demographers need to think about the age structure of each country as well as the number of people with fatal diseases, including AIDS.

© Pearson Education, Inc., publishing as Pearson Prentice Hall.

Population Size

Population size is the number of individuals that make up a population. Immigration and births increase population size. Emmigration and deaths decrease population size.

The table below shows how several different populations have changed over a one-year time span. Look at each population and determine whether the overall population size has increased or decreased. If the population size has increased, draw an arrow that points upward (↑) in the population size column. If it has decreased, draw an arrow that points downward (↓). The first one has been done for you.

Factors that Affect Population Size

Population	Births	Deaths	Number of Individuals that Emigrated	Number of Individuals that Immigrated	Population Size
A	200	100	0	0	↑
B	10	10	100	0	
C	1	1	1	50	
D	10	100	100	10	
E	100	200	0	0	
F	50	1	1	50	
G	10	10	0	100	

Use the table to answer the question.

1. Look at population G. How would the population size have changed if 100 individuals had also emigrated?

_____

_____

2. A food shortage causes many members of a population to leave an area. What type of population movement does this describe? Circle the correct answer.

emigration   immigration

© Pearson Education, Inc., publishing as Pearson Prentice Hall.

Population Density

Population density is the number of individuals in a population in a unit area.

The grid below represents an ecosystem. Use the statements to map three populations that live in the ecosystem. Draw in each individual. Use an X to represent an oak tree. Use an O to represent an owl. Use an M to represent a mouse.

- Boxes 1, 2, 6, and 7 each have five oak trees.
- Boxes 8, 13, 15, 22, and 24 each have one oak tree.
- Boxes 6, 15, and 23 have one owl.
- Every box has two mice.

1	2	3	4	5
6	7	8	9	10
11	12	13	14	15
16	17	18	19	20
21	22	23	24	25

Use the diagram to answer the questions.

1. Which population has the lowest population density in this

   ecosystem? _____

2. In which boxes is the population density of oak trees the highest?

   _____

© Pearson Education, Inc., publishing as Pearson Prentice Hall.

Exponential and Logistic Growth Curves

Exponential growth occurs when individuals in a population are reproducing at a constant rate. Logistic growth occurs when a population's growth slows or stops after a period of exponential growth.

The graphs below represent two different types of population growth. Use the graphs to answer the questions that follow.

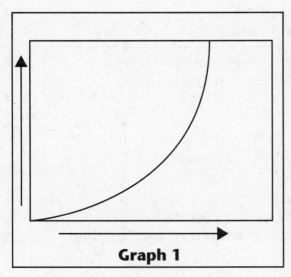

Graph 1

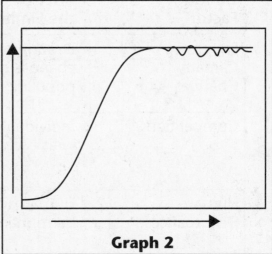

Graph 2

_____ _____

1. On the blank lines below the graphs, give each graph a title based on the type of population growth it depicts.

2. Which graph shows a population that has reached its carrying capacity?

_____

3. Which graph represents a population that is growing under ideal conditions with unlimited resources?

_____

4. What is a population's carrying capacity?

_____

_____

© Pearson Education, Inc., publishing as Pearson Prentice Hall.

Density-Dependent and Density-Independent Limiting Factors

Density-dependent limiting factors limit a population when the population density reaches a certain level. Density-independent limiting factors affect a population in the same way no matter how big or small it is.

Read the information in the table.

Limiting Factor	Brief Description of the Limiting Factor
Extreme Climate Changes	Drought and other extreme climate changes can cause members of a population to die off rapidly.
Competition	Individuals of the same species compete with each other for resources.
Human Disturbances	Human activity, like damming a river, can harm many populations in an ecosystem.
Parasitism	Parasites limit the growth of a population by taking nourishment from their hosts.

In the spaces provided, label each limiting factor as either density-dependent *or* density-independent.

Extreme climate changes _____

Competition _____

Human disturbances _____

Parasitism _____

Use the table to answer the question.

1. Give another example of an extreme climate change that might limit the growth of a population.

   _____

   _____

© Pearson Education, Inc., publishing as Pearson Prentice Hall.

Predator-Prey Relationships

A predator is an animal that eats other animals. Prey is the animal that gets eaten. Predator-prey interactions can affect the population growth of both the predator and the prey. In the graph below, the wolves are the predators and the moose are the prey.

Follow the prompts to help you analyze the graph.
- Circle the part of the line representing the moose population from the years 1964 to 1974 in red.
- Circle the part of the line representing the wolf population from the years 1969 to 1980 in blue.

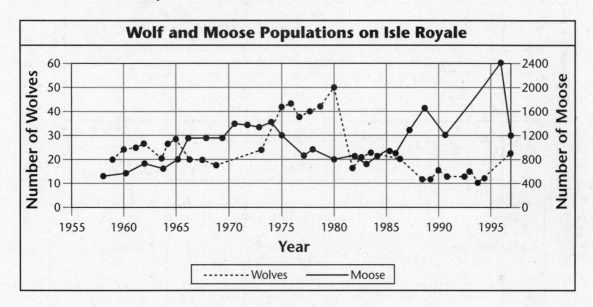

Wolf and Moose Populations on Isle Royale

Use the graph to answer the questions.

1. Was the moose population increasing or decreasing from 1964 to 1974?

_____

2. Was the wolf population increasing or decreasing from 1969 to 1980?

_____

3. Why might changes in the moose population from 1964 to 1974 relate to changes in the wolf population from 1969 to 1980?

_____

_____

© Pearson Education, Inc., publishing as Pearson Prentice Hall.

Human Population Growth

Several events in human history have influenced the size of the human population. The table below identifies some of these events and the approximate size of the population at this time. Graph the changes in the human population size using the data in the table.

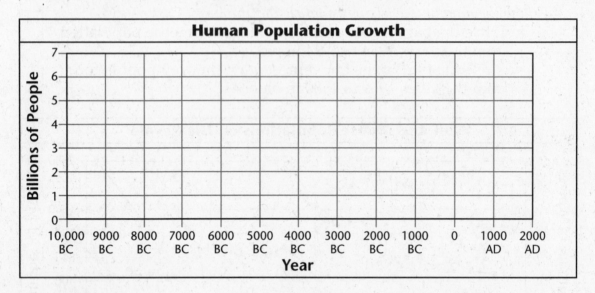

Event	Approximate Date	Human Population Size
Agriculture begins	8500 B.C.	.1 billion
Plowing and irrigation	3400 B.C.	.2 billion
Bubonic plague	1300 A.D.	.4 billion
Industrial Revolution begins	1800 A.D.	1 billion
Present day	2000 A.D.	6.3 billion

Use the graph and table to answer the questions. Circle the correct answer.

1. Which term best describes the human population growth trend?

   exponential   logistic

2. Did industry have a negative or positive affect on human population growth? Explain.

   _____

   _____

   _____

© Pearson Education, Inc., publishing as Pearson Prentice Hall.

Age-Structure Diagrams

Age-structure diagrams show the numbers of people, by gender, in different age groups in a population. They can be used to predict future population growth.

Follow the prompts to color the age-structure diagrams.

- Color the bars that represent the percentage of the population for females ages 5–9 red, and, males 5–9 orange.
- Color the bars that represent the percentage of the population for females ages 40–44 yellow, and, males 40–44 green.
- Color the bars that represent the percentage of the population for females ages 70–74 blue, and, males 70–74 purple.

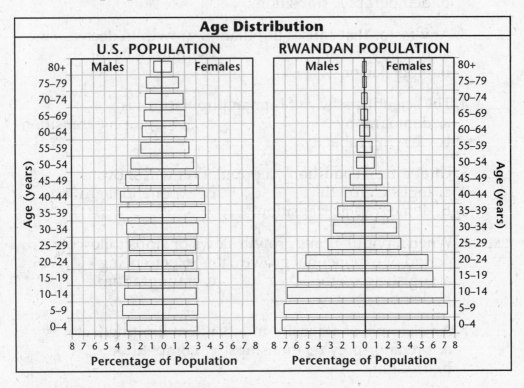

Use the graphs to answer the questions.

1. Which country do you predict will experience a slow and

   steady growth rate in the near future? _____

2. Which population will likely experience a large population growth? Explain.

   _____

   _____

   _____

© Pearson Education, Inc., publishing as Pearson Prentice Hall.

Chapter 5   Populations

Vocabulary Review

Multiple Choice   *In the space provided, write the letter of the term that best completes each sentence.*

_____ 1. The movement of individuals into an area is
   a. demography.   **c.** emigration.
   b. immigration.

_____ 2. The number of individuals of a particular species that an environment can support is the
   a. population density.   **c.** carrying capacity.
   b. demographic transition.

_____ 3. Any factor that causes population growth to decrease is a
   a. primary factor.   **c.** limiting factor.
   b. biotic factor.

_____ 4. The scientific study of human populations is
   a. demography.   **c.** demographic transition.
   b. carrying capacity.

_____ 5. Under ideal conditions, a population will show
   a. logistic growth.   **c.** exponential growth.
   b. demographic transition.

_____ 6. When a population's growth slows or stops following a period of exponential growth, it is experiencing
   a. logistic growth.   **c.** immigration.
   b. demography.

_____ 7. An example of a density-independent limiting factor is
   a. predator-prey relationships. **c.** competition.
   b. drought.

_____ 8. A change in a population from high birth and death rates to low birth and death rates is known as
   a. logistic growth.   **c.** demographic transition.
   b. exponential growth.

_____ 9. The movement of individuals out of an area is
   a. demography.   **c.** emigration.
   b. immigration.

© Pearson Education, Inc., publishing as Pearson Prentice Hall.

Chapter 6   Humans in the Biosphere

Summary

6–1 A Changing Landscape

Earth's organisms share limited resources. They rely on ecological processes, such as the water cycle, to sustain the resources. Understanding how humans interact with the biosphere can help to protect these resources and processes.

Humans are the main source of environmental change. **Among human activities that affect the biosphere are hunting and gathering, agriculture, industry, and urban development.**

- Prehistoric hunters and gatherers changed the environment by hunting some animal species to extinction.
- Farming increased the amount of food produced. This allowed cities to develop. People in the cities produced wastes. Later advances in agriculture included use of pesticides and monoculture. **Monoculture** is the planting of fields with the same crop year after year. Such advances led to the green revolution, a great increase in the world food supply. Agricultural advances also caused problems, such as pollution from pesticides.
- After the Industrial Revolution, human impact on the biosphere grew. Industry used more resources. It also produced more pollution than ever before.

6–2 Renewable and Nonrenewable Resources

Resources may be classified as either renewable or nonrenewable.

- **Renewable resources** are those that natural processes can replace. For example, forests can regrow. Water and oxygen can be replaced by biochemical cycles.
- **Nonrenewable resources** are those that cannot be replaced by natural processes. An example is fossil fuels. Fossil fuels take hundreds of millions of years to form. They are a limited resource and can be used up by humans.

© Pearson Education, Inc., publishing as Pearson Prentice Hall.

Human activities threaten many resources. These activities can affect the quality and supply of renewable resources such as land, forests, fisheries, air, and fresh water.

Sustainable development is a way of using natural resources without depleting them. It also provides for human needs without causing long-term environmental harm.

Soil erosion is the wearing away of surface soil by water and wind. Plowing removes roots that hold soil in place. This can lead to soil erosion. In some places, plowing methods and other activities have changed good soils into deserts. This process is called **desertification.** Contour plowing can reduce soil erosion.

Deforestation is loss of forests. Forests supply wood, oxygen, and other resources. Sustainable development of forests includes planting trees to replace those that are cut down.

Overfishing causes fish populations to decline. **Aquaculture** is the raising of aquatic animals for food. It helps to sustain fish resources.

Smog is a mixture of chemicals that forms a gray-brown haze in the air. It is mainly caused by emissions from cars and industry. Smog is a pollutant. A **pollutant** is a material that harms land, air, or water. Burning fossil fuels releases harmful compounds to the air. Some of these join with water vapor in air to form **acid rain.** Acid rain kills plants and causes other damage. Emission controls have improved air quality and reduced acid rain.

Sewage and discarded chemicals can pollute water. Sustainable development of water includes protecting the water cycle. Wetlands are vital to the water cycle. Thus, protecting wetlands helps sustain water resources.

6–3 Biodiversity

Biological diversity, or **biodiversity,** is the sum of all the kinds of organisms in the biosphere. There are several types of diversity:

- **Ecosystem diversity** is all of the habitats, communities, and ecological processes in ecosystems.
- **Species diversity** is the number of different species in the biosphere.
- **Genetic diversity** is the genetic information carried in all living things on Earth.

© Pearson Education, Inc., publishing as Pearson Prentice Hall.

Biodiversity is one of Earth's great natural resources. Human activity can reduce biodiversity by altering habitats, hunting species to extinction, introducing pollution into food webs, or introducing foreign species into new environments.

- As humans destroy habitats, the species living in those habitats may die out. Development can split habitats, a process called **habitat fragmentation.** The smaller the pieces of habitat, the less likely its species can survive.
- **Extinction** is the disappearance of a species from all or part of its range. An **endangered species** is one whose population size is declining in a way that places it in danger of extinction.
- Toxic compounds build up in the tissues of organisms. These concentrations get larger in living things at higher trophic levels. This is called **biological magnification.**
- Plants and animals brought into an area from other places can become **invasive species.** Invasive species can multiply quickly if their new habitat lacks parasites and predators to control their numbers.

Conservation is the wise management of natural resources. Today, conservation efforts focus on protecting entire ecosystems as well as single species. Protecting an ecosystem will ensure that the natural habitats and the interactions of many different species are preserved at the same time.

6–4 Charting a Course for the Future

Researchers are gathering data to monitor and evaluate the effects of human activities on the ozone layer and the global climate system.

- The **ozone layer** is an area high in the atmosphere where ozone gas is concentrated. This layer protects Earth from harmful radiation. Compounds in some products have damaged the ozone layer. These compounds have now been banned.
- **Global warming** is an increase in the average temperature of the biosphere. It is mainly a result of the burning of fossil fuels. Burning fuels adds gases to the atmosphere that cause it to hold more heat. Continued global warming may lead to rising sea levels and coastal flooding.

People can help look after the health of the biosphere by conserving resources. For example, they can avoid using more water than necessary. They can also reuse or recycle trash.

© Pearson Education, Inc., publishing as Pearson Prentice Hall.

Earth's Resources

Write one way humans can reduce their effect on each resource. One row has been completed for you.

How Humans Affect Earth's Resources

Resource	How Humans Affect the Resource	How Humans Can Reduce the Effect
Land	Plowing land removes roots and leads to soil erosion and desertification.	Contour plowing reduces the amount of erosion.
Forests	Logging leads to deforestation.	
Air	The burning of fossil fuels leads to air pollution.	
Fresh Water	Pollution from sewage leads to the growth of algae and bacteria.	

Answer the question.

1. Describe sustainable development.

_____

_____

_____

© Pearson Education, Inc., publishing as Pearson Prentice Hall.

Biological Magnification

The diagram below shows biological magnification. It shows how the concentration of DDT in organisms increases as the DDT moves through the levels of a food chain.

Follow the prompts to color the diagram.
- Color the trophic level with the lowest concentration of DDT blue.
- Color the trophic level with the highest concentration of DDT red.
- Draw an arrow showing how the concentration of DDT increases in organisms.

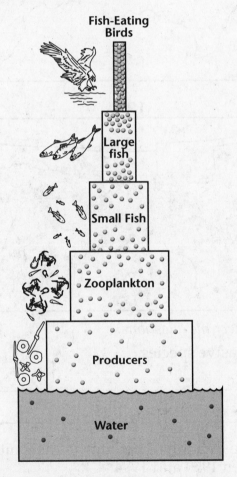

Use the diagram to answer the questions.

1. Circle the organism that would have a higher concentration of

   DDT in its body.   zooplankton   small fish

2. Think about your answer to question 1. Why is this so?

   _____

   _____

© Pearson Education, Inc., publishing as Pearson Prentice Hall.

Invasive Species

Fire ants are a species of ant that scientists believe came to the United States on a ship from South America. The shaded areas on the maps show where the fire ant population lived in 1953 and 1994.

1953

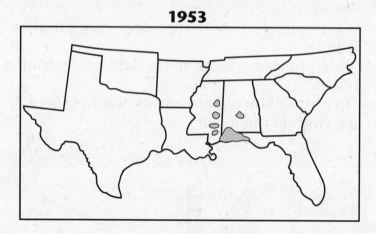

1994

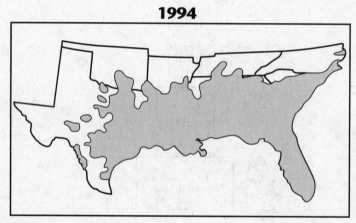

Use the maps to answer the questions.

1. Describe an invasive species.

_____

_____

2. Explain how the location of fire ants in the United States changed between 1953 and 1994.

_____

3. How do invasive species often affect ecosystems?

_____

_____

_____

© Pearson Education, Inc., publishing as Pearson Prentice Hall.

Global Temperature Changes

The graph shows how global temperature changed between 1850 and 2000. On the *y*-axis, the unit 0.0 represents the temperature in 1850. The other numbers show how much the temperature increased or decreased from that temperature.

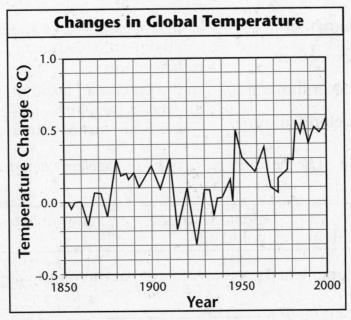

Use the graph to answer the questions.

1. What was the difference in global temperature between 1850 and 1880?

   _____

   _____

2. Describe the overall trend in global temperature since 1850.

   _____

   _____

3. Which of the following may have helped cause the trend in overall global temperatures shown above? Circle the correct answer.

   burning fossil fuels   melting polar ice caps

4. Suppose the trend in overall global temperatures shown above continues. How might this affect Earth in the future?

   _____

   _____

   _____

© Pearson Education, Inc., publishing as Pearson Prentice Hall.

Chapter 6   Humans in the Biosphere

Vocabulary Review

Matching   *In the space provided, write the letter of the definition that best matches each term.*

_____ **1.** agriculture

_____ **2.** extinction

_____ **3.** desertification

_____ **4.** deforestation

a. disappearance of a species within all or part of its range

b. loss of forests

c. the practice of farming

d. process by which once-productive lands are turned into deserts

Completion   *Use the words below to fill in the blanks with terms from the chapter.*

acid rain conservation	global warming pollutant	renewable resource

5. An environmental good or service that can regenerate and be

replaced is a(an) _____.

6. A harmful material that enters the biosphere through air,

water, or land is a(an) _____.

7. _____ is the wise management of natural resources.

8. The trend of an increasing average temperature of the

biosphere is _____.

9. Rain that contains nitric and sulfuric acids is called

_____.

© Pearson Education, Inc., publishing as Pearson Prentice Hall.

Chapter 7   Cell Structure and Function

Summary

7–1 Life Is Cellular

Since the 1600s, scientists have made many discoveries about the cells of living things. These discoveries are summarized in the cell theory. **The cell theory states:**

- **All living things are made up of cells.**
- **Cells are the basic units of structure and function in living things.**
- **New cells are produced from existing cells.**

All cells share two characteristics:

- a barrier called a cell membrane that surrounds the cell, and
- at some point in their lives they contain DNA. DNA is the molecule that carries biological information.

Cells fall into two broad groups, based on whether they have a nucleus. A **nucleus** is a membrane-enclosed structure that holds the cell's genetic material (DNA). The nucleus controls many of the cell's activities.

- **Prokaryotes** do not have nuclei. **They have genetic material that is not contained in a nucleus.** Bacteria are prokaryotes.
- **Eukaryotes** are cells that have nuclei. **Eukaryotes have a nucleus in which their genetic material is separated from the rest of the cell.** Plants, animals, fungi, and protists are eukaryotes.

7–2 Eukaryotic Cell Structure

Cell biologists divide the eukaryotic cell into two main parts: the nucleus and the cytoplasm. The **cytoplasm** is the part of the cell outside the nucleus.

<u>In the Nucleus</u>
   The nucleus contains most of a cell's DNA. The DNA contains the coded instructions for making proteins and other important molecules.

- The nucleus is surrounded by a double membrane called a **nuclear envelope.**
- Inside the nucleus is granular material called **chromatin.** Chromatin is made up of DNA bound to proteins. When the cell divides, this chromatin condenses into chromosomes. **Chromosomes** are threadlike structures. They contain the genetic information that is passed from one generation of cells to the next.
- Most nuclei also have a small, dense region known as the **nucleolus** where the assembly of ribosomes begins.

© Pearson Education, Inc., publishing as Pearson Prentice Hall.

In the Cytoplasm

Eukaryotic cells have structures called **organelles** within the cytoplasm.

- **Ribosomes** are small particles of RNA and protein spread throughout the cytoplasm. **Proteins are made on ribosomes.**
- The **endoplasmic reticulum (ER)** is an internal membrane system. **The ER is where lipid components of the cell membrane are assembled, along with proteins and other materials that are exported from the cell.** The part of the ER involved in the protein synthesis is called rough ER. Rough ER has ribosomes on its surface. Smooth ER does not have ribosomes on its surface. Smooth ER helps make lipids.
- **Golgi apparatus** appear as closely grouped membranes. **The job of the Golgi apparatus is to change, sort, and package proteins and other materials from the ER for storage in the cell or secretion outside the cell.**
- **Lysosomes** are small organelles filled with enzymes. Lysosomes help break down lipids, carbohydrates and proteins into small molecules that can be used by the rest of the cell.
- **Vacuoles** are saclike structures that are used to store materials.
- Almost all eukaryotic cells contain **mitochondria. Mitochondria convert the chemical energy stored in food into compounds that are more convenient for the cell to use.**
- Plants and some other organisms contain **chloroplasts. Chloroplasts capture the energy in sunlight and convert it into chemical energy.**
- The structure that helps support the cell is called the **cytoskeleton. The cytoskeleton is a network of protein filaments that helps the cell maintain its shape. The cytoskeleton is also involved in movement.**

7–3 Cell Boundaries

A thin, flexible barrier known as the **cell membrane** surrounds all cells. The makeup of most cell membranes is a double-layered sheet called a lipid bilayer. **The cell membrane**

- **controls what enters and leaves the cell, and**
- **protects and supports the cell.**

Cells of plants, algae, fungi, and many prokaryotes also have a strong supporting layer called a **cell wall** surrounding the cell membrane. **The main job of the cell wall is to support and protect the cell.**

© Pearson Education, Inc., publishing as Pearson Prentice Hall.

One of the most important functions of the cell membrane is to control the movement of dissolved molecules from the liquid on one side of the membrane to the liquid on the other side.

The cytoplasm of a cell is a solution of many substances in water. Particles in a solution move constantly. Particles tend to move from an area where they are more concentrated to an area where they are less concentrated. This process is called **diffusion. Diffusion does not require energy.**

- Water passes easily across most membranes. **Osmosis is the diffusion of water through a selectively permeable membrane.** A selectively permeable membrane is a membrane that some substances can pass through, while others cannot.
- Many cell membranes have protein channels that let certain molecules cross the membranes. These protein channels facilitate, or help, the diffusion of the molecules across the membrane. This process is called **facilitated diffusion**. It does not require the cell to use energy.

Active transport requires energy. **Active transport** occurs when cells move materials from one side of a membrane to the other side against the concentration difference. Four types of active transport are:

- **endocytosis:** the process of taking material into the cell by means of infolding of the cell membrane
- **phagocytosis:** the extension of cytoplasm to surround a particle and package it within a food vacuole
- **pinocytosis:** the taking up of liquids from the environment
- **exocytosis:** the release of materials from the cell

7–4 The Diversity of Cellular Life

A *unicellular organism* is made up of only one cell. Unicellular organisms carry out all the essential functions of life. Multicellular organisms are made up of many cells. **Cells throughout an organism can develop in different ways to perform different tasks.** This process is called **cell specialization.**

Multicellular organisms have several levels of organization.

- Individual **cells** are the first level.
- Similar cells form units called **tissues.** A tissue is a group of cells that carry out a particular function.
- Groups of tissues that work together form an **organ.**
- A group of organs that work together to perform a specific function is an **organ system.**

© Pearson Education, Inc., publishing as Pearson Prentice Hall.

Prokaryotic and Eukaryotic Cells

Look at the diagrams below. Label the prokaryotic cell *and the* eukaryotic cell.

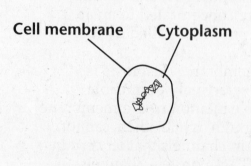

Cell membrane   Cytoplasm

_____

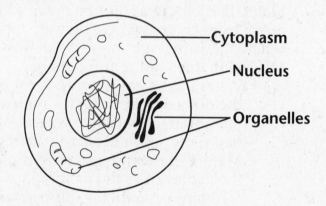

Cytoplasm

Nucleus

Organelles

_____

Use the diagrams to answer the question.

1. Explain why you labeled each diagram as you did.

_____

_____

Compare and contrast the two types of cells by completing the table.

	Prokaryotic Cell	Eukaryotic Cell
Cell membrane	present	
Nucleus		present
Cell size		large
Complexity	simple	

Answer the questions. Circle the correct answer.

2. What type of cells makes up your body?

    prokaryotic   eukaryotic

3. What type of cell is a bacterial cell?

    prokaryotic   eukaryotic

© Pearson Education, Inc., publishing as Pearson Prentice Hall.

Plant Cell

Use the words below to label the plant cell. Some structures have already been labeled for you.

cell wall	mitochondrion	ribosome
chloroplast	nucleus	vacuole

Plant Cell

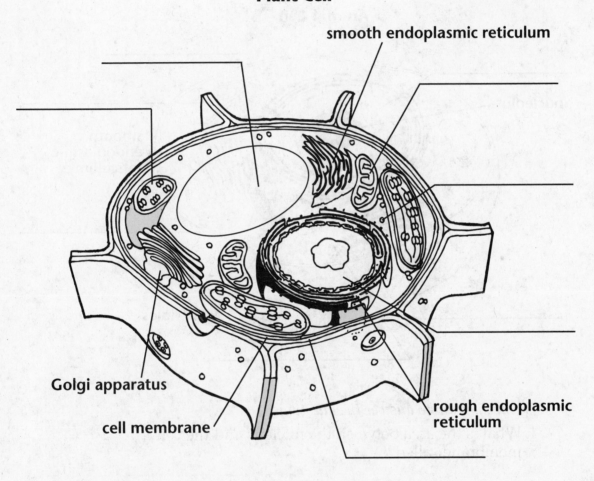

smooth endoplasmic reticulum

Golgi apparatus

cell membrane

rough endoplasmic reticulum

Use the diagram to answer the questions.

1. Which structure is found in a plant cell but not in an animal cell? Circle the correct answer.

   chloroplast   cell membrane   ribosome

2. What is the main function of vacuoles?

   _____

© Pearson Education, Inc., publishing as Pearson Prentice Hall.

Animal Cell

*Use the words below to label the animal cell. Some structures have
already been labeled for you.*

cell membrane	mitochondrion	rough endoplasmic reticulum
Golgi apparatus	nucleus	ribosome

Animal Cell

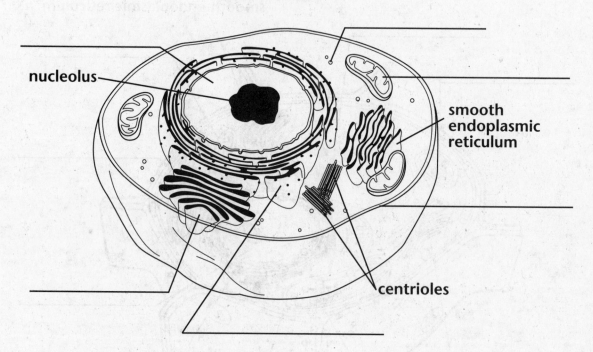

nucleolus

smooth
endoplasmic
reticulum

centrioles

Use the diagram to answer the questions.

1. What is the area between the nucleus and the cell
membrane called?

_____

2. What cell structures are found on the surface of rough endoplasmic reticulum but not on smooth endoplasmic reticulum?

_____

© Pearson Education, Inc., publishing as Pearson Prentice Hall.

Organelle Function

An organelle is a specialized cell structure. Each organelle functions in a different way to help the cell carry out life processes.

A mitochondrion, nucleus, endoplasmic reticulum, *and* Golgi apparatus *are pictured and described below. Write the name of the organelle underneath its picture.*

Organelle	Function
	controls most cell processes and stores genetic material
	makes membrane lipids that will be exported out of the cell
	modifies, sorts, and packages materials from the endoplasmic reticulum
	converts the energy stored in food into a more useable form

Use the table to answer the question.

1. Which of the structures shown above contains a nucleolus?

_____

© Pearson Education, Inc., publishing as Pearson Prentice Hall.

Cell Membranes

The cell membrane controls what enters and leaves the cell. Most cell membranes are made up of a phospholipid bilayer. This bilayer usually contains membrane proteins embedded in it.

Draw a diagram of a portion of a cell membrane. Label the cytoplasm and the area outside the cell. A sample phosolipid and membrane protein have been diagrammed for you.

phospholipid

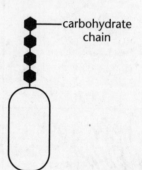

membrane protein

carbohydrate chain

Answer the question.

1. What do the carbohydrate chains on some membrane proteins do?

_____

_____

© Pearson Education, Inc., publishing as Pearson Prentice Hall.

Diffusion and Osmosis

Diffusion is the movement of particles from an area of high concentration to an area of low concentration. Osmosis is the diffusion of water through a selectively permeable membrane.

Look at the beakers on the left. In the beakers on the right, draw in any changes in water level or number of solute particles on each side of the membrane that occur as a result of the described process.

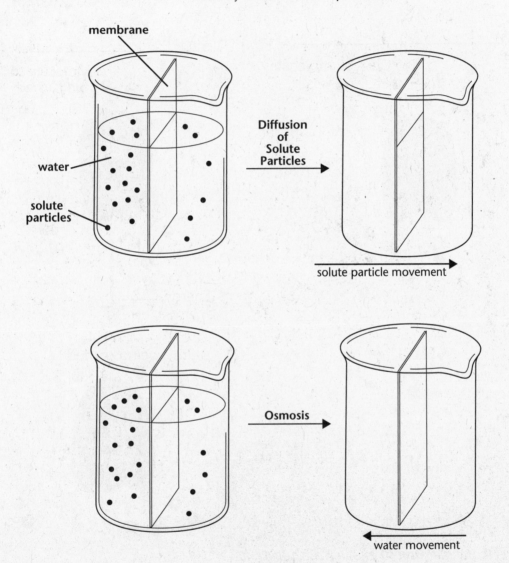

Use the diagrams to answer the question.

1. Look at the top left beaker. What would happen if the membrane did not allow water or solute particles to pass through it?

_____

_____

© Pearson Education, Inc., publishing as Pearson Prentice Hall.

Facilitated Diffusion and Active Transport

Facilitated diffusion occurs when a substance diffuses across the cell membrane through a protein channel. Active transport occurs when the cell uses energy to carry a substance across the cell membrane.

Look at the diagrams. Label each as either facilitated diffusion *or* active transport.

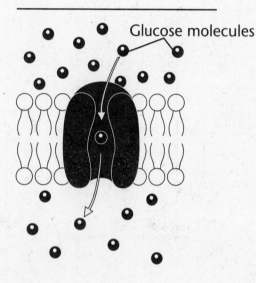

Glucose molecules

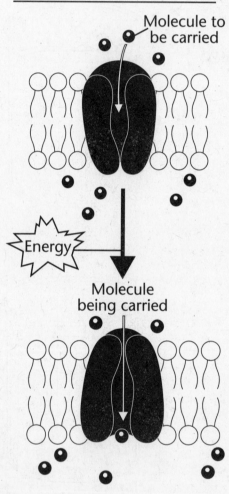

Molecule to be carried

Energy

Molecule being carried

Use the diagram to answer the questions.

1. Which process can move molecules from a lower concentration solution on one side of the membrane to a higher concentration solution on the other side?

_____

2. Which process does not require energy?

_____

© Pearson Education, Inc., publishing as Pearson Prentice Hall.

Multicellular Organisms—Levels of Organization

The levels of organization in a multicellular organism are cells, tissues, organs, and organ systems.

Draw arrows that show how the levels are organized. Start with the lowest level, and draw an arrow to the next higher level of organization. Continue until you reach the highest level of organization.

Organ system

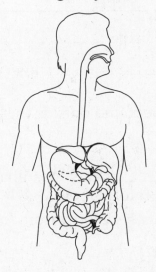

Tissue

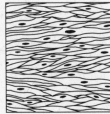

Cell

Organ

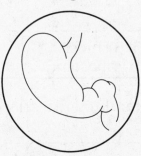

Use the diagram to answer the questions.

1. What is a group of cells that perform a particular function called?

_____

2. What is a group of tissues that work together called?

_____

© Pearson Education, Inc., publishing as Pearson Prentice Hall.

Chapter 7   Cell Structure and Function

Vocabulary Review

Completion   *Use the words below to fill in the blanks with terms from the chapter.*

cell	chromosome	mitochondrion
cell wall	cytoplasm	prokaryote

1. The basic unit of life is the _____.

2. A _____ is a unicellular organism that lacks a nucleus.

3. The support structure found outside the cell membrane is the

   _____.

4. A _____ is the threadlike nuclear structure that contains genetic information.

5. An organelle that releases energy from food molecules is a

   _____.

6. The material inside the cell membrane that surrounds the

   nucleus is the _____.

Completion   *Use the words below to fill in the blanks with terms from the chapter.*

nucleus	osmosis	tissue
organ	ribosome	

7. The diffusion of water through a selectively permeable

   membrane is _____.

8. A group of similar cells that work together to perform a

   specific function is called a(an) _____.

9. Proteins are made on a(an) _____.

10. A group of tissues that work together to perform a similar

    function is called a(an) _____.

11. The _____ is the structure in eukaryotic cells that controls cell activities and contains genetic material.

© Pearson Education, Inc., publishing as Pearson Prentice Hall.

Chapter 8   Photosynthesis

Summary

8–1 Energy and Life

Plants and some other living things can use light energy from the sun to make food. These organisms are called **autotrophs.** Many organisms cannot use the sun's energy directly. These organisms, called **heterotrophs**, get energy from their food.

   Adenosine triphosphate, or ATP, is a compound cells use to store and release energy. **ATP is the basic energy source of all cells.** Cells use energy from ATP to carry out many activities. These include active transport, synthesis of proteins and nucleic acids, and responses to chemical signals at the cell surface. ATP is made up of adenine, a 5-carbon sugar called ribose, and three phosphate groups.

   Adenosine diphosphate (ADP) is a compound similar to ATP. Unlike ATP, ADP has only two phosphate groups. When energy is available, a cell can store small amounts of energy by adding a phosphate group to ADP to form ATP (ADP + P → ATP). Energy stored in ATP is released by breaking the bond between the second and third phosphate groups (ATP → ADP + P).

8–2 Photosynthesis: An Overview

Research into photosynthesis began centuries ago. **The experiments of van Helmont, Priestly, and Ingenhousz led to work by other scientists. These scientists found that in the presence of light, plants change carbon dioxide and water into carbohydrates and give off oxygen.** This process is called **photosynthesis.**

   The overall equation for photosynthesis is:

$$6CO_2 + 6H_2O \xrightarrow{\text{light}} C_6H_{12}O_6 + 6O_2$$

$$\text{carbon dioxide} + \text{water light} \xrightarrow{\text{light}} \text{sugars} + \text{oxygen}$$

Photosynthesis uses the energy of sunlight to convert water and carbon dioxide into high-energy sugars and oxygen. Plants get the carbon dioxide needed for photosynthesis from the air or from the water in which they grow. Plants use the sugars produced during photosynthesis to make complex carbohydrates such as starches.

© Pearson Education, Inc., publishing as Pearson Prentice Hall.

Photosynthesis also requires light and chlorophyll. Plants gather the sun's energy with light-absorbing molecules called **pigments.** The main pigment in plants is **chlorophyll.** A compound that absorbs light also absorbs the light's energy. When chlorophyll absorbs sunlight, much of the light energy is sent directly to electrons in the chlorophyll molecules. This raises the energy levels of the electrons.

The visible spectrum is made up of wavelengths of light you can see. This spectrum contains all the colors. Chlorophyll absorbs light in the blue-violet and red regions of the visible spectrum well. Chlorophyll does not absorb light in the green region well. Plants look green because their leaves reflect this green light.

8–3 The Reactions of Photosynthesis

In plants and other photosynthetic prokaryotes, photosynthesis takes place inside the chloroplasts. Chloroplasts have saclike photosynthetic membranes called **thylakoids.** Proteins in the thylakoid membrane organize chlorophyll and other pigments into clusters known as **photosystems.** The photosystems are the light-collecting units of chlorophyll.

When sunlight excites electrons in chlorophyll, the electrons gain energy. The electron transfers its energy to another molecule. The energy continues to move from molecule to molecule until it gets to the end of the chain.

The reactions of photosynthesis occur in two parts: light-dependent reactions and light-independent reactions.

1. **The light-dependent reactions produce oxygen gas and convert ADP and NADP$^+$ into ATP and NADPH.** These reactions need light and they occur in the thylakoid membranes. The light-dependent reactions can be divided into four processes: light absorption, oxygen production, electron transport, and ATP formation. The light-dependent reactions use water, ADP, and NADP$^+$. They produce oxygen, ATP, and NADPH.

2. The light-independent reactions are also called the Calvin cycle. These reactions do not need light. **The Calvin cycle uses ATP and NADPH from the light-dependent reactions to produce high-energy sugars.** The Calvin cycle takes place in the **stroma** of chloroplasts. The Calvin cycle uses carbon dioxide in its reactions. As photosynthesis proceeds, the Calvin cycle works steadily to remove carbon dioxide from the atmosphere and turn out energy-rich sugars. Six carbon dioxide molecules are needed to make a single 6-carbon sugar.

Many factors affect the rate of photosynthesis. Such factors include water availability, temperature, and the intensity of light.

© Pearson Education, Inc., publishing as Pearson Prentice Hall.

ATP

ATP is the basic energy source of all cells. Energy is stored by cells when ADP is converted into ATP. Energy is released when ATP loses a phosphate and becomes ADP.

Label the energy storing *reaction and the* energy releasing *reaction.*

ADP   +   Phosphate ⟶   ATP

_____

ATP   ADP   +   Phosphate

_____

Answer the questions.

1. How many phosphate groups are in one molecule of ATP?

_____

2. How many phosphate groups are in one molecule of ADP?

_____

3. What are the three parts of an ATP molecule?

_____

© Pearson Education, Inc., publishing as Pearson Prentice Hall.

The Chloroplast

In plants, photosynthesis takes place in chloroplasts. Inside chloroplasts are saclike membranes called thylakoids. These thylakoids are arranged in stacks. A stack of thylakoids is called a granum. The region outside of the thylakoids, but inside the chloroplast is called the stroma.

In the diagram of the chloroplast, label a thylakoid, *the* stroma, *and the* granum.

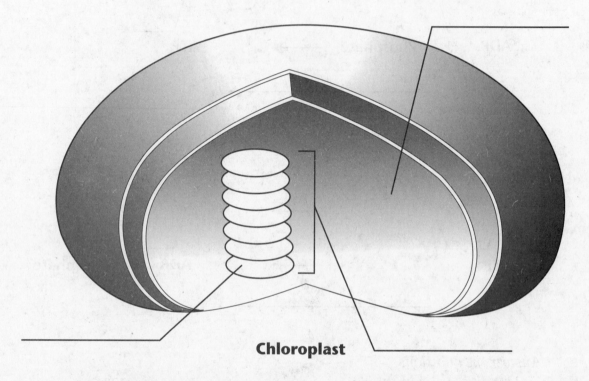

Chloroplast

Answer the following questions. Circle the correct answer.

1. Where are the photosystems, or light-collecting units of photosynthesis, found?

   thylakoid membranes   stroma

2. In what part of the chloroplast does the Calvin cycle take place?

   thylakoid membranes   stroma

3. In what part of the chloroplast do the light-dependent reactions of photosynthesis take place?

   thylakoid membranes   stroma

© Pearson Education, Inc., publishing as Pearson Prentice Hall.

Photosynthesis Overview

Photosynthesis uses light energy to convert water and carbon dioxide into oxygen and high-energy sugars. The picture below shows an overall view of the process of photosynthesis.

Use the words below to label the diagram.

Calvin cycle	light energy	sugars
light-dependent reactions	oxygen	

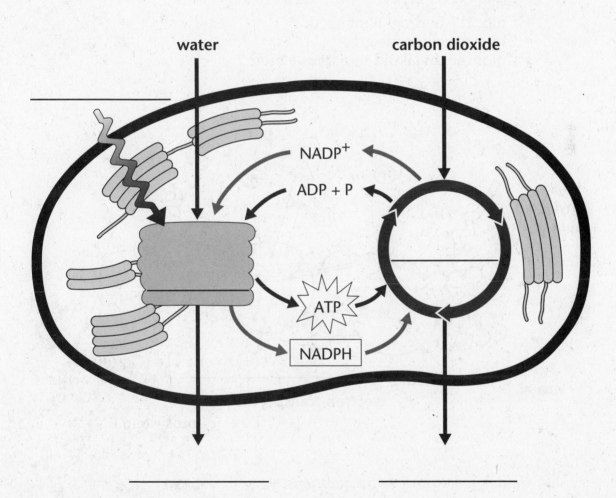

Use the diagram to answer the questions.

1. Finish the equation for photosynthesis.

carbon dioxide + water $\xrightarrow{\text{light}}$ _____

2. Which of the following is also called the light-independent reactions of photosynthesis? Circle the correct answer.

Calvin cycle   electron transport chain

© Pearson Education, Inc., publishing as Pearson Prentice Hall.

Photosystems I and II

Photosystems I and II are important parts of the light-dependent reactions of photosynthesis. In photosystem II, light energy is absorbed by electrons. These high-energy electrons are then passed down an electron transport chain. The electrons are then passed to photosystem I. In photosytem I, the electrons are reenergized by light energy and used to make NADPH.

Color the diagram according to the prompts below.
- Color the two places where light energy enters the reactions yellow.
- Color the hydrogen ions red.
- Color the electrons green.
- Color the thylakoid membrane blue.

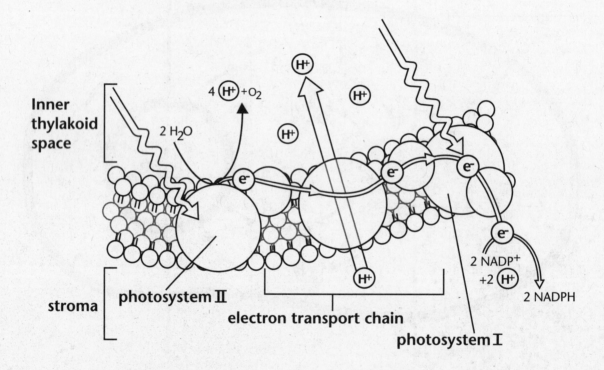

Use the diagram to answer the questions.

1. Where does light energy enter the system?

_____

2. What uses energy from the high-energy electrons to transport hydrogen across the thylakoid membrane? Circle the correct answer.

photosystem II   electron transport chain

© Pearson Education, Inc., publishing as Pearson Prentice Hall.

ATP Formation in the Light-Dependent Reactions of Photosynthesis

In the light-dependent reactions of photosynthesis, the electron transport chain transports hydrogen ions across the thylakoid membrane. ATP synthase uses these hydrogen ions to power the formation of ATP. Hydrogen ions move through ATP synthase and cause it to spin. As it spins, it forms ATP from ADP and a phosphate.

Color the arrow that shows how ATP synthase spins. Then, draw in the formation of ATP from ADP.

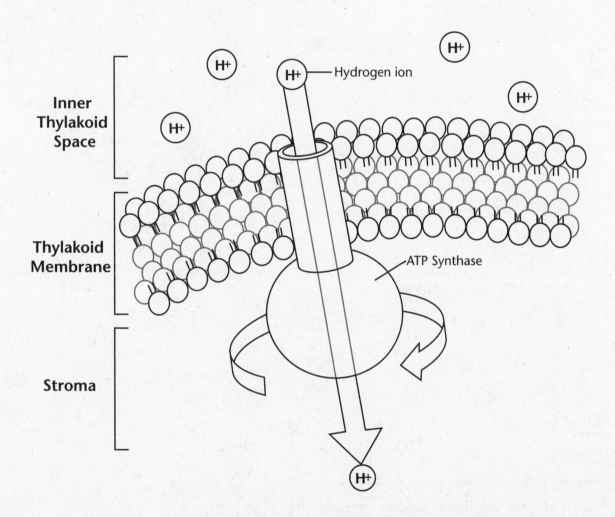

Use the diagram to answer the question. Circle the correct answer.

1. Where does the formation of ATP take place?

  inner thylakoid space   stroma

© Pearson Education, Inc., publishing as Pearson Prentice Hall.

The Calvin Cycle

ATP and NADPH are both produced by the light-dependent reactions of photosynthesis. The Calvin cycle uses the energy in ATP and NADPH to produce high-energy sugars.

Circle the places where ATP and NADPH are used. Then, draw an X over the 6-carbon high-energy sugar produced by the Calvin cycle.

Calvin Cycle

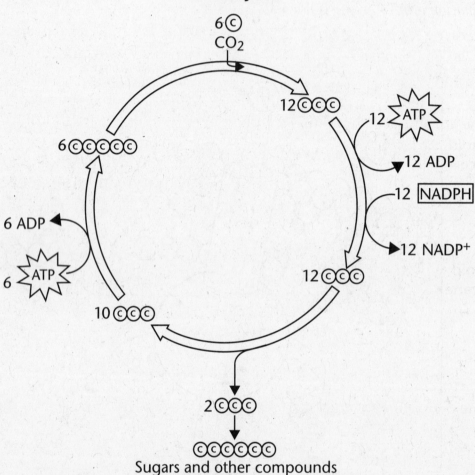

Sugars and other compounds

Use the diagram to answer the question.

1. How many molecules of carbon dioxide are used to produce one 6-carbon sugar molecule?

_____

2. What is formed as a result of the Calvin cycle? Circle the correct answer.

six-carbon sugar   carbon dioxide

© Pearson Education, Inc., publishing as Pearson Prentice Hall.

Chapter 8   Photosynthesis

Vocabulary Review

Completion   *Use the words below to fill in the blanks with terms from the chapter.*

ATP	light-dependent
Calvin cycle	thylakoid

1. During the _____ reactions of photosynthesis, energy from sunlight is used to form ATP, NADPH, and oxygen.

2. _____ is one of the main chemical compounds that cells use to store and release chemical energy.

3. The light-dependent reactions of photosynthesis take place in

the _____ membranes of chloroplasts.

4. The stage of photosynthesis that uses ATP and NADPH to form

high-energy sugars is the _____.

Completion   *Use the words below to fill in the blanks with terms from the chapter.*

autotroph	photosynthesis
chlorophyll	stroma

5. A plant or other organism that is able to make its own food is

a(an) _____.

6. _____ is the overall process in which sunlight is used to convert carbon dioxide and water into oxygen and high-energy sugars.

7. The region of the chloroplast in which the Calvin cycle occurs

is the _____.

8. The principle pigment in plants is called

_____.

© Pearson Education, Inc., publishing as Pearson Prentice Hall.

Chapter 9   Cellular Respiration

Summary

9–1 Chemical Pathways

Food is the energy source for cells. The energy in food is measured in calories. A **calorie** is the amount of energy needed to raise the temperature of 1 gram of water 1 degree Celsius. The Calorie (capital C) used on food labels is equal to 1000 calories.

Cells do not burn glucose or other food compounds. They gradually release the energy. The process begins with a pathway called **glycolysis.**

Glycolysis is the process in which a glucose molecule is split in half. This forms two molecules of pyruvic acid, a 3-carbon compound. Glycolysis takes place in the cytoplasm of a cell. Through glycolysis, the cell gains 2 ATP molecules. In addition, the electron carrier NAD^+ accepts a pair of high-energy electrons, producing NADH. By doing this, NAD^+ helps pass energy from glucose to other pathways in the cell.

When oxygen is not present, fermentation follows glycolysis. **Fermentation** releases energy from food molecules by forming ATP. Fermentation does not need oxygen, so it is said to be **anaerobic.** During fermentation, cells convert NADH back into the electron carrier NAD^+ that is needed for glycolysis. This lets glycolysis continue to make a steady supply of ATP. **The two types of fermentation are alcoholic fermentation and lactic acid fermentation.**

- Yeasts and a few other microorganisms carry out alcoholic fermentation. The equation for alcoholic fermentation after glycolysis is:

  pyruvic acid + NADH → alcohol + CO_2 + NAD^+

- Lactic acid fermentation occurs in muscles during rapid exercise. The equation for lactic acid fermentation after glycolysis is:

  pyruvic acid + NADH → lactic acid + NAD^+

If oxygen is present, the Krebs cycle and electron transport chain follow glycolysis. Together, these pathways make up **cellular respiration. Cellular respiration is the process that releases energy by breaking down glucose and other food molecules in the presence of oxygen.** Cellular respiration takes place in mitochondria. The equation for cellular respiration is:

$6O_2 + C_6H_{12}O_6 \rightarrow 6CO_2 + 6H_2O$ + Energy

oxygen + glucose → carbon dioxide + water + Energy

© Pearson Education, Inc., publishing as Pearson Prentice Hall.

9–2 The Krebs Cycle and Electron Transport

Cellular respiration requires oxygen, so it is said to be **aerobic.**
The **Krebs cycle** is the second stage of cellular respiration.
**During the Krebs cycle, pyruvic acid is broken down into
carbon dioxide in a series of energy-extracting reactions.**
The Krebs cycle is also known as the citric acid cycle, because
citric acid is one of its first products.

Here are the stages of the Krebs cycle.
- The Krebs cycle starts when pyruvic acid formed by
  glycolysis enters the mitochondrion.
- The pyruvic acid is broken down into carbon dioxide and
  a 2-carbon acetyl group.
- The two carbons of the acetyl group join a 4-carbon compound to produce citric acid. The Krebs cycle continues in
  a series of reactions. In these reactions, two energy carriers
  accept high-energy electrons. NAD^+ is changed to NADH,
  and FAD is changed to $FADH_2$. These molecules carry the
  high-energy electrons to the electron transport chain. The
  carbon dioxide is released as a waste product.

**The electron transport chain uses the high-energy electrons
to change ADP into ATP.** In the electron transport chain, high-
energy electrons move from one carrier protein to the next. At
the end of the chain, oxygen pulls electrons from the final carrier
molecule. These electrons join with hydrogen ions, forming water.

Each transfer along the chain releases a small amount of energy.
ATP synthase uses the energy to produce ATP.

Glycolysis produces 2 ATP molecules from one molecule
of glucose. The Krebs cycle and the electron transport chain let the
cell form 34 ATP molecules per glucose molecule. The total, then,
for cellular respiration is 36 ATP molecules per glucose molecule.

The energy flows in photosynthesis and cellular respiration
occur in opposite directions. On a global level, photosynthesis and
cellular respiration are also opposites. Photosynthesis removes
carbon dioxide from the atmosphere and puts back oxygen.
Cellular respiration removes oxygen from the atmosphere and
puts back carbon dioxide.

© Pearson Education, Inc., publishing as Pearson Prentice Hall.

The Mitochondrion

In plant and animal cells, the final stages of cellular respiration take place in mitochondria. A mitochondrion has two membranes. The inner membrane is folded up inside the outer membrane. The space between the inner and outer membranes is called the inter-membrane space. The space inside the inner membrane is called the matrix.

Label the inner membrane, intermembrane space, matrix, *and* outer membrane.

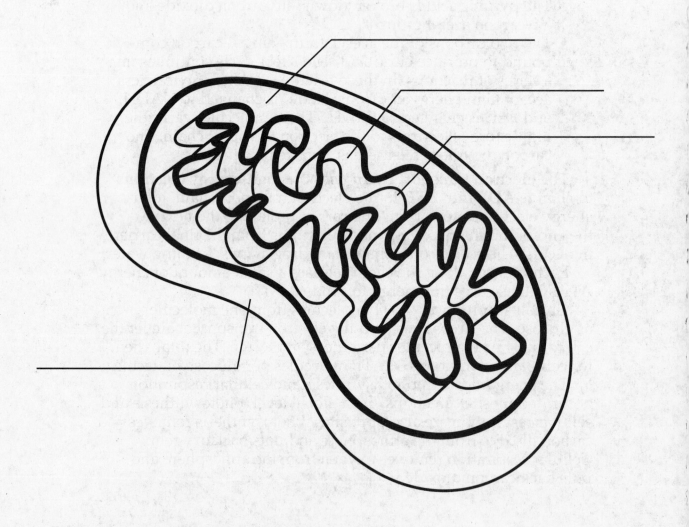

Answer the questions. Circle the correct answer.

1. In which membrane is the electron transport chain located?

outer membrane   inner membrane

© Pearson Education, Inc., publishing as Pearson Prentice Hall.

Cellular Respiration Overview

Cellular respiration is the process that releases energy from food in the presence of oxygen.

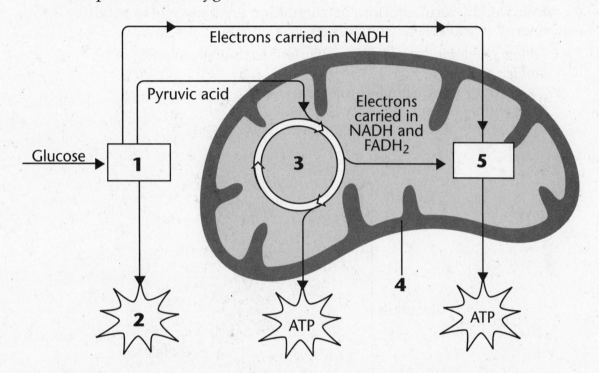

Use the words below to label the diagram of cellular respiration on the lines provided.

ATP	glycolysis	mitochondrion
electron transport chain	Krebs cycle	

1. _____

2. _____

3. _____

4. _____

5. _____

Use the diagram to answer the questions.

1. Where does glycolysis take place?

_____

2. Where do the Kreb cycle and electron transport chain take place?

_____

© Pearson Education, Inc., publishing as Pearson Prentice Hall.

Glycolysis and Fermentation

Glycolysis uses ATP to break a molecule of glucose in half, producing pyruvic acid. When oxygen is not present, glycolysis is followed by fermentation. Fermentation enables cells to produce energy in the absence of oxygen.

Follow the prompts to identify important parts of glycolysis and fermentation.

- Color the carbon atoms blue.
- Circle the place where ATP is formed.
- Mark an X on the place where ATP is used.

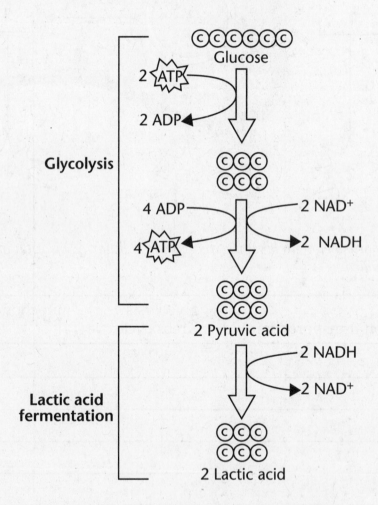

Answer the questions.

1. How many carbon atoms are in one molecule of glucose?

_____

2. What is the product of glycolysis? _____

© Pearson Education, Inc., publishing as Pearson Prentice Hall.

The Krebs Cycle

If oxygen is present, the pyruvic acid formed during glycolysis moves into the Krebs cycle. The Krebs cycle converts pyruvic acid into carbon dioxide. As carbon dioxide is formed, high energy electrons are accepted by NAD^+ and FAD. This results in the formation of NADH and $FADH_2$. NADH and $FADH_2$ will be used later to produce ATP.

Follow the prompts to identify important parts of the Krebs cycle.
- Color the carbon atoms blue.
- Circle the electron carriers in green.
- Circle ATP in orange.

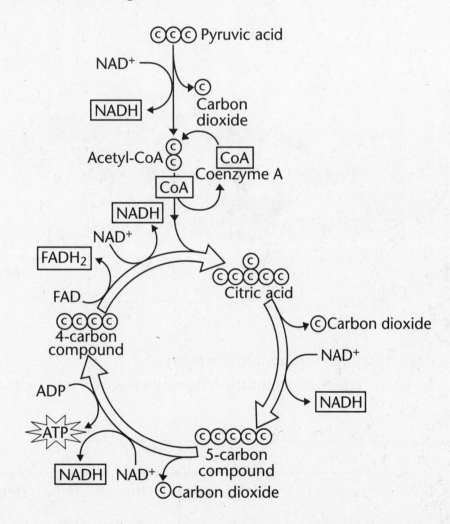

Use the diagram to answer the question. Circle the correct answer.

1. Which of the following is formed during the Krebs cycle?

$FADH_2$ pyruvic acid

© Pearson Education, Inc., publishing as Pearson Prentice Hall.

Electron Transport Chain

The electron transport chain uses the high-energy electrons
produced by the Krebs cycle to move hydrogen ions from one
side of the inner membrane to the other.

Label the diagram with the following terms: electron, hydrogen ion,
and inner membrane.

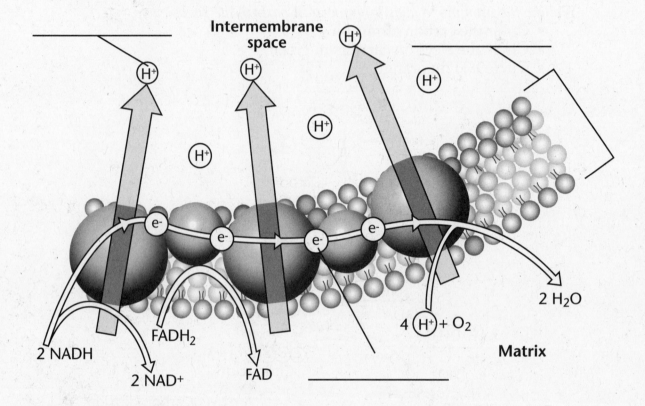

Use the diagram to answer the questions.

1. Where in the mitochondrion does the electron transport chain
   take place?

   _____

   _____

2. What happens to the high-energy electrons from the Krebs cycle?

   _____

   _____

© Pearson Education, Inc., publishing as Pearson Prentice Hall.

Cellular Respiration and Photosynthesis

Cellular respiration and photosynthesis can be thought of as opposite processes. Energy flows in opposite directions in the two processes.

Complete the table using the words below. Some cells have been completed for you. Some words may be used more than once.

carbon dioxide	energy release	mitochondria	water

	Photosynthesis	**Cellular Respiration**
Function	energy capture	
Location	chloroplasts	
Reactants		glucose; oxygen
Products	oxygen; glucose	

Use the table to answer the questions.

1. Which process releases energy for the cell? Circle the correct answer.

   cellular respiration   photosynthesis

2. For which reaction is $6CO_2 + 6H_2O \rightarrow C_6H_{12}O_6 + 6O_2$ the correct equation? Circle the correct answer.

   cellular respiration   photosynthesis

3. How do the products of photosynthesis compare to the reactants of cellular respiration?

   _____

© Pearson Education, Inc., publishing as Pearson Prentice Hall.

Chapter 9 Cellular Respiration

Vocabulary Review

Matching   *In the space provided, write the letter of the definition that best matches each term.*

_____ **1.** anaerobic

_____ **2.** aerobic

_____ **3.** calorie

_____ **4.** cellular respiration

a. process that releases energy by breaking down food in the presence of oxygen

b. amount of energy needed to raise the temperature of 1 g of water 1°C

c. chemical process that does not require oxygen

d. chemical process that requires oxygen

Matching   *In the space provided, write the letter of the definition that best matches each term.*

_____ **5.** fermentation

_____ **6.** glycolysis

_____ **7.** Krebs cycle

_____ **8.** NAD⁺

a. electron carrier of glycolysis

b. process that releases energy from food molecules when no oxygen is present

c. stage of cellular respiration in which pyruvic acid is broken down into carbon dioxide in a series of energy-extracting reactions

d. process in which glucose is broken down into two molecules of pyruvic acid

© Pearson Education, Inc., publishing as Pearson Prentice Hall.

Chapter 10   Cell Growth and Division

Summary

10–1 Cell Growth

In most cases, living things grow by producing more cells. There are two main reasons why cells divide:

1. **The larger a cell gets, the more demands it places on its DNA.**

2. **As a cell gets larger, it has more trouble moving enough nutrients (food) and wastes across its cell membrane.** The rates at which materials move through the cell membrane depend on the cell's surface area—the total area of its cell membrane. However, the rate at which food and oxygen are used up and waste products are formed depends on the cell's volume. As a cell grows, its volume increases faster than its surface area. That is, as a cell becomes larger, its ratio of surface area to volume decreases.

Before a cell gets too large, it divides, forming two "daughter" cells. **Cell division** is the process by which a cell divides into two new daughter cells.

10–2 Cell Division

A cell must copy its genetic information before cell division begins. Each daughter cell then gets a complete copy of that information.

- In most prokaryotes, the rest of cell division is a simple matter of separating the contents of the cell into two parts.
- In eukaryotes, cell division occurs in two main stages, mitosis and cytokinesis. **Mitosis** is the division of the nucleus. **Cytokinesis** is the division of the cytoplasm.

The **cell cycle** is a series of events cells go through as they grow and divide. **During the cell cycle, a cell grows, prepares for division, and divides to form two daughter cells. Each daughter cell then begins the cycle again.** The phases of the cell cycle include interphase and cell division.

- **Interphase** is divided into three phases: G_1, S, and G_2.
  - During the G_1 phase, cells increase in size and make new proteins and organelles.
  - In the S phase, replication (copying) of chromosomes takes place.
  - During the G_2 phase, many of the organelles and molecules needed for cell division are produced.
- The M phase, or cell division includes mitosis and cytokinesis.

© Pearson Education, Inc., publishing as Pearson Prentice Hall.

Biologists divide the events of mitosis into four phases: prophase, metaphase, anaphase, and telophase.

1. **Prophase.** During prophase, the chromosomes condense and become visible. There are two tiny structures located in the cytoplasm near the nuclear envelope. These structures are called centrioles. The centrioles separate and move to opposite sides of the nucleus. The spindle is a structure that helps move chromosomes apart. During prophase, the chromosomes attach to fibers in the spindle. At the end of prophase, the nuclear envelope breaks down.

2. **Metaphase.** During metaphase, chromosomes line up across the center of the cell. The centromere of each chromosome attaches to the spindle.

3. **Anaphase.** During anaphase, the centromeres joining the sister chromatids split. The sister chromotids become individual chromosomes. The two sets of chromosomes move apart.

4. **Telophase.** During telophase, the chromosomes move to opposite ends of the cell. They lose their distinct shapes. Two new nuclear envelopes form.

Cytokinesis usually occurs at the same time as telophase. In most animal cells, the cell membrane pinches the cytoplasm into two nearly equal parts. In plant cells, a cell plate forms midway between the divided nuclei. A cell wall then begins to form in the cell plate.

10–3 Regulating the Cell Cycle

In a multicellular organism, cell growth and cell division are carefully controlled. For instance, when an injury such as a cut in the skin occurs, cells at the edge of the cut divide rapidly. When the healing process is nearly complete, the rate of cell division slows and then returns to normal.

Cyclins—a group of proteins—regulate the timing of the cell cycle in eukaryotic cells. Cyclins are one group of proteins involved in cell cycle regulation. Other proteins, called regulatory proteins, regulate the cell cycle in different ways.

Controls on cell growth can be turned on and off by the body. **Cancer** is a disorder in which some of the body's cells lose the ability to control growth. **Cancer cells do not respond to the signals that control the growth of most cells.** As a result, cancer cells divide uncontrollably. Cancer cells do not stop growing when they touch other cells. Instead, they continue to grow and divide until their supply of nutrients is used up.

© Pearson Education, Inc., publishing as Pearson Prentice Hall.

Surface Area and Volume

Use what you know about surface area and volume to complete the table.

Cell	1 cm, 1 cm, 1 cm	3 cm, 3 cm, 3 cm
What is the surface area? (length × width × 6)	__cm × __cm × 6 = __cm²	__cm × __cm × 6 = __ cm²
What is the volume? (length × width × height)	__cm × __cm × __cm = __cm³	__cm × __cm × __cm = __ cm³

Use the table to answer the questions.

1. Suppose you had enough smaller cells to fill the larger cell. What would their combined surface area be?

   _____ smaller cells × _____ cm² for one cell =

   _____ cm² total

2. Which has a greater surface area? Circle the best answer.

   one large cell   27 smaller cells

© Pearson Education, Inc., publishing as Pearson Prentice Hall.

Cell Cycle

Cell growth and division occur in a regular cycle. This cycle is divided into four phases: G_1, S, G_2, and M. The diagram shows this cycle, along with events that occur in each phase.

Follow the prompts below.
- Color the phase in which most cell growth occurs blue.
- Color the phase in which DNA replication occurs red.
- Color the phase in which preparation for mitosis occurs yellow.
- Color the phase in which mitosis and cytokinesis occur orange.

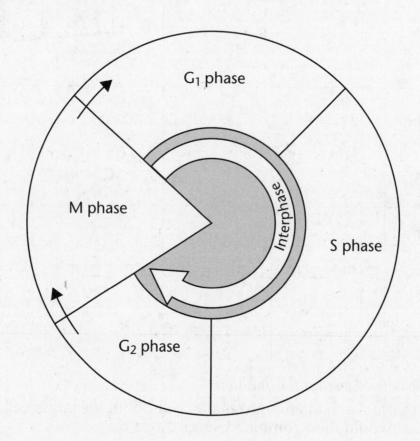

Use the diagram to answer the questions.

1. Which three phases make up interphase?

_____

2. Many organelles and molecules needed for cell division are formed after DNA replication and before mitosis. In which phase are they formed?

_____

© Pearson Education, Inc., publishing as Pearson Prentice Hall.

Mitosis

Mitosis is the process by which the nucleus of most eukaryotic cells divides. Mitosis has four phases: prophase, metaphase, anaphase, and telophase.

Color each chromosome in prophase a different color. Follow each of these chromosomes through mitosis. Show this by coloring the correct structures in each phase of mitosis.

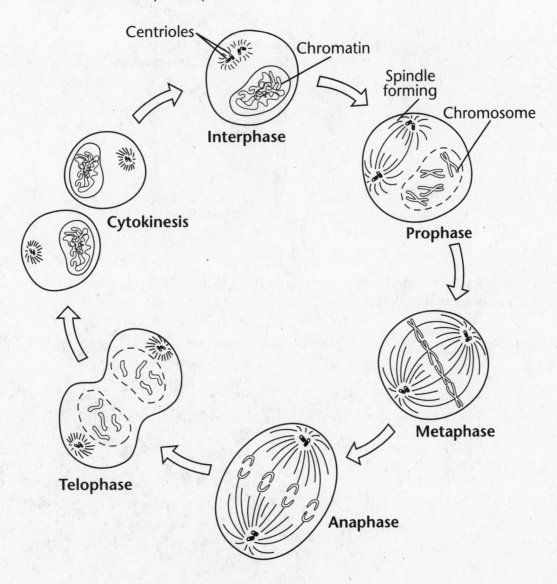

Use the diagram to answer the questions.

1. In which phase do the chromosomes line up in the middle of

   the cell? _____

2. In which process are two daughter cells formed?

_____

© Pearson Education, Inc., publishing as Pearson Prentice Hall.

Cytokinesis

Cytokinesis is the final step of cell division. During cytokinesis in plant cells, a cell plate forms between the two daughter cells.

The diagram shows plant cytokinesis in progress.

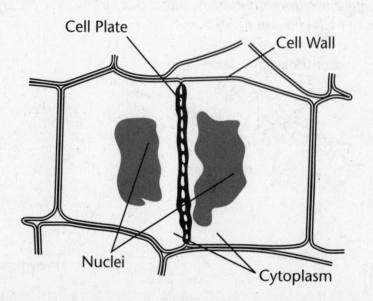

In the space provided below, draw how the cells will look when cytokinesis is complete.

Use the diagram to answer the questions. Circle the correct answer.

1. What structure forms in the cell plate?

   cell wall   cytoplasm

2. What divides during cytokinesis?

   cytoplasm   nucleus

© Pearson Education, Inc., publishing as Pearson Prentice Hall.

Controls on Cell Division

When cells come in contact with one another, molecules on their surfaces signal them to stop growing. This prevents cells from growing uncontrollably and disrupting nearby tissues.

Circle the dish(es) in which cells would be stimulated to grow. Mark an X over the dish(es) in which cells would not be growing.

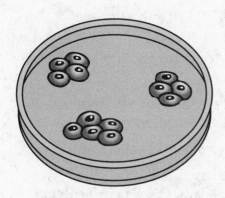

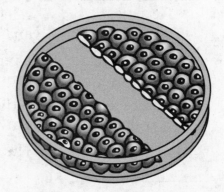

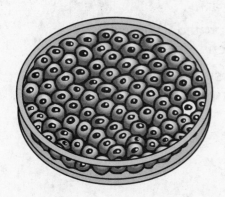

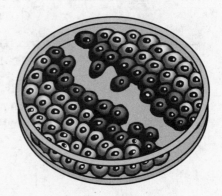

Answer the questions.

1. What happens when there is a gap between two groups of cells?

_____

2. Which of the following best describes cancer? Circle the correct answer.

uncontrolled cell growth   cells stop growing

© Pearson Education, Inc., publishing as Pearson Prentice Hall.

Chapter 10 Cell Growth and Division

Vocabulary Review

True or False *If the statement is true, write* true. *If it is false, write* false.

_____ 1. One of two identical "sister" parts of a copied chromosome is called a chromatid.

_____ 2. The final phase of mitosis in which the nuclear envelope re-forms is called anaphase.

_____ 3. Division of the cytoplasm takes place during prophase.

_____ 4. A disorder in which some of the body's cells grow uncontrollably is called cancer.

_____ 5. The first phase of mitosis is called prophase.

_____ 6. The part of the cell cycle in which the cell grows and replicates its DNA is interphase.

_____ 7. The third stage of mitosis during which the sister chromatids separate and become individual chromosomes is cytokinesis.

_____ 8. The division of the cell nucleus occurs during interphase.

_____ 9. A tiny structure located in the cytoplasm near the nuclear envelope is a centriole.

_____ 10. The stage of mitosis in which the chromosomes line up across the center of the cell is metaphase.

© Pearson Education, Inc., publishing as Pearson Prentice Hall.

Chapter 11   Introduction to Genetics

Summary

11–1 The Work of Gregor Mendel

Every living thing inherits traits, or characteristics, from its parents. People have long wondered how these traits are passed from one generation to the next. **Genetics** is the scientific study of heredity.

Gregor Mendel did experiments with pea plants to study inheritance. Pea plants are usually self-pollinating, meaning that sperm cells fertilize egg cells in the same flower. The pea plants he studied were true-breeding. **True-breeding** plants produce offspring identical to themselves.

Mendel wanted seeds that inherited traits from two different parent plants. He crossed two plants with different forms of the same trait. A **trait** is a specific characteristic, such as height or seed color. Mendel then grew plants from the seeds formed by each cross. These plants were hybrids. **Hybrids** are the offspring of crosses between parents with different traits. The first generation of a cross is called the F_1 generation. The second generation is called F_2, and so on.

Each group of Mendel's hybrid plants looked like only one of its parents. In one case, all of the offspring were tall. In another, all of the offspring had yellow seeds. From these results, Mendel drew two conclusions:

- Biological inheritance is determined by factors that are passed from one generation to the next. These factors are called **genes.** One gene with two different forms controlled each trait. Each form of the gene is called an **allele.**
- Mendel also formed the **principle of dominance, which states that some alleles are dominant and others are recessive.** A living thing with a dominant allele, for a trait always shows the trait. Recessive alleles are not seen if the dominant allele is present.

Mendel wondered what happened to the recessive allele. To find out, he let the F_1 plants self-pollinate. Some of F_2 plants showed the recessive trait. The recessive alleles had not disappeared. Instead, the dominant allele had masked them. From this, Mendel concluded that **when each F_1 plant flowers and produces gametes, or sex cells, the two alleles segregate, or separate, from each other. As a result, each gamete carries only a single copy of each gene. Therefore, each F_1 plant produces two types of gametes—those with the allele for tallness and those with the allele for shortness.**

© Pearson Education, Inc., publishing as Pearson Prentice Hall.

11–2 Probability and Punnett Squares

Probability is the likelihood that a specific event will occur. **The principles of probability can be used to predict the outcomes of genetic crosses.** This is because the ways in which alleles segregate is completely random. There are two important points to remember with probabilities:

- Past outcomes do not affect future events.
- Probabilities predict the average outcome of many events. They do not predict what will happen in a single event. Therefore, the more trials there are, the closer the numbers will get to the predicted values.

Punnett squares are diagrams that model genetic crosses. **Punnett squares can be used to predict and compare the genetic variations that will result from a cross.** They help predict the chances an offspring will be **homozygous** or **heterozygous** for a trait.

- Organisms that have two identical alleles for a particular trait are called **homozygous.**
- Organisms that have two different alleles for the same trait are called **heterozygous.**

11–3 Exploring Mendelian Genetics

Mendel wondered if genes that determine different traits affect one another. He did an experiment to find out. Mendel found that the gene for seed shape did not affect how the gene for seed color sorted. He summarized his conclusions as the principle of **independent assortment. The principle of independent assortment states that genes for different traits can segregate independently during the formation of gametes. Independent assortment helps account for the many genetic variations observed in plants, animals, and other organisms.**

Not all genes show simple patterns of dominant and recessive alleles. **Some alleles are neither dominant nor recessive, and many traits are controlled by multiple alleles or multiple genes.** Some of these patterns are described below.

- In **incomplete dominance,** one allele is not completely dominant over another.
- In **codominance,** both alleles appear as part of the phenotype of the heterozygous offspring.
- Genes that have more than two alleles are said to have **multiple alleles.**
- A single trait can be controlled by more than one gene. These are called **polygenic traits.**

Genes do not control all characteristics. Some are due to interactions between genes and the environment.

© Pearson Education, Inc., publishing as Pearson Prentice Hall.

11–4 Meiosis

Living things inherit a single copy of each gene from each parent. These copies are separated when gametes form. The process in which this happens is called **meiosis. Meiosis is a process in which the number of chromosomes per cell is divided in half through the separation of homologous chromosomes in a diploid cell.**

- A cell that has both sets of homologous chromosomes is said to be diploid. **Diploid** means "two sets."
- Gametes have half the number of chromosomes as their parent cells. Cells that have only one set of chromosomes are said to be **haploid.** Gametes are genetically different from the parent cell and from one another.

Before meiosis begins, cells undergo DNA replication forming duplicate chromosomes. Meiosis then occurs in two stages.

Meiosis I:
- Two cells form.
- Each cell has sets of chromosomes and alleles that are different from each other and from the original cell.

Meiosis II:
- The cells divide again, but this time the DNA is not copied first.
- Four daughter cells form.
- Each daughter cell contains half the number of chromosomes as the original cell.

Although they sound the same, meiosis and mitosis are different. **Mitosis makes two identical cells. These cells are exactly like the parent cell. Meiosis, however, forms four cells. Each cell has only half the number of chromosomes as the parent cell. The cells are also genetically different from one another.**

11–5 Linkage and Gene Maps

Some genes are usually inherited together. These genes are linked. A chromosome is a group of linked genes. **When gametes form, it is the chromosomes that sort independently, not individual genes.** The location of genes on a chromosome can be determined by studying crossover events. The farther apart two genes are, the more likely they will be separated by crossover events. Scientists collect data on how often crossing-over separates certain genes. These data are used to find the distance between the genes on a chromosome. Scientists can then make a **gene map** of the chromosome.

© Pearson Education, Inc., publishing as Pearson Prentice Hall.

Dominance

Mendel's principle of dominance states that some alleles are dominant and others are recessive. An organism with a dominant allele will show the dominant form of the trait. An organism will only express the recessive form of a trait when a dominant allele is not present.

In the space provided, fill in the genotype of the offspring. The first one has been done for you.

Dominant and Recessive Forms of Pea Plant Traits			
Trait	Parent Plants (P Generation)		Offspring (F₁ Generation)
Seed Color	Yellow YY	Green yy	Yellow Yy
Seed Coat Color	White gg	Gray GG	Gray ___
Pod Shape	Constricted ss	Smooth SS	Smooth ___
Pod Color	Green CC	Yellow cc	Green ___
Plant Height	Tall TT	Short tt	Tall ___

Use the table to answer the questions. Circle the correct answer.

1. What is the dominant shape of a pea pod?

   constricted   smooth

2. What is the recessive color of a pea plant's seed coat?

   white   gray

© Pearson Education, Inc., publishing as Pearson Prentice Hall.

Homozygous or Heterozygous?

Homozygous organisms have two identical alleles for a particular trait. Heterozygous organisms have two different alleles for the same trait.

Color the homozygous recessive plant yellow. Color the homozygous dominant plant red. Color the heterozygous plant orange. In the space provided, fill in the missing genotype.

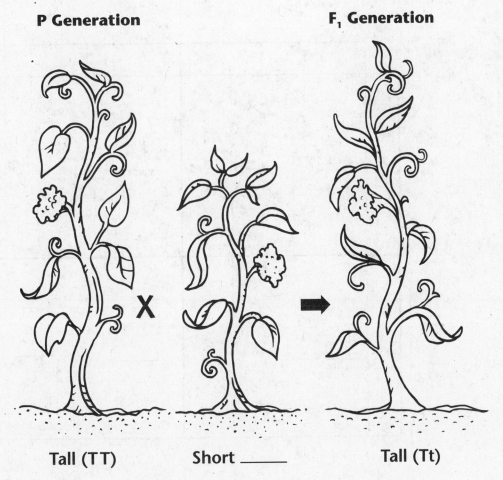

P Generation   **F₁ Generation**

Tall (TT)   Short _____   Tall (Tt)

Use the diagram to answer the questions.

1. Does the tall offspring plant look like the tall parent plant? Explain.

_____

_____

2. Why did you color the offspring plant a different color than the tall parent plant?

_____

_____

© Pearson Education, Inc., publishing as Pearson Prentice Hall.

F₂ Generation Punnett Square

In the space provided, fill in the missing genotypes as either Tt or tt. In this example, T = tall and t = short.

Tt

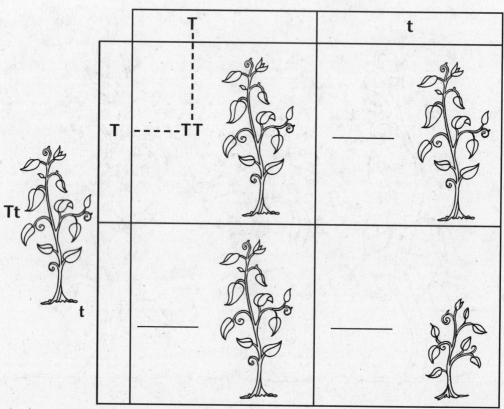

Use the Punnett square to answer the questions.

1. Write the phenotypes of the three genotypes shown above.

TT _____   tt _____

Tt _____

2. If two heterozygous plants create four offspring, how many do you predict would be tall? How many do you predict would be short?

_____

_____

© Pearson Education, Inc., publishing as Pearson Prentice Hall.

Meiosis

At the beginning of meiosis, two homologous chromosomes pair
up. These two homologous chromosomes are separated during
meiosis I.

*Look at the labeled pair of homologous chromosomes in the original cell.
Color one chromosome red. Color the other chromosome blue. Follow
these two chromosomes through meiosis. Show this by coloring the
correct structures in the cells that result from meiosis I and II.*

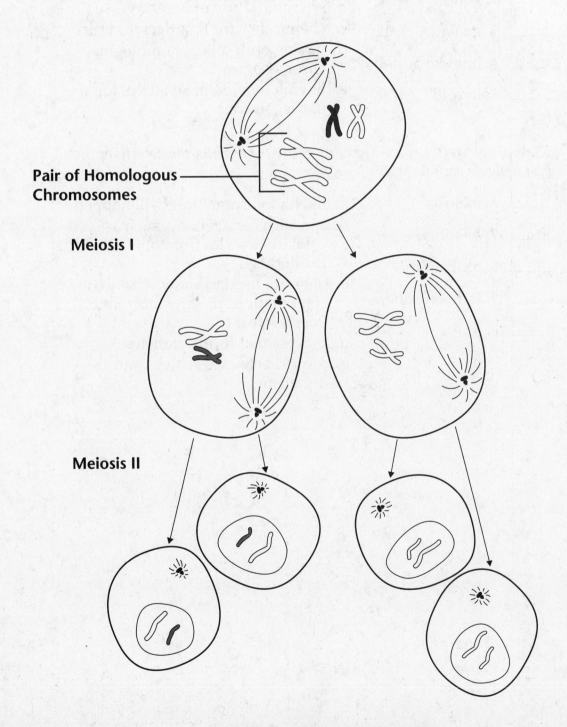

Pair of Homologous Chromosomes

Meiosis I

Meiosis II

© Pearson Education, Inc., publishing as Pearson Prentice Hall.

Chapter 11   Introduction to Genetics

Vocabulary Review

Matching   *In the space provided, write the letter of the definition that best matches each term.*

_____ **1.** diploid

_____ **2.** gene

_____ **3.** genetics

_____ **4.** homozygous

_____ **5.** hybrid

a. offspring of crosses between parents with different traits

b. scientific study of heredity

c. chemical factor that decides traits

d. having both sets of homologous chromosomes

e. having two identical alleles for a particular trait

Matching   *In the space provided, write the letter of the definition that best matches each term.*

_____ **6.** meiosis

_____ **7.** phenotype

_____ **8.** probability

_____ **9.** Punnett square

_____ **10.** trait

a. likelihood something will happen

b. specific characteristic, such as seed color, that varies from one individual to another

c. diagram used to show what gene combinations may result from a genetic cross

d. process that forms gametes

e. physical characteristics of an organism

© Pearson Education, Inc., publishing as Pearson Prentice Hall.

Chapter 12   DNA and RNA

Summary

12–1 DNA

To understand genetics, biologists had to learn the chemical makeup of the gene. Scientists discovered that genes are made of DNA. **Scientists also found that DNA stores and transmits the genetic information from one generation of an organism to the next.** Scientists began studying DNA structure to find out how it carries information, decides traits, and replicates itself.

- DNA is a long molecule made up of units called **nucleotides.** Each nucleotide is made up of a 5-carbon sugar, a phosphate group, and a nitrogen-containing base.
- There are four kinds of bases: adenine (A), guanine (G), cytosine (C), and thymine (T).

Watson and Crick made a three-dimensional model of DNA. Their model was a double helix, in which two strands were wound around each other. A double helix is like a twisted ladder. Sugar and phosphates make up the sides of the ladder. Hydrogen bonds between the bases hold the strands together. Bonds form only between certain base pairs: between adenine and thymine, and between guanine and cytosine. This is called **base pairing.**

12–2 Chromosomes and DNA Replication

Most prokaryotes have one large DNA molecule in their cytoplasm. Eukaryotes have DNA in chromosomes in their nuclei. Before a cell divides, it copies its DNA in a process called **replication. During DNA replication,**

- **the DNA molecule separates into two strands. Each strand of the DNA molecule serves as a model for the new strand.**
- Following the rules of base pairing, new bases are added to each strand. For example, if the base on the original strand is adenine, thymine is added to the newly forming strand. Likewise, cytosine is always added to guanine.
- The end result is two identical strands.

© Pearson Education, Inc., publishing as Pearson Prentice Hall.

12-3 RNA and Protein Synthesis

For a gene to work, the genetic instructions in the DNA molecule must be decoded. The first step is to copy the DNA sequence into RNA. RNA is a molecule which contains instructions for making proteins. RNA is similar to DNA, except for three differences:
- The sugar in RNA is ribose instead of deoxyribose.
- RNA is single-stranded.
- RNA has uracil in place of thymine.

Most RNA molecules are involved in making proteins. **There are three main kinds of RNA:**
- **Messenger RNA** has the instructions for joining amino acids to make a protein.
- Proteins are assembled on ribosomes. Ribosomes are made up of proteins and **ribosomal RNA.**
- **Transfer RNA** carries each amino acid to the ribosome according to the coded message in messenger RNA.

RNA is copied from DNA in a process called **transcription**. **During transcription:**
- **The enzyme RNA polymerase binds to DNA and separates the two DNA strands.**
- **RNA polymerase builds a strand of RNA using one strand of DNA as the template.**
- The DNA is transcribed into RNA following base-pairing rules except that uracil binds to adenine.

The directions for making proteins are in the order of the four nitrogenous bases. This code is read three letters at a time. Each **codon,** or group of three nucleotides, stands for an amino acid. Some amino acids are specified by more than one codon. One codon is a start signal for translation. Three codons signal the end of a protein.

Translation is the process in which the cell uses information from messenger RNA to make proteins. Translation takes place on ribosomes.
- Before translation can begin, messenger RNA is transcribed from DNA.
- The messenger RNA moves into the cytoplasm and attaches to a ribosome.
- As each codon of the messenger RNA moves through the ribosome, the proper amino acid is brought into the ribosome by transfer RNA. The ribosome joins together each amino acid. In this way, the protein chain grows.
- When the ribosome reaches a stop codon, it releases the newly formed polypeptide and the process of translation is complete.

© Pearson Education, Inc., publishing as Pearson Prentice Hall.

12–4 Mutations

Mutations are mistakes made when cells copy their own DNA. Mutations are changes in the genetic material of a cell.

- Gene mutations are changes in a single gene. A **point mutation** occurs at a single point in the DNA sequence of a gene. When a point mutation causes one base to replace another, only one amino acid is affected. If a nucleotide is added or removed, it causes a **frameshift mutation.** All the groupings of codons are changed. This can cause the gene to make a completely different protein.
- In a chromosome mutation, there is a change in the number or the structure of chromosomes. There are four kinds of chromosomal mutations: *deletions, duplications, inversions,* and *translocations.*

12–5 Gene Regulation

Genes can be turned on and off as different proteins are needed. In prokaryotes, some genes are turned on and off by a chromosome section called an operon. An **operon** is a group of genes that work, or operate, together. In bacteria, one operon controls whether the organism can use the sugar lactose as food. It is called the *lac* operon. **The *lac* genes are turned off by repressors and turned on by the presence of lactose.** Operators and promoters are DNA sequences in the operon that control when genes are turned on and off.

- When the cell needs a certain protein, RNA polymerase attaches to the promoter and makes a messenger RNA that is translated into the needed protein.
- When the cell no longer needs the protein, it makes another protein called the repressor. The repressor attaches to the operator. This blocks the promoter so RNA polymerase cannot attach to it. This turns the genes of the operon off.

Most eukaryotic genes are controlled individually and have regulatory sequences that are much more complex than those of the *lac* operon. In eukaryotes, genes are regulated by enhancer sequences located before the point at which transcription begins. Some proteins can bind directly to these DNA sequences. Ways in which these proteins affect transcription include:

- increasing the transcription of certain genes
- attracting RNA polymerase
- blocking access to genes

© Pearson Education, Inc., publishing as Pearson Prentice Hall.

Genetic Material

The Hershey-Chase experiment was designed to find out whether DNA or protein carried a virus's genetic information. The scientists used radioactive substances to label the DNA in some viruses and the protein coat in other viruses. Then they let the viruses inject their genetic material into bacteria.

Label the DNA with radioactive label, *and the* DNA without radioactive label.

DNA with radioactive label

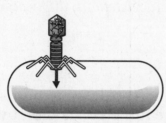 

Phage infects bacteria

_____

Protein coat with radioactive label

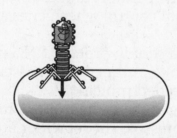 

Phage infects bacteria

_____

Use the diagram to answer the question. Circle the best answer.

1. What did Hershey and Chase conclude was the genetic material of the virus?

   DNA   protein

© Pearson Education, Inc., publishing as Pearson Prentice Hall.

Base Pairing

Four nucleotides make up DNA: adenine, cytosine, guanine, and thymine. These nucleotides always occur in pairs called base pairs.

Write the missing letter to complete each base pair. The first two have been done for you.

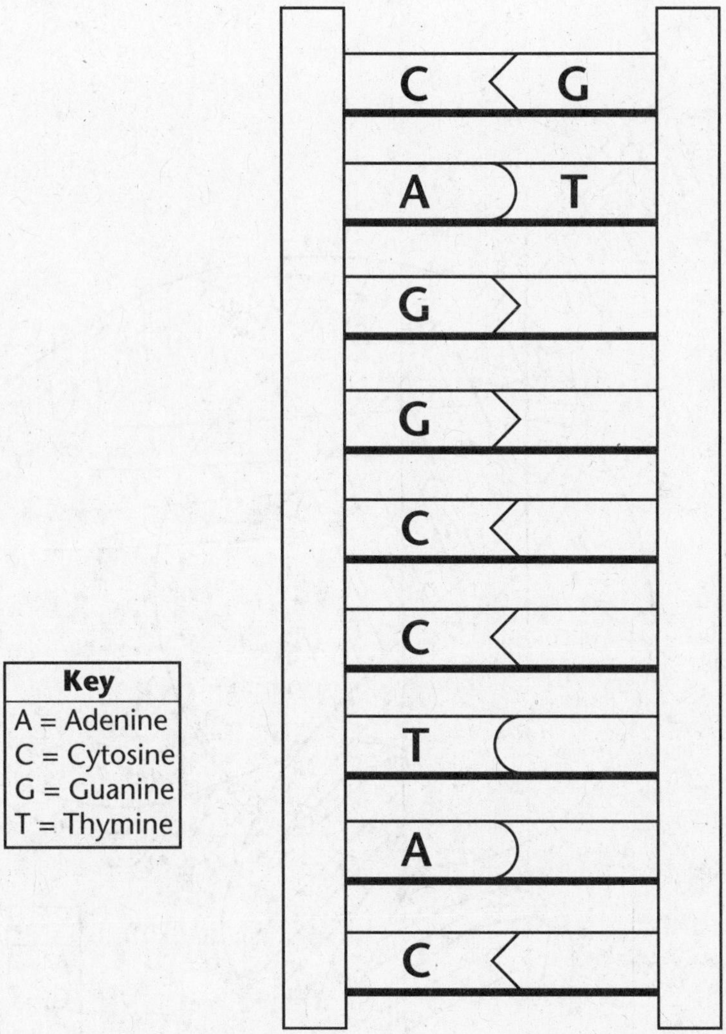

Key
A = Adenine
C = Cytosine
G = Guanine
T = Thymine

Use the diagram to answer the questions.

1. What nucleotide is always paired with thymine?

_____

2. What nucleotide is always paired with guanine?

_____

© Pearson Education, Inc., publishing as Pearson Prentice Hall.

Transcription

In transcription, RNA polymerase splits the two halves of a strand of DNA. RNA then uses one half as a template to make a copy of the other half. RNA contains the nucleotide uracil instead of the nucleotide thymine.

Label the DNA *and* RNA. *Then, label the missing nucleotides marked on the diagram.*

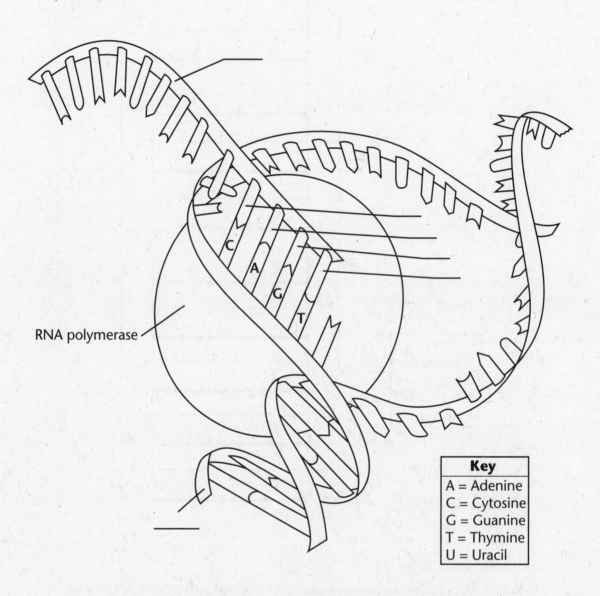

RNA polymerase

Key
A = Adenine
C = Cytosine
G = Guanine
T = Thymine
U = Uracil

Use the diagram to answer the question. Circle the correct answer.

1. In RNA, which nucleotide is always paired with uracil?

adenine   guanine

© Pearson Education, Inc., publishing as Pearson Prentice Hall.

Comparing DNA Replication and Transcription

DNA replication is the process by which a cell copies its DNA. During replication, both strands of the double helix are used as templates to make complementary, or matching, strands of DNA. DNA transcription is the process by which a single strand of DNA is used as a template to generate a strand of mRNA.

Fill in the missing information. One row has been completed for you.

Template DNA	Complementary DNA	Messenger RNA (mRNA)
TTACG	AATGC	AAUGC
	GGCGG	
		ACGUAGC
AGACTC		
	GATAAGA	
		CUGGCUAC

Use the table to answer the question.

1. Give another example of a template DNA code that is at least four base pairs long. Then, give its matching complementary DNA and mRNA codes.

_____

_____

© Pearson Education, Inc., publishing as Pearson Prentice Hall.

Decoding mRNA

The diagram shows the mRNA codes that correspond to amino acids and stop codons. Read the diagram from the center outwards. For example, the mRNA code UAC corresponds to the amino acid tyrosine.

Write the name of the amino acid that corresponds to each mRNA code. The first one has been done for you.

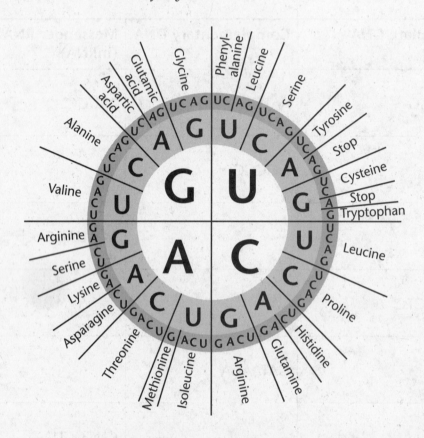

mRNA Code	Amino Acid
AAA	lysine
GCG	
GAU	
CAA	

Use the diagram to answer the questions.

1. Which two mRNA codes correspond to histidine?

_____

2. How many different mRNA codes correspond to arginine?

_____

© Pearson Education, Inc., publishing as Pearson Prentice Hall.

Translation

During translation, transfer RNA (tRNA) anticodons match to messenger RNA (mRNA) codons. Each tRNA molecule can carry one particular amino acid. The amino acids are joined to form a polypeptide.

Number the four tRNA anticodons in the order in which they should appear to match the codons in the mRNA strand.

mRNA

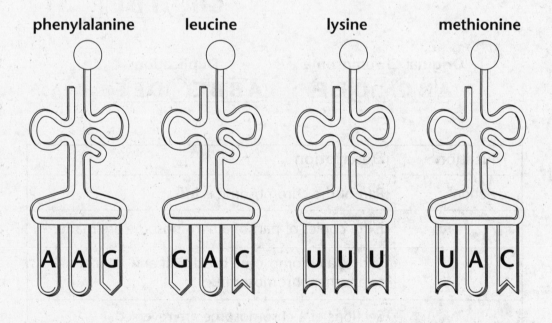

phenylalanine   leucine   lysine   methionine

A A G   G A C   U U U   U A C

_____   _____   _____   _____

Use the diagrams to answer the question.

1. List the amino acids in the order they would appear in the polypeptide coded for by the mRNA.

_____

_____

© Pearson Education, Inc., publishing as Pearson Prentice Hall.

Chromosomal Mutations

Each diagram represents a possible mutation of the chromosome shown below. Use the diagrams and descriptions below to help you complete the table. One row has been completed for you.

Original Chromosome (A B C D E F)

Deletion (A C D E F)

Original Chromosome (A B C D E F)

Inversion (A E D C B F)

Original Chromosome (A B C D E F)

Translocation (A B C J K L) (G H I D E F)

Original Chromosome (A B C D E F)

Duplication (A B B C D E F)

Mutation	Description
deletion	Part of the chromosome is lost.
	Extra copies of part of a chromosome are made.
	Part of a chromosome breaks off and attaches to another chromosome.
	Sections of a chromosome are reversed.

Use the table to answer the question.

1. Which types of mutation can add genes to a chromosome?

_____

_____

© Pearson Education, Inc., publishing as Pearson Prentice Hall.

Gene Regulation

Repressors are proteins that bind to areas of DNA called operators. They prevent RNA polymerase from transcribing the genes on the DNA strand. The diagram shows how repressors work with *lac* genes in the *E. coli* bacterium. The *lac* genes are turned on when lactose is present.

Label the repressor, operators, *and* genes *in each diagram.*

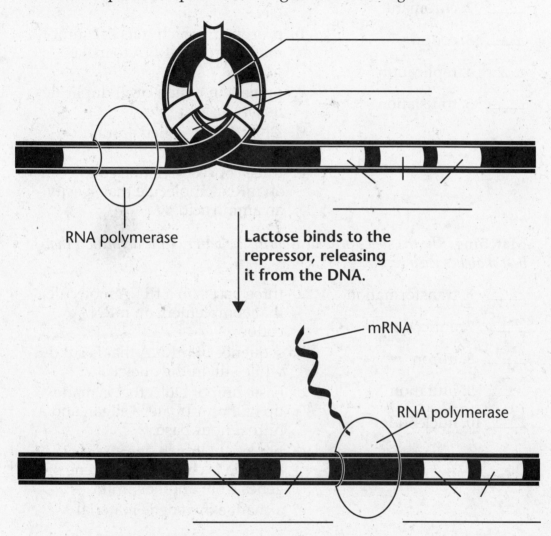

RNA polymerase

Lactose binds to the repressor, releasing it from the DNA.

mRNA

RNA polymerase

Use the diagram to answer the questions.

1. In which strand is a repressor present?

_____

_____

2. In which strand is transcription occurring?

_____

_____

Chapter 12   DNA and RNA

Vocabulary Review

Matching   *In the space provided, write the letter of the definition that best matches each term.*

_____ **1.** transcription

_____ **2.** chromatin

_____ **3.** codon

_____ **4.** replication

_____ **5.** translation

a. process in which an mRNA molecule is made by copying DNA

b. process in which cells use information from mRNA to make proteins

c. process in which a cell duplicates its DNA

d. DNA tightly coiled around proteins

e. three consecutive nucleotides on an mRNA molecule that specify an amino acid

Matching   *In the space provided, write the letter of the definition that best matches each term.*

_____ **6.** transformation

_____ **7.** anticodon

_____ **8.** intron

_____ **9.** mutation

_____ **10.** nucleotide

a. three bases on a tRNA molecule that complement an mRNA codon

b. sequence of mRNA that is cut out while still in the nucleus

c. basic unit of DNA that is made up of a phosphate, a sugar, and a nitrogenous base

d. process in which one strain of bacteria is changed by a gene or genes from another strain

e. a change in genetic material

© Pearson Education, Inc., publishing as Pearson Prentice Hall.

Chapter 13 Genetic Engineering

Summary

13–1 Changing the Living World

For thousands of years, people have bred animals and plants that have desired traits. This technique is called **selective breeding**. **Humans use selective breeding, which takes advantage of naturally occurring genetic variation, to pass desired traits on to the next generation of organisms.**

- Hybridization is a tool used by selective breeders. In **hybridization**, individuals with different traits are crossed. The goal is to produce offspring that have the best traits of both parents. These offspring, called hybrids, are often hardier than the parents.
- Breeders use inbreeding to maintain a group of plants or animals with desired traits. In **inbreeding**, individuals with similar traits are crossed. A disadvantage of inbreeding is the risk of bringing together two recessive alleles for a genetic defect.

Selective breeding would be nearly impossible without many variations in traits. **Breeders can increase the genetic variation in a population by inducing mutations.** Mutations are inheritable changes in DNA. Mutations do occur naturally. However, breeders can boost the rate of mutation through use of radiation and chemicals. Many mutations are harmful. However, with luck, breeders can produce useful mutations.

13–2 Manipulating DNA

To increase variation, scientists can make changes directly to DNA. *Genetic engineering* is the intentional changing of an organism's DNA. **Scientist use their knowledge of the structure of DNA and its chemical properties to study and change DNA molecules.**

- **Extracting DNA.** Scientists can extract, or separate, DNA from the other cell parts using a chemical procedure.
- **Cutting DNA.** Scientists can cut DNA into smaller pieces using restriction enzymes.
- **Separating DNA.** Scientists use **gel electrophoresis**, a method in which DNA fragments are put at one end of a porous gel. When an electric current is applied to the gel, DNA molecules move toward the positive end of the gel. This technique allows scientists to compare the gene composition of different organisms or different individuals.

© Pearson Education, Inc., publishing as Pearson Prentice Hall.

Scientists also use different techniques to read, change, and copy the DNA sequence.

- Scientists can read the order of nucleotide bases in a DNA fragment. They make a copy of a single strand of DNA with colored nucleotides inserted at random places. Reading the order of colored bands in a gel gives the nucleotide sequence of the DNA fragment.
- Scientists can change DNA sequences. Short sequences of DNA made in the laboratory can be joined to the DNA molecule of an organism. DNA from one organism can be attached to the DNA of another organism. These DNA molecules are called **recombinant DNA** because combining DNA from different sources makes them.
- Scientists often need many copies of a certain gene to study it. A technique called **polymerase chain reaction** (PCR) allows scientists to do that. PCR is a chain reaction in which DNA copies become templates to make more DNA copies.

13–3 Cell Transformation

DNA fragments do not work by themselves. They must be part of the DNA molecule in an organism. **During transformation, a cell takes in DNA from outside the cell. This external DNA becomes a component of the cell's DNA.** Bacterial, plant, and animal cells can be transformed.

To add DNA fragments to bacteria, the fragment is placed in a plasmid. A **plasmid** is a small, circular DNA molecule that occurs naturally in some bacteria. These plasmids with added DNA fragments are recombinant DNA. The plasmids are mixed in a solution with other bacteria. Some of the bacteria take up the plasmids. These bacteria are transformed.

Plant cells can be transformed in several ways.

- Some plant cells in culture can take up DNA on their own. These plant cells have had their cell walls removed.
- Scientists can also insert a DNA fragment into a plasmid. This plasmid is transformed into a bacterium that infects plants.
- Scientists can also inject DNA directly into some plant cells.

If transformation is successful, the recombinant DNA is integrated into one of the chromosomes of the cell.

Animal cells can be transformed in ways similar to plant cells. An egg cell may be large enough to inject DNA directly into its nucleus. Once inside, the repair enzymes may help insert the DNA fragment into the chromosomes of the egg.

© Pearson Education, Inc., publishing as Pearson Prentice Hall.

13–4 Applications of Genetic Engineering

Scientists wondered if genes from one organism could work in a different organism. Some scientists isolated the gene from fireflies that allows them to glow. Then they inserted this gene into the DNA of plants. The plants glowed in the dark. This showed that both plants and animals use the same process to translate DNA into proteins. The glowing plant is **transgenic** because it has a gene from another species.

Genetic engineering has spurred the growth of biotechnology, which is changing the way we interact with the living world. Some examples of genetic engineering include:

- Human genes have been added to bacteria. These transgenic bacteria are used to make human proteins such as insulin, human growth hormone, and clotting factor.
- Scientists have made transgenic animals to study the role of genes and to improve the food supply. Transgenic animals may be used to supply us with human proteins that can be collected in the animal's milk.
- Transgenic plants that can make their own insecticide have been formed. Others are resistant to weed killers. Some have been engineered to contain vitamins needed for human health.

A *clone* is a member of a population of genetically identical cells that were produced from a single cell. Clones are useful in making copies of transgenic organisms. It is easy to produce cloned bacteria and plants. Animals are difficult to clone. However, in the 1990s, scientists in Scotland successfully cloned a sheep. Animal cloning has risks. Studies suggest that cloned animals may have genetic defects and other health problems. The use of cloning also raises serious ethical and moral issues.

© Pearson Education, Inc., publishing as Pearson Prentice Hall.

Selective Breeding

In selective breeding, a person decides which traits he or she would like an animal to have. The breeder then chooses a male and female animal that have those traits and breeds them. The breeder expects that they will have offspring with the same traits.

Identify the parents a breeder would select in order to breed offspring with the traits listed.

Female Rabbits   **Male Rabbits**

Offspring Traits	Parents
black fur, floppy ears	3 and 5
white fur, short ears	
black fur, short ears	
white fur, floppy ears	

Use the diagrams and table to answer the question. Circle the correct answer.

1. A breeder breeds rabbits 2 and 8. What trait is the breeder most likely interested in?

     black fur   short ears

© Pearson Education, Inc., publishing as Pearson Prentice Hall.

EcoR I

A restriction enzyme cuts DNA at a specific sequence of nucleotides. The enzyme *Eco*R I cuts a DNA strand when it encounters the nucleotide sequence CTTAAG.

Circle the place(s) on the DNA strands where EcoR I would recognize and cut the DNA. Note: There may be more than one nucleotide sequence on each DNA strand. The first one has been done for you.

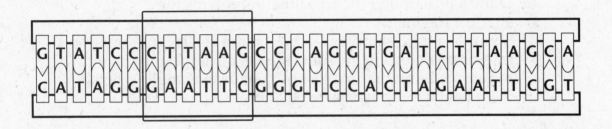

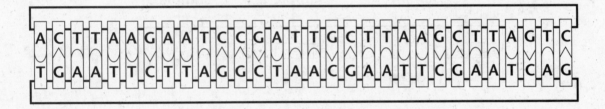

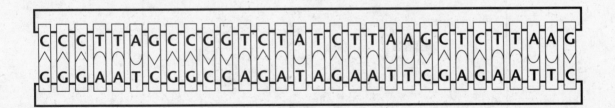

Use the diagram to answer the question. Circle the correct answer.

1. What is the term that describes the sequence of DNA that a restriction enzyme finds and cuts?

recognition sequence   template sequence

© Pearson Education, Inc., publishing as Pearson Prentice Hall.

Gel Electrophoresis

In gel electrophoresis, DNA fragments are placed in wells at one end of a gel. A current is run through the gel. The negatively charged DNA molecules move toward the positive end. The smallest fragments move farthest.

Two DNA samples have been separated on this gel. Follow the prompts to analyze the gel.

- Circle the band that represents the longest fragments.
- Draw a box around the band that represents the shortest fragments.
- Suppose a third sample was run on the gel. It contained fragments that were the same size as the largest fragments in Sample 2 and the smallest fragments in Sample 1. Draw these bands in the lane labeled Sample 3.

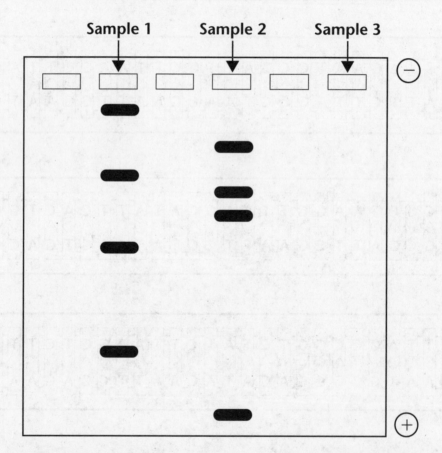

Use the diagram to answer the question. Circle the correct answer.

1. Which of the following best describes how scientists use gel electrophoresis?

cutting DNA   separating DNA

© Pearson Education, Inc., publishing as Pearson Prentice Hall.

Bacterial Transformation

During transformation, plasmids are taken out of bacterial cells. Plasmids are small circular pieces of bacterial DNA. These plasmids are cut using restriction enzymes. A foreign gene is inserted into the plasmids. The plasmids, which are now recombinant DNA, are then inserted into other bacteria cells.

Use the words below to label the diagram.

foreign DNA	recombinant DNA
plasmid	transformed bacterium

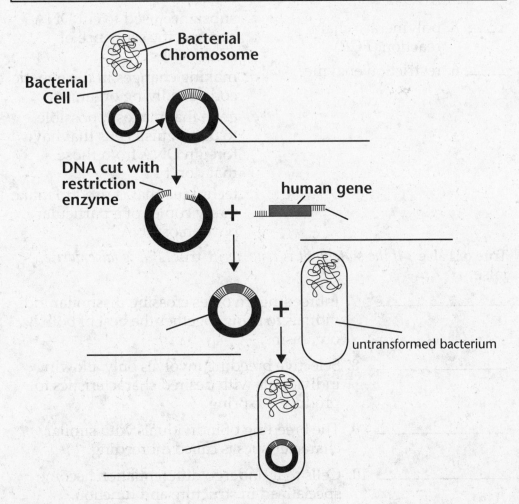

Answer the question.

1. Why might a scientist insert a gene that codes for a human growth hormone into bacteria cells?

_____

_____

© Pearson Education, Inc., publishing as Pearson Prentice Hall.

Chapter 13   Genetic Engineering

Vocabulary Review

Matching   *In the space provided, write the letter of the description that best matches each term.*

_____ **1.** recombinant DNA

_____ **2.** genetic engineering

_____ **3.** genetic marker

_____ **4.** gel electrophoresis

_____ **5.** polymerase chain reaction (PCR)

_____ **6.** restriction enzyme

a. technique that uses electric voltage and a gel to separate and analyze DNA fragments

b. molecule produced by combining DNA from two different sources

c. substance used to cut DNA at a specific sequence of nucleotides

d. making changes in the genetic code of a living organism

e. gene that makes it possible to distinguish cells that have foreign DNA from those that don't

f. technique that is used to make many copies of a particular portion of DNA

True or False   *If the statement is true, write* true. *If it is false, write* false.

_____ **7.** Inbreeding involves crossing dissimilar individuals to bring together the best of both organisms.

_____ **8.** Selective breeding involves only allowing individuals with desired characteristics to produce offspring.

_____ **9.** The breeding of individuals with similar characteristics is called inbreeding.

_____ **10.** Cells that undergo differentiation become specialized in structure and function.

© Pearson Education, Inc., publishing as Pearson Prentice Hall.

Chapter 14   The Human Genome

Summary

14–1 Human Heredity

In order to learn more about humans, biologists often use a karyotype to analyze human chromosomes. A **karyotype** is a picture of a cell's chromosomes grouped in homologous pairs. Humans have 46 chromosomes. Two of these, X and Y, are **sex chromosomes.** Females have two X chromosomes (XX). Males have one X and one Y chromosome (XY). The other 44 chromosomes are known as **autosomes. All human egg cells carry a single X chromosome. Sperm cells carry either X or Y chromosomes. Half of all sperm cells carry an X chromosome and half carry a Y chromosome. This ensures that just about half of the zygotes will be female and half will be male.**

To study human inheritance, biologists use pedigree charts. A **pedigree chart** shows relationships within a family. The inheritance of a trait can be traced through the family. From this, biologists may determine the genotypes of family members.

It is difficult to link an observed human trait with a specific gene. Many human traits are polygenic, or controlled by many genes. The environment also affects some traits.

The genes controlling blood type were among the first human genes to be identified. A number of genes are responsible for blood groups, but the two best known are the ABO blood groups and the Rh blood group.

- Red blood cells can carry two antigens—A and B. Antigens are molecules the immune system can recognize. A person who has only antigen A has type A blood. A person who has only antigen B has type B blood. A person who has both antigens has type AB blood. A person who does not have either antigen has type O blood. A single gene with three alleles determines the ABO blood types.

- Red blood cells can also have the Rh antigen. People with the Rh antigen are Rh positive. Those without it are Rh negative. A single gene with two alleles determines the Rh blood group.

There are many human genetic disorders. Some, including PKU and Tay-Sachs disease are caused by recessive alleles. Individuals must inherit a recessive allele from each parent. Other disorders, such as Huntington disease, are caused by a dominant allele. Huntington disease is expressed in any person who has the allele. Still other disorders, such as sickle cell disease, are caused by a codominant allele.

© Pearson Education, Inc., publishing as Pearson Prentice Hall.

Scientists are starting to learn which changes in the DNA sequence cause certain genetic disorders. **Sometimes, a small change in the DNA of a single gene affects the structure of a protein and causes a serious genetic disorder.** This is the case with cystic fibrosis and sickle cell disease.

14–2 Human Chromosomes

Genes on the X and Y chromosomes are said to be **sex-linked.** They are inherited in a different pattern than are genes on autosomes. **Males have just one X chromosome. Thus all X-linked alleles are expressed in males, even if they are recessive.** Some examples of sex-linked disorders are color-blindness and hemophilia.

Most of the time, the mechanisms that separate chromosomes in meiosis work well, but sometimes errors happen. The most common error during meiosis is nondisjunction. **Nondisjunction** is the failure of chromosomes to separate properly during meiosis. **If nondisjunction occurs, abnormal numbers of chromosomes may find their way into gametes, and a disorder of chromosome numbers may result.**

- Down syndrome is an example of autosomal nondisjunction. In this disorder, there is an extra copy of chromosome 21.
- Nondisjunction can also occur in sex chromosomes. Turner's syndrome and Klinefelter's syndrome are two examples.

14–3 Human Molecular Genetics

Biologists use molecular biology techniques to read, analyze, and change the DNA code of human genes. DNA analysis techniques can be used in different ways.

- DNA analysis can be used to test parents for recessive alleles that code for genetic disorders.
- **DNA fingerprinting** is a DNA analysis technique that can be used to identify individuals.

The Human Genome Project is an ongoing effort to analyze the human DNA sequence. Scientists are using the results of the human genome project to help locate genes on human chromosomes. In addition, information about the human genome may be used to help diagnose and treat disease.

Data from the human genome may be used to cure genetic disorders by gene therapy. **In gene therapy, an absent or faulty gene is replaced by a normal, working gene.** In one method of gene therapy, a normal, working copy of a gene is attached to viral DNA. Virus particles deliver this copy of the gene to human cells. The human cells can then make proteins that correct genetic defects.

© Pearson Education, Inc., publishing as Pearson Prentice Hall.

Pedigree Charts

A pedigree chart is a diagram that shows family relationships. This pedigree chart shows how the trait of a white lock of hair has been inherited in a family. The allele that codes for a white lock of hair is dominant.

Study the chart. Then, answer the questions below.

A White Lock of Hair

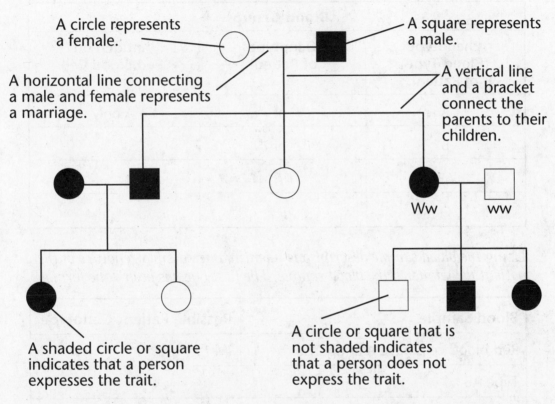

A circle represents a female.

A square represents a male.

A horizontal line connecting a male and female represents a marriage.

A vertical line and a bracket connect the parents to their children.

Ww   ww

A shaded circle or square indicates that a person expresses the trait.

A circle or square that is not shaded indicates that a person does not express the trait.

1. How many males shown in the chart have a white lock of hair?

_____

2. The alleles of two of the people in the chart are provided. What are the alleles of their three children?

Son without white lock: _____

Son with white lock: _____

Daughter with white lock: _____

© Pearson Education, Inc., publishing as Pearson Prentice Hall.

Human Blood Types

The ABO blood group gene codes for different antigens on the surface of a person's red blood cells. There are three alleles for this gene, I^A, I^B, and i. Depending on a person's alleles, they can have A antigens, B antigens, both, or none.

Label which blood types have A only, B only, A and B, or no antigens on their red blood cells. The first one has been done for you.

Blood Groups		
Phenotype (Blood Type) of Patient	**Genotype of Patient**	**Antigen on Red Blood Cell**
A	$I^A I^A$ or $I^A i$	A only
B	$I^B I^B$ or $I^B i$	
AB	$I^A I^B$	
O	ii	

Using the blood sample descriptions, identify one possible genotype of the patient who donated the blood sample. The first one has been done for you.

Blood Sample	Possible Patient Genotype
Red blood cells have A antigens.	$I^A i$, $I^A I^A$, or $I^A I^B$
Type AB	
Red blood cells have no antigens.	
Type B	

Use the tables to answer the questions.

1. Which alleles are codominant? _____

2. Which allele is recessive? _____

© Pearson Education, Inc., publishing as Pearson Prentice Hall.

Sex-Linked Disorders

The X and Y chromosomes are the sex chromosomes. Females have two X chromosomes. Males have one X and one Y chromosome. Because males have only one allele for X-linked genes, the allele is expressed, even if it is recessive.

The pedigree below shows the offspring of a female carrier of hemophilia and a male who does not suffer from the disorder.

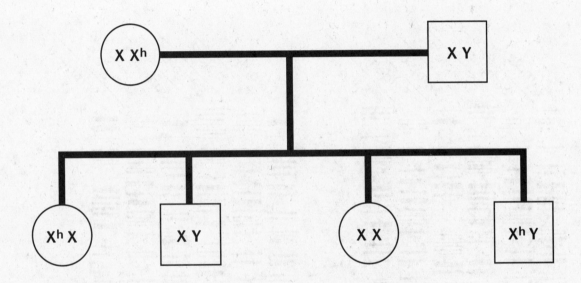

Use the pedigree to answer the questions.

1. Color each square or circle that indicates an individual who is a carrier of the hemophilia trait in red.

2. Color each square or circle that indicates an individual who has hemophilia in blue.

3. Could these parents have a daughter with hemophilia? Explain.

_____

_____

_____

4. Why are sex-linked diseases more common in males than in females?

_____

_____

© Pearson Education, Inc., publishing as Pearson Prentice Hall.

DNA Fingerprinting

No two people have exactly the same genetic code, except for identical twins. DNA fingerprinting is a technique used to identify individuals based on their genetic code. Using DNA fingerprinting, DNA from blood and other materials left at a crime scene can be compared to a suspect's DNA. If the samples match, it is likely that the DNA found at the crime scene is the suspect's DNA.

Look at the DNA fingerprints and answer the following questions.

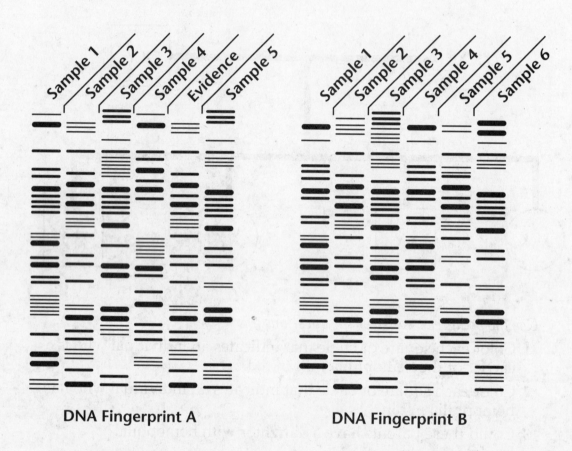

DNA Fingerprint A   **DNA Fingerprint B**

1. In DNA Fingerprint A, which sample matches the evidence?

_____

2. In DNA Fingerprint B, which two samples match?

_____

3. In DNA fingerprint B, which two samples may be from a set of identical twins?

_____

© Pearson Education, Inc., publishing as Pearson Prentice Hall.

Gene Therapy

Gene therapy is the process by which genes that cause a disorder are replaced by normal, working genes. Often, viruses are used during gene therapy. The diagram below shows how a virus might be used to deliver a gene to a bone marrow cell.

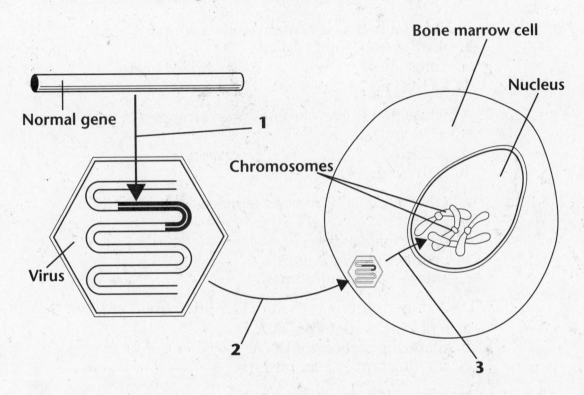

Arrange the following steps in the correct order.

_____ Virus infects human cell.

_____ Normal gene is inserted into viral DNA.

_____ Virus delivers its DNA to human cell.

Answer the question.

1. Why are viruses used in gene therapy?

_____

_____

© Pearson Education, Inc., publishing as Pearson Prentice Hall.

Name_____ Class_____ Date_____

Vocabulary Review

Multiple Choice   *In the space provided, write the letter of the term that best completes each sentence.*

_____ 1. In addition to two sex chromosomes, humans have 44 other chromosomes called
   a. autosomes.   **c.** sex-linked genes.
   b. karyotypes.

_____ 2. A picture that shows chromosomes arranged in pairs is a
   a. pedigree.   **c.** karyotype.
   b. DNA fingerprint.

_____ 3. Whether a human is male or female is determined by his or her
   a. sex chromosomes.
   b. pedigree chromosomes.
   c. autosomal chromosomes.

_____ 4. DNA fingerprinting is used to identify individuals by
   a. replacing sections of DNA.
   b. analyzing sections of DNA.
   c. charting family relationships.

_____ 5. A pedigree is a chart that shows
   a. the separation of chromosomes during meiosis.
   b. sections of an individual's DNA.
   c. relationships within a family.

_____ 6. Nondisjunction occurs when
   a. homologous chromosomes fail to separate in meiosis.
   b. humans analyze DNA.
   c. males have a recessive gene on their X chromosome.

_____ 7. A sex-linked gene is a gene that
   a. is located on an autosome.
   b. causes nondisjunction.
   c. is located on an X or a Y chromosome.

© Pearson Education, Inc., publishing as Pearson Prentice Hall.

Chapter 15   Darwin's Theory of Evolution

Summary

15–1 The Puzzle of Life's Diversity

Evolution, or change over time, is the process by which modern organisms have descended from ancient organisms. The theory of evolution can explain Earth's biodiversity. A scientific **theory** is an explanation of natural events that is supported by evidence and can be tested with new evidence.

Charles Darwin added the most to our understanding of evolution. In the 1830s, Charles Darwin sailed around the world. **Darwin made many observations and collected evidence.** Darwin observed many organisms. He saw that many plants and animals were very well suited to their environment. Darwin collected **fossils,** or the preserved remains of ancient organisms. Some of the fossils were unlike any creatures he had ever seen. He wondered why the species in the fossils had disappeared.

Darwin's observations on the Galápagos Islands influenced him most. The islands are near one another but have different climates. **Darwin saw that the characteristics of many animals and plants varied noticeably among the different islands.** He wondered whether animals on different islands had once belonged to the same species. According to this hypothesis, these separate species would have evolved from an original ancestor species after becoming isolated from one another.

15–2 Ideas That Shaped Darwin's Thinking

In Darwin's day, most Europeans thought that Earth and all of its life-forms had existed for only a few thousand years. They also thought that species did not change. Some scientists of Darwin's time began challenging these ideas. These scientists influenced the development of Darwin's theory of evolution.

- **Hutton and Lyell helped scientists recognize that Earth is many millions of years old, and that it had changed over time.** These ideas helped Darwin realize that life might change as well. Knowing that Earth was very old convinced Darwin that there had been enough time for life to evolve.

© Pearson Education, Inc., publishing as Pearson Prentice Hall.

- Jean-Baptiste Lamarck was one of the first scientists to see that evolution occurred. He also recognized that organisms adapt to their environments. **Lamarck proposed that by selective use or disuse of organs, organisms acquired or lost certain traits during their lifetime. These traits could then be passed on to their offspring.** Over time, this process led to change in a species. Scientists now know that some of Lamarck's ideas are wrong. However, his general ideas about evolution and adaptation are correct. These ideas influenced Darwin.
- Economist Thomas Malthus also influenced Darwin. **Malthus thought that if the human population kept growing, sooner or later there would be insufficient living space and food for everyone.** Darwin thought this was true for all organisms.

15-3 Darwin Presents His Case

Darwin was hesitant to publish his ideas because they were so extreme. When he learned that scientist Alfred Russel Wallace had the same ideas, Darwin published *On the Origin of Species* in 1859. In the book, Darwin supplied evidence that evolution has occurred. He also explained his ideas about how evolution occurs.

Darwin's theory was based on **artificial selection. In artificial selection, nature provided the variation, and humans selected those variations that they found useful.** For example, animal breeders used only the largest hogs, fastest horses, or cows that produced the most milk for breeding.

Darwin thought that a similar process occurs in nature. He called this **natural selection.** This process can be summed up as follows.

- Individuals differ, and some of the differences can be passed on to their offspring.
- More offspring are produced than can survive and reproduce.
- There is competition for limited resources, or a struggle for existence.
- Individuals best suited to their environment survive and reproduce most successfully. In other words, there is **survival of the fittest. Fitness** is the ability to survive and reproduce in a given environment. It results from adaptations. **Adaptations** are inherited traits that increase an organism's chance of survival. Only the fittest organisms pass on their traits. Because of this, a species changes over time.

© Pearson Education, Inc., publishing as Pearson Prentice Hall.

Darwin argued that species alive today descended with modification from species of the past. Darwin also introduced the principle of **common descent**. This principle holds that all species come from common ancestors. The principle of common descent links all organisms on Earth into a single tree of life.

Darwin argued that living things have been evolving on Earth for millions of years. He presented four types of evidence in support of evolution.

- **The fossil record**   Comparing fossils from older and younger rock layers provides evidence that evolution has taken place.
- **Geographic distribution of living species**   The presence of similar but unrelated organisms in similar environments suggests the action of natural selection.
- **Homologous structures of living organisms**   **Homologous structures** have different mature forms but develop from the same embryonic tissues. They provide strong evidence that organisms have descended, with modifications, from common ancestors.
- Some homologous structures no longer serve major roles in descendants. If the structures are greatly reduced in size, they are called **vestigial organs.** For example, the appendix in humans is a vestigial organ. It carries out no function in digestion.
- **Similarities in early development**   The early stages, or embryos, of many animals are very similar. These similarities are evidence that the animals share common ancestors.

Scientific advances have upheld most of Darwin's hypotheses. However, evolutionary theory continues to change as new data are gathered and new ways of thinking arise.

© Pearson Education, Inc., publishing as Pearson Prentice Hall.

Galápagos Tortoises

When Charles Darwin visited the Galápagos Islands, he discovered that similar animals that lived on separate islands had different features.

Look at the drawings of tortoises. Use the drawings to answer the questions.

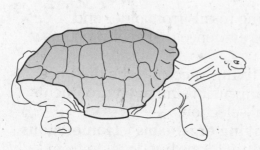

Pinta Island tortoise

Hood Island tortoise

Isabela Island tortoise

1. The tortoises eat plants. On one island, plants grow very close to the ground. Which island is this most likely to be? Circle the correct answer.

   Isabela Island   Hood Island

2. Explain your answer to question 1. Why did you choose the island you did?

   _____

   _____

3. Which island most likely has sparse vegetation that is hard to reach? Circle the correct answer.

   Pinta Island   Hood Island

© Pearson Education, Inc., publishing as Pearson Prentice Hall.

Natural Selection

An adaptation is an inherited characteristic that helps an organism survive and reproduce in its environment. Over time, adaptations become more common in the population. For example, suppose that the water in a pond gets darker over a period of four years. The table below shows what might happen to a frog population living in the pond.

Look at the pictures showing how a population of frogs changed over time.

Complete the table.

Year	Light-Colored Frogs	Dark-Colored Frogs
1		
2		
3		
4		

Use the table to answer the question.

1. How did the numbers of light- and dark-colored frogs change over time?

_____

_____

© Pearson Education, Inc., publishing as Pearson Prentice Hall.

The Fossil Record

In the fossil record, an intermediate form is a fossil that shows some characteristics of an earlier related organism and some characteristics of a later related organism. The illustrations below show organisms whose fossils make up part of the fossil record. The organisms are in order from oldest (organism 1) to most recent (organism 4).

Draw an animal that might have been an intermediate form between organism 1 and organism 2. Then, draw an animal that might have been an intermediate form between organism 3 and organism 4.

Organism 1

Organism 3

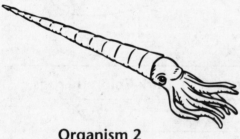

Organism 2

Organism 4

Use the illustrations to answer the questions.

1. Describe one change you see between organism 1 and organism 2.

_____

2. How might these fossils provide evidence for evolution?

_____

© Pearson Education, Inc., publishing as Pearson Prentice Hall.

Evidence for Evolution

Use the words below and your knowledge of the evidence for evolution to complete the table. The first one has been done for you.

> fossil record
> geographic distribution of living species
> similarities in embryo development

Type of Evidence	What It Reveals
homologous body structures	Animals with different limb structures that develop from the same embryonic tissues evolved from a common ancestor.
	Vertebrates share a common ancestor, as shown by how these organisms develop.
	Intermediate forms show that organisms have evolved over time.
	Species have adapted over time to local conditions.

Answer the question.

1. Give an example of homologous body structures.

_____

_____

© Pearson Education, Inc., publishing as Pearson Prentice Hall.

Chapter 15   Darwin's Theory of Evolution

Vocabulary Review

Matching   *In the space provided, write the letter of the definition that best matches each term.*

_____ **1.** evolution

_____ **2.** artificial selection

_____ **3.** vestigial organs

_____ **4.** survival of the fittest

a. change over time

b. structures that serve no useful function in an organism

c. process in which individuals that are best suited to their environment live and reproduce most successfully

d. process in which humans breed organisms with desired variations of specific traits

Completion   *Use the words below to fill in the blanks with terms from the chapter.*

adaptation	natural selection	theory
common descent	struggle for existence	

5. The idea that members of each species compete for necessities

of life is known as _____.

6. A(An) _____ is a well-supported, testable

explanation of events that occur in the natural world.

7. The concept of survival of the fittest is also known as

_____.

8. Any inherited characteristic that increases an organism's

chance of survival is a(an) _____.

9. The idea that all species have evolved from shared ancestors is

called _____.

© Pearson Education, Inc., publishing as Pearson Prentice Hall.

Chapter 16   Evolution of Populations

Summary

16-1 Genes and Variation

Darwin's theory of evolution by natural selection explained how life on Earth changed, or evolved, over many generations. What Darwin did not know was how heritable traits were passed down through each generation. The study of genetics helps scientists understand the relationship between inheritance and evolution.

Genetics supports Darwin's ideas. Scientists know that genes control traits and that many genes have at least two forms, or alleles. They also know that members of all species are heterozygous for many genes. **In genetic terms, evolution is any change in the relative frequency of alleles in a population.** A population is a group of individuals of the same species that can interbreed. Members of a population share a gene pool. A **gene pool** is all the genes, and their alleles, in the population. The number of times the allele occurs in a gene pool compared to the number of times that other alleles for the same gene occur is the **relative frequency** of the allele.

The two main sources of genetic variation are mutations and gene shuffling.
- A mutation is any change in a sequence of DNA.
- Gene shuffling occurs during gamete formation. It can produce millions of different gene combinations.

Both mutations and gene shuffling increase genetic variation by increasing the number of different genotypes.

The number of phenotypes for a trait depends on how many genes control the trait.
- A **single-gene trait** is a trait controlled by only one gene. If there are two alleles for the gene, two or three genotypes are possible. An example in humans of a single-gene trait is the presence of a widow's peak—a downward dip in the center of the hairline. The allele for a widow's peak is dominant over the allele for a hairline with no peak. As a result, there are only two phenotypes—having a widow's peak or not having one.
- A **polygenic trait** is controlled by two or more genes. Each gene of a polygenic trait may have more than one allele. Polygenic traits form many phenotypes. Variation in a polygenic trait in a population often forms a bell-shaped curve with most members near the middle. An example of a polygenic trait is height in humans.

16–2 Evolution as Genetic Change

Evolution of populations results from the effects of natural selection on individuals. **Natural selection on single-gene traits can lead to changes in allele frequencies and thus to evolution.** The process can cause an increase or a decrease in the relative frequency of an allele.

Natural selection on polygenic traits is more complex. **Natural selection on polygenic traits can occur in three ways:**

- **Directional selection** occurs when individuals at one end of the bell-shaped curve have higher fitness than individuals near the middle or other end of the curve. Directional selection causes a shift in the curve toward the higher fitness end.
- **Stabilizing selection** occurs when individuals near the middle of the curve have higher fitness than those at either end. Stabilizing selection leads to a narrowing of the curve near the middle.
- **Disruptive selection** occurs when individuals at the upper and lower ends of the curve have higher fitness than those near the middle. Disruptive selection forms a curve with a peak at each end and a low point in the middle.

Natural selection is not the only source of evolutionary change. In small populations, chance can cause alleles to become more or less common. This kind of change in allele frequency is called **genetic drift. Genetic drift occurs when individuals with a specific allele leave more descendants than other individuals, just by chance. Over time, this can cause an allele to become more or less common in a population.** Genetic drift may also occur when a small group of individuals moves into a new habitat. By chance, the small group may have different relative allele frequencies than did the original population. When this happens, it is called the **founder effect.**

To understand how evolution occurs, scientists first ask, "Under what conditions does evolution *not* occur?" The **Hardy-Weinberg principle** answers this question. The principle states that allele frequencies in a population stay the same unless one or more factors change the frequencies. **Genetic equilibrium** is the condition in which allele frequencies remain constant. **Five conditions are needed for a population to be in genetic equilibrium:**

- **random mating**
- **large population size**
- **no migrations**
- **no mutations**
- **no natural selection**

If all five conditions are met, relative allele frequencies will not change. Evolution will not occur.

© Pearson Education, Inc., publishing as Pearson Prentice Hall.

16–3 The Process of Speciation

Speciation is the formation of new species. For one species to evolve into two new species, the gene pools of two populations must be separated. **As new species evolve, populations become reproductively isolated from one another.** When members of two populations can no longer interbreed and produce fertile offspring, **reproductive isolation** has occurred. Reproductive isolation takes three forms.

- **Behavioral isolation** occurs when populations have different courtship or reproductive behaviors.
- **Geographic isolation** occurs when geographic barriers separate populations. Such barriers can include mountains or rivers.
- **Temporal isolation** occurs when populations reproduce at different times.

Peter and Rosemary Grant proved that natural selection is still causing finches on the Galápagos Islands to evolve. The Grants showed that there was enough heritable variation in finch beaks to provide raw material for natural selection. The couple also showed that beak differences led to fitness differences. These fitness differences have brought about directional selection.

Combining the Grants' work and Darwin's ideas, scientists have come up with a hypothetical scenario for the evolution of Galápagos finches. **Speciation in the Galápagos finches occurred by**

- **Founding of a new population**   A few finches may have traveled from the mainland to one of the islands. There, they survived and reproduced.
- **Geographic isolation**   Some birds then moved to a second island. The two populations were geographically isolated. They no longer shared a gene pool.
- **Changes in the new population's gene pool**   Seed sizes on the second island favored birds with larger beaks. So this bird population evolved into a population with larger beaks.
- **Reproductive isolation**   In time, the large-beaked birds were reproductively isolated from birds on other islands and evolved into a new species.
- **Ecological competition**   If birds from the second island cross back to the first, they live in competition. Individuals that are most different from one another compete less and are most able to reproduce. In time, this may lead to the evolution of yet another species.

Evolution continues today. For example, some bacteria are evolving resistance to certain drugs. Evolutionary theory can help us understand these changes.

© Pearson Education, Inc., publishing as Pearson Prentice Hall.

Gene Pools

A homozygous black mouse has two alleles for black fur. A heterozygous black mouse has one allele for black fur and one allele for brown fur. A homozygous brown mouse has two alleles for brown fur.

Sample Population

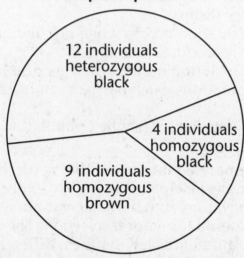

12 individuals heterozygous black

4 individuals homozygous black

9 individuals homozygous brown

Each rectangle represents one mouse. Each mouse has two alleles, represented by circles, for fur color. Use the graph to color the gene pool of the sample population. Color alleles for black fur black and alleles for brown fur brown.

Gene Pool

Use the diagram to answer the questions.

1. How many black alleles are in the gene pool? _____

2. How many brown alleles are in the gene pool? _____

© Pearson Education, Inc., publishing as Pearson Prentice Hall.

Polygenic Traits

Follow the prompts to make a graph showing the frequency of different heights in a group of students.

- Draw one bar for each height range. The bar should show how many students have heights in that range.
- Draw a curve connecting the tops of the bars.

Height in cm	Number of Students
155–159	1
160–164	2
165–169	6
170–174	10
175–179	10
180–184	6
185–189	2
190–194	1

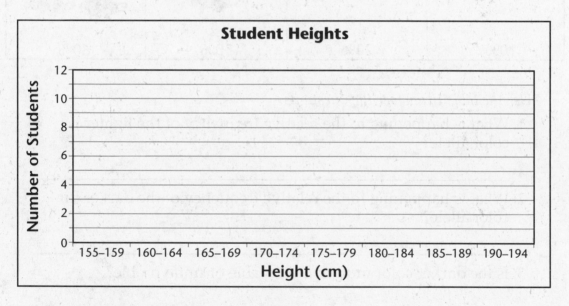

Student Heights

Use the graph to answer the questions.

1. What shape is the curve you drew?

_____

2. What type of trait is height? Circle the correct answer.

single-gene   polygenic

© Pearson Education, Inc., publishing as Pearson Prentice Hall.

Natural Selection on a Single-Gene Trait

A color mutation occurred in a brown mouse population, causing darker fur. The table below shows how the population changed over the next 30 generations.

Initial Population	Generation 10	Generation 20	Generation 30
90%	80%	70%	40%
10%	20%	30%	60%

Use the table to answer the questions.

1. What is happening to the relative frequency of the lighter fur color allele?

   _____

2. What is happening to the relative frequency of the darker fur color allele?

   _____

3. Is the darker color mutation favorable or unfavorable?

   _____

4. What might cause the change shown in the table?

   _____

   _____

5. How do you predict the mouse population will look after 40 generations?

   _____

   _____

© Pearson Education, Inc., publishing as Pearson Prentice Hall.

Directional Selection

A population of birds eats seeds. Small seeds can be eaten by birds with small beaks. Larger, thicker seeds can be eaten only by birds with larger, thicker beaks. Suppose there is a shortage of small seeds but that there are still many large seeds.

Draw a new curve on the graph to show how the distribution of beak sizes might change as a result of selection in this environment.

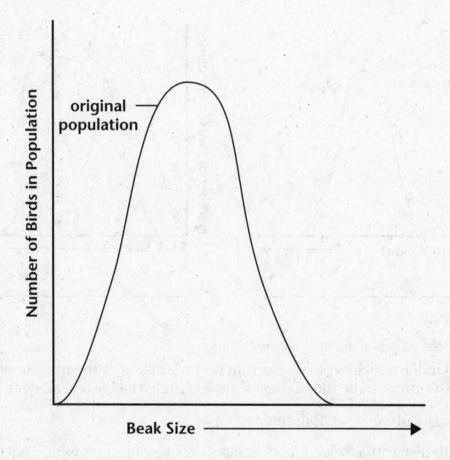

Use the graph to answer the questions.

1. Which birds in this population have the highest fitness? Circle the best answer.

   small-beaked birds   large-beaked birds

2. Explain how natural selection could lead to the change you predicted.

   _____

   _____

   _____

© Pearson Education, Inc., publishing as Pearson Prentice Hall.

Stabilizing and Disruptive Selection

In most populations, a trait that has higher fitness leads to greater numbers of organisms with that trait. On the graphs, dotted lines represent the original population. The solid lines represent the population after selection has taken place.

Identify whether each graph shows stabilizing selection or disruptive selection. Write the type of selection shown below each graph.

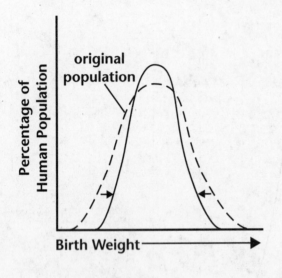

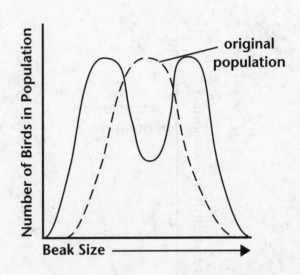

_____   _____

Use the graphs to answer the questions.

1. Under which type of selection do organisms in the middle of the curve have the highest fitness? Circle the correct answer.

disruptive   stabilizing

2. In disruptive selection, organisms represented by which part of the curve have the lowest fitness? Circle the correct answer.

middle of the curve   ends of the curve

3. Describe a situation that might lead to the changes shown in the graph on the right.

_____

_____

_____

_____

© Pearson Education, Inc., publishing as Pearson Prentice Hall.

Genetic Drift

In a small population, an individual with particular alleles may
have more descendants than another individual, by chance. This
kind of chance can, over time, lead to an allele's becoming more
common in a population.

*Draw what the descendants of these populations might look like. Draw
12 descendants for each population.*

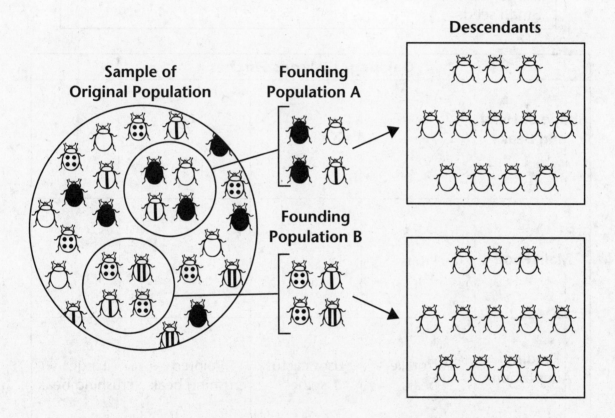

Use the diagrams to answer the questions.

1. Draw a beetle that could be found in both descendant
populations.

2. Why are the beetles in the two descendant populations
different?

_____

_____

© Pearson Education, Inc., publishing as Pearson Prentice Hall.

Galápagos Island Finches

Finches in the Galápagos Islands have beaks adapted to eat the foods available in the birds' habitats.

Use the words below to match each finch with the food it is adapted to eat. The first one is done for you.

Insects that live inside dead wood
Large, thick-shelled seeds
Small seeds

Galápagos Islands Finches

Shape of Head and Beak				
Main Food	Fruits			
Feeding Adaptation	Parrotlike beak	Uses cactus spines	Pointed crushing beak	Large crushing beak
Habitat	Trees	Trees	Ground	Ground

Use the table to answer the questions.

1. How does the large crushing beak help the fourth finch survive?

_____

2. Circle the finch that would be least likely to survive if the insect population decreased.

© Pearson Education, Inc., publishing as Pearson Prentice Hall.

Speciation

Use the words below to identify each process that leads to speciation. One row has been completed for you.

Changes in the gene pool	Geographic isolation
Ecological competition	Reproductive isolation

Process	How It Leads to Speciation
Founders arrive	A population arrives in a new place.
	Populations are separated by a geographic barrier and do not share a gene pool.
	Populations evolve new traits in response to natural selection in their environments.
	Populations reproduce only within their own group, leading to the development of new species.
	Species evolve in a way that reduces competition between them.

Use the table to answer the question.

1. Do populations that are geographically isolated from one another share a gene pool? Explain.

_____

_____

© Pearson Education, Inc., publishing as Pearson Prentice Hall.

Chapter 16　Evolution of Populations

Vocabulary Review

True or False　*If the statement is true, write* true. *If it is false, write* false.

_____ 1. All of the genes in a population make up the relative frequency of the population.

_____ 2. When two related species live in the same area but mate during different seasons, they are separated by directional selection.

_____ 3. Traits controlled by two or more genes are polygenic traits.

_____ 4. Reproductive isolation occurs when members of two populations cannot interbreed and produce fertile offspring.

_____ 5. The separation of two populations by barriers such as rivers or mountains results in temporal isolation.

_____ 6. The Hardy-Weinberg principle states that allele frequency in a population will remain constant unless one or more factors cause those frequencies to change.

_____ 7. When two populations can breed but do not because of differences in mating rituals or other similar behaviors, behavioral isolation exists.

_____ 8. Genetic drift is the formation of new species.

_____ 9. Geographic isolation is a random change in the allele frequencies of a small population.

_____ 10. Genetic equilibrium occurs when the allele frequencies in a population remain constant.

© Pearson Education, Inc., publishing as Pearson Prentice Hall.

Chapter 17   The History of Life

Summary

17-1 The Fossil Record

Fossils are preserved traces and remains of ancient life. Most fossils form in sedimentary rock. **Paleontologists** study fossils to learn what past life-forms were like. Data from fossils forms the **fossil record. The fossil record provides evidence about the history of life on Earth. It also shows how different groups of organisms have changed over time.** The fossil record shows that more than 99 percent of all of Earth's species have become extinct, or died out.

To determine the age of a fossil, paleontologists use relative dating and radioactive dating.

- **Relative dating allows paleontologists to estimate a fossil's age compared with that of other fossils.** Fossils in deeper rock layers are assumed to be older than fossils from rock layers nearer the surface. **Index fossils** represent species that lived for a short time over a wide geographic range. Index fossils can help decide the relative ages of fossils from different places.

- **In radioactive dating, scientists calculate the age of a sample according to the amount of remaining radioactive isotopes it contains.** Radioactive elements in fossils decay, or break down, at a steady rate. This rate is called a half-life. A **half-life** is the time needed for half of the radioactive atoms in a sample to decay. A fossil's age is calculated from the half-life and the amount of radioactive atoms still in the fossil.

Once the age of a fossil is determined, paleontologists may want to find out the portion of Earth's history in which the fossil formed. To do this, they use the **geologic time scale.** The geologic time scale shows evolutionary time. The scale begins with Precambrian Time. **After Precambrian Time, the scale is divided into three eras: the Paleozoic, Mesozoic, and Cenozoic.** Each era is further divided into smaller lengths of time, called periods.

17-2 Earth's Early History

Earth is about 4.6 billion years old. At first, Earth was very hot. **Earth's early atmosphere probably contained hydrogen cyanide, carbon dioxide, carbon monoxide, nitrogen, hydrogen sulfide, and water.** About 3.8 billion years ago, Earth's surface cooled enough for water to remain a liquid. Water vapor condensed and rain soaked the surface, forming oceans.

© Pearson Education, Inc., publishing as Pearson Prentice Hall.

In the 1950s, Stanley Miller and Harold Urey did an experiment to try and learn how life on Earth began. They filled a container with water and gases from Earth's early atmosphere. They passed electric sparks through the mixture to simulate lightning. Soon, organic compounds formed. **The experiment showed that molecules needed for life could have formed under early Earth conditions.**

Sometimes large organic molecules form tiny bubbles called **proteinoid microspheres.** Structures similar to these microspheres may have become the first living cells. RNA and DNA also could have formed from simple organic molecules.

The first known life-forms evolved about 3.5 billion years ago. They were unicellular and looked like modern bacteria. Some were preserved as microscopic fossils, or microfossils. In time, photosynthetic bacteria evolved. During photosynthesis, the bacteria gave off oxygen. **The rise of oxygen in the atmosphere drove some life-forms to extinction. Other life-forms evolved new, more efficient metabolic pathways that used oxygen for respiration.**

The first eukaryotes—organisms with nuclei—evolved about 2 billion years ago. The **endosymbiotic theory** is one account of how eukaryotes evolved. **This theory suggests that eukaryotic cells arose from living communities formed by prokaryotic organisms.**

Sexual reproduction was an important step in the evolution of life. Sexual reproduction increases genetic variation. This process allows evolution to occur more quickly.

17–3 Evolution of Multicellular Life

A few hundred million years after the evolution of sexual reproduction, multicellular organisms evolved. These first multicellular organisms then experienced a large increase in diversity. The events in the evolution of multicellular organisms are described below.

During Precambrian time, eukaryotes appeared. Some eukaryotes gave rise to multicellular forms. This life existed in the oceans. Few fossils exist from the Precambrian because the animals lacked hard parts.

Fossil evidence shows that early in the Paleozoic Era, there was a diversity of marine life. Animals with hard parts, such as trilobites, evolved. **During the Devonian period of this era, vertebrates began to invade the land.** Evolution of land plants, insects, amphibians, and reptiles also occurred. The Paleozoic ended with a mass extinction. This mass extinction affected both plants and animals on land and in the seas. As much as 95 percent of the complex life in the ocean disappeared.

© Pearson Education, Inc., publishing as Pearson Prentice Hall.

During the Mesozoic Era, flowering plants appeared and dinosaurs dominated. Reptiles were so successful that the Mesozoic is called the Age of Reptiles. The Mesozoic Era also ended with a mass extinction.

During the Cenozoic Era, mammals evolved adaptations that allowed them to live in various environments. This era is called the Age of Mammals. The first humans evolved about 200,000 years ago in Africa. Today, humans live everywhere.

17–4 Patterns of Evolution

Biologists use the term **macroevolution** to describe large-scale evolution that takes place over long periods of time. It is evolution above the species level. **Six important topics in macroevolution include extinction, adaptive radiation, convergent evolution, coevolution, punctuated equilibrium, and changes in developmental genes.**

- **Extinction** is the disappearance, or dying out, of a species. Most extinction occurs when species cannot compete for resources or adapt to changing environments. By contrast, mass extinctions may occur from combinations of events, such as volcanoes erupting and asteroids striking Earth.

- **Adaptive radiation** is the process in which one species evolves into diverse species that live in different ways. Darwin's finches are an example of adaptive radiation. More than a dozen species evolved from a single species of finch.

- **Convergent evolution** is a process in which unrelated species come to look alike because they have evolved similar adaptations to similar environments. For example, penguins and dolphins have similar body shapes. They are both streamlined to help them swim through the water. However, penguins are birds and dolphins are mammals.

- **Coevolution** is the process by which two species evolve in response to changes in each other. For example, some plants have evolved poisons to protect themselves from insects. In response, insects have evolved ways to protect themselves from the poisons.

- **Punctuated equilibrium** is a pattern of evolutionary change. In this pattern, long periods of little or no change are interrupted by short periods of rapid change. The fossil record sometimes shows punctuated equilibrium.

- **Changes in developmental genes** may explain some large-scale evolutionary change. For example, some scientists believe that small changes in the development of an embryo can have a large affect on the adult organism.

© Pearson Education, Inc., publishing as Pearson Prentice Hall.

Relative Age

Sedimentary rock layers form in order by age. The oldest layers are on the bottom, and more recent layers lie above them in the order in which they formed.

Number the rock layers in the order that they formed. The first one has been done for you.

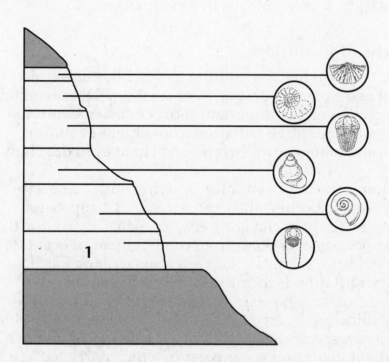

Use the diagram of the rock layers to number the fossils in order. The oldest fossil, labeled 1, has been done for you.

_____ _____1_____ _____ _____ _____ _____

Use the diagram to answer the question.

1. Suppose that you found a fossil of the same species as fossil 1 in a rock layer in another location. What could you conclude about that rock layer?

_____

_____

© Pearson Education, Inc., publishing as Pearson Prentice Hall.

Geologic Time Scale

Follow the prompts below to make a timeline of geologic time.
- Use the information in the table to divide the timeline into periods.
- Label each period.
- Color the Cenozoic Era red.
- Color the Mesozoic Era yellow.
- Color the Paleozoic Era blue.
- Color Precambrian Time orange.

Geologic Time Scale

Era	Period	Time (millions of years ago)
Cenozoic	Quaternary	1.8–present
Cenozoic	Tertiary	65–1.8
Mesozoic	Cretaceous	145–65
Mesozoic	Jurassic	208–145
Mesozoic	Triassic	245–208
Paleozoic	Permian	290–245
Paleozoic	Carboniferous	360–290
Paleozoic	Devonian	410–360
Paleozoic	Silurian	440–410
Paleozoic	Ordovician	505–440
Paleozoic	Cambrian	544–505
Precambrian Time	Vendian	650–544

Time (millions of years ago)

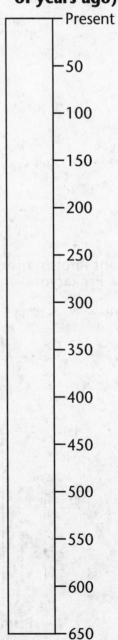

- Present
- 50
- 100
- 150
- 200
- 250
- 300
- 350
- 400
- 450
- 500
- 550
- 600
- 650

© Pearson Education, Inc., publishing as Pearson Prentice Hall.

Endosymbiotic Theory

The endosymbiotic theory is one theory that explains the evolution of eukaryotic cells. According to the theory, ancient prokaryotes developed a symbiotic relationship with smaller prokaryotes that lived inside them. Some of these smaller prokaryotes could use oxygen to generate ATP. These aerobic prokaryotes evolved into mitochondria. Others could perform photosynthesis. These evolved into chloroplasts.

Draw the final step in the endosymbiotic theory. Your drawing should show a primitive eukaryotic cell that can perform photosynthesis. Label the chloroplast in your drawing.

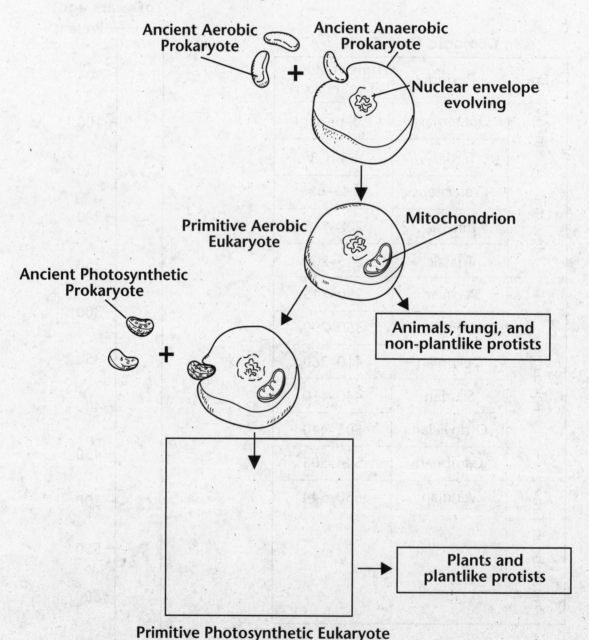

Primitive Photosynthetic Eukaryote

© Pearson Education, Inc., publishing as Pearson Prentice Hall.

Evolution of Multicellular Life

Use the words below to fill in examples of life-forms that existed in each period. Then, mark an X at two times when mass extinctions occurred.

early birds	reptiles and giant ferns
early human ancestors	trilobites and worms
first land plants	*Tyrannosaurus rex*

Era	Period(s)	Life-forms
Cenozoic	Quaternary	
	Tertiary	whales and dolphins
Mesozoic	Cretaceous	
	Jurassic	
	Triassic	first dinosaurs and small mammals
Paleozoic	Permian and Carboniferous	
	Devonian	insects, fishes, first amphibians
	Silurian and Ordovician	
	Cambrian	
Precambrian Time	Vendian	soft-bodied prokaryotes and eukaryotes

© Pearson Education, Inc., publishing as Pearson Prentice Hall.

Adaptive Radiation

The diagram shows the evolutionary relationships between some mammals. The dotted lines and question marks show places where scientists are not sure when groups of animals branched from earlier groups.

Follow the prompts.
- Color the group most closely related to the sirenians blue.
- Color the group most closely related to cetaceans yellow.

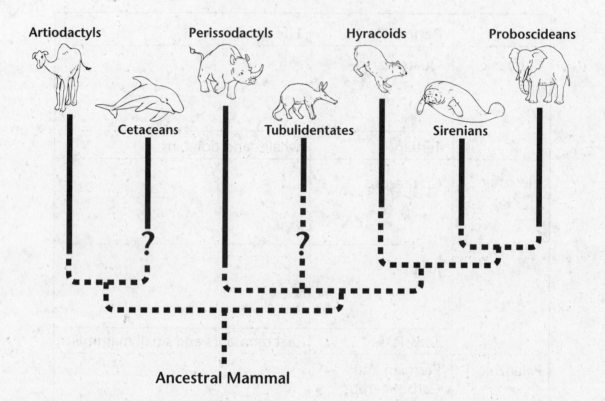

Use the diagram to answer the questions.

1. What is adaptive radiation?

_____

_____

2. Why are scientists not sure of all the evolutionary relationships shown in the diagram above?

_____

_____

3. Which two groups are least closely related to artiodactyls?

_____

© Pearson Education, Inc., publishing as Pearson Prentice Hall.

Punctuated Equilibrium

The theory of punctuated equilibrium is one explanation of how evolution occurs. It describes a pattern of long periods of stability interrupted, or punctuated, by shorter periods of rapid evolution. The diagram shows one possible model for the evolution of horses that follows this theory.

Look at the four circled areas. Put a check mark next to the circled areas that show periods of rapid evolution. Put an X next to the circled areas that show a relatively stable period.

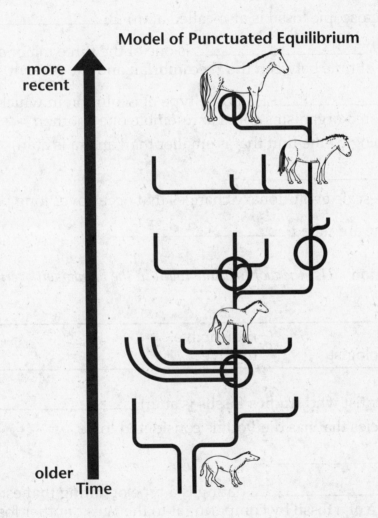

Model of Punctuated Equilibrium

Use the diagram to answer the question.

1. What on the diagram indicates that rapid evolution was taking place?

_____

_____

© Pearson Education, Inc., publishing as Pearson Prentice Hall.

Chapter 17 The History of Life

Vocabulary Review

Completion *Use the words below to fill in the blanks with terms from the chapter.*

convergent	macroevolution	period
era	microfossil	

1. A microscopic fossil is also called a(an) _____.

2. A(An) _____ is one of the three major subdivisions of time between the Precambrian and the present.

3. _____ is one type of evolution in which unrelated organisms come to resemble one another.

4. A geologic time unit that is smaller than an era is a(an) _____.

5. Large-scale evolutionary changes that occur over long periods of time are called _____.

Completion *Use the words below to fill in the blanks with terms from the chapter.*

extinct	radioactive
paleontologist	relative

6. A scientist who studies fossils is a(an) _____.

7. A species that has died out is considered to be _____.

8. _____ dating is a type of dating that estimates the age of a fossil by comparing it to the ages of other fossils.

9. _____ dating is the type of dating that uses the half-life of an isotope to determine the age of a sample.

© Pearson Education, Inc., publishing as Pearson Prentice Hall.

Chapter 18   Classification

Summary

18-1 Finding Order in Diversity

There are millions of species on Earth. **To study the diversity of life, biologists use a classification system to name organisms and group them in a logical manner.** A good classification system groups together organisms that are more similar to one another than they are to organisms in other groups.

To name organisms, scientists needed to use names that could be understood and used worldwide. By the 1700s, scientists tried to solve this problem by agreeing to use one name for each species. They began using Latin or Greek names that described the physical characteristics of organisms. At first, the names were very long. Then, Carolus Linnaeus developed a naming system called **binomial nomenclature.** This system is still in use. **In binomial nomenclature, each species is assigned a two-part scientific name.**

- The first part of the name refers to a genus (plural: genera). A **genus** is a group of closely related species. For example, the genus *Ursus* refers to bears.
- The second part of the name refers to one species. A species is a group of individuals that can interbreed. The name *Ursus maritimus*, for example, refers to the polar bear species.

The first letter of the genus name is always capitalized, while the species name is always in lowercase. Both names are printed in italics to make the names easy to recognize.

Linnaeus also developed a system for grouping organisms. Organisms that shared important traits were classified in the same taxon, or group. **Linnaeus's classification system has seven groups, or taxon. From smallest to largest, the taxon are as follows:**

- **Species,** a group of individuals that can interbreed
- **Genus,** a group of closely related species
- **Family,** a group of similar genera
- **Order,** a group of similar families
- **Class,** a group of similar orders
- **Phylum,** a group of similar classes
- **Kingdom,** a group of similar phyla

Linnaeus named two kingdoms of living things: Animalia (animal) and Plantae (plant).

© Pearson Education, Inc., publishing as Pearson Prentice Hall.

18–2 Modern Evolutionary Classification

Early classification was based on visible similarities. **Biologists now group organisms according to evolutionary relationships.** This is called **evolutionary classification.** Species within one genus are more closely related to one another than to species in another genus. All members of a genus share a recent common ancestor.

All genera in a family also share a common ancestor. However, this ancestor is farther in the past than the common ancestor of the species within a genus. In fact, the higher the taxon level, the farther back in time is the common ancestor of the organisms in that taxon.

To decide evolutionary relationships, many biologists use cladistic analysis. Cladistic analysis is a classification method that is based on derived characters. **Derived characters** are new traits that arise as a group evolves. Derived traits are found in closely related organisms but not in their distant ancestors. Derived characters are used to make a cladogram. A **cladogram** is a diagram that shows the evolutionary relationships among a group of organisms. A cladogram is a type of evolutionary tree, much like a family tree. One type of evidence that can be used to determine evolutionary relationships is genetic evidence.

The genes of many organisms show important similarities at the molecular level. **Similarities in DNA can be used to help determine classification and evolutionary relationships.**

- The more similar the molecules in species, the more recently the species shared a common ancestor. Thus, the more closely related they are.
- Comparisons of DNA also are used to estimate how long two species have been evolving independently. This is done using a model called a **molecular clock.** The model assumes that neutral mutations—those not affecting phenotype— accumulate in gene pools. Two species evolving independently from each other will accumulate different neutral mutations over time. The more different neutral mutations that are present, the longer the two species have been evolving independently.

© Pearson Education, Inc., publishing as Pearson Prentice Hall.

18–3 Kingdoms and Domains

Biologists realized that Linnaeus's two kingdoms did not include all life-forms. This led to a system with additional kingdoms.

- First, microorganisms such as bacteria were discovered. Microorganisms did not fit into the plant or animal kingdom. They were placed in their own kingdom, called Protista.
- Next, mushrooms, yeast, and molds were separated from plants. They were placed in the kingdom Fungi.
- Later, bacteria were separated from other Protista. They were placed in a new kingdom, called Monera.
- Most recently, the Monera were divided into two kingdoms: Eubacteria and Archaebacteria.

In the 1990s, a six-kingdom system of classification was proposed. **The six-kingdom system of classification includes the kingdoms Eubacteria, Archaebacteria, Protista, Fungi, Plantae, and Animalia.**

Many biologists now use a new taxon—the domain. The **domain** is one level higher than the kingdom. **There are three domains: Bacteria, Archaea, and Eukarya.**

- The domain **Bacteria** includes only the kingdom Eubacteria. All members of this domain are unicellular organisms without a nucleus. They have cell walls that contain peptidoglycan.
- The domain **Archaea** includes only the kingdom Archaebacteria. All members of the domain Archaea are unicellular organisms without a nucleus. They have cell walls that do not contain peptidoglycan.
- The domain **Eukarya** includes the kingdoms Protista, Fungi, Plantae, and Animalia. All members of this domain have cells with a nucleus.
  - Most members of the kingdom **Protista** are unicellular. Some Protista are autotrophs, and others are heterotrophs.
  - Most members of the kingdom **Fungi** are multicellular. All are heterotrophs.
  - All members of the kingdom **Plantae** are multicellular autotrophs. Most plants cannot move about, and their cells have cell walls.
  - All members of the kingdom **Animalia** are multicellular heterotrophs. Most animals can move about. Their cells lack cell walls.

© Pearson Education, Inc., publishing as Pearson Prentice Hall.

Linnaeus's System of Classification

Linnaeus developed a system of classification to name and group organisms in a logical manner. This made it easier to study the many forms of life.

The diagrams show the classification of a grizzly bear, but the items are out of order. Number the groups from largest (1) to smallest (7). The first one has been done for you.

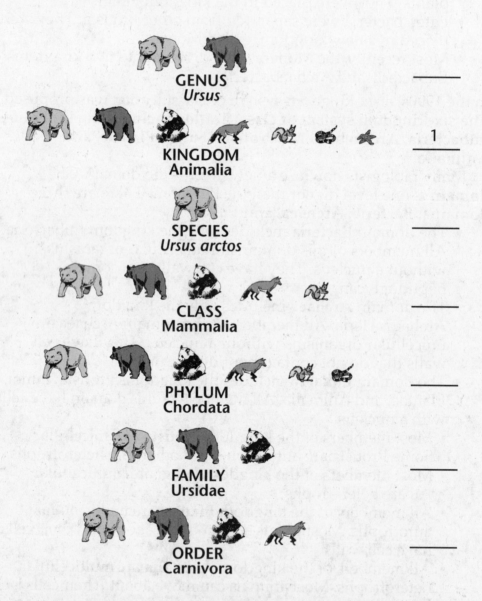

GENUS
Ursus   _____

KINGDOM
Animalia   __1__

SPECIES
Ursus arctos   _____

CLASS
Mammalia   _____

PHYLUM
Chordata   _____

FAMILY
Ursidae   _____

ORDER
Carnivora   _____

Use the diagram to answer the question.

1. Using binomial nomenclature, what is the scientific name of the grizzly bear?

_____

© Pearson Education, Inc., publishing as Pearson Prentice Hall.

Understanding Cladograms

A cladogram shows evolutionary relationships between species.

Follow the prompts to interpret the cladogram.

- Color the organisms that have a molted external skeleton blue. Color the organism without a molted external skeleton red.
- Circle the point on the cladogram that shows the most recent common ancestor of the crab and the barnacle.
- Mark an X on the point on the cladogram that shows the most recent common ancestor of mollusks and crustaceans.

CLADOGRAM

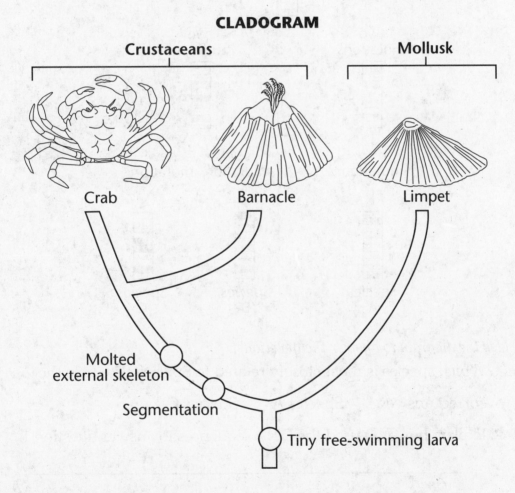

Use the cladogram to answer the questions. Circle the correct answer.

1. Which organism shows segmentation?

   barnacle   limpet

2. What do all three organisms shown have in common?

   tiny free-swimming larva   molted external skeleton

© Pearson Education, Inc., publishing as Pearson Prentice Hall.

Genetic Evidence of Common Ancestors

Biologists compare DNA sequences to determine evolutionary relationships. The more similar the DNA sequences of two species are, the more recently the two species shared a common ancestor. Each picture in the diagram below represents a gene. Each shaded portion of a gene represents a mutation.

A gene in an ancestral species

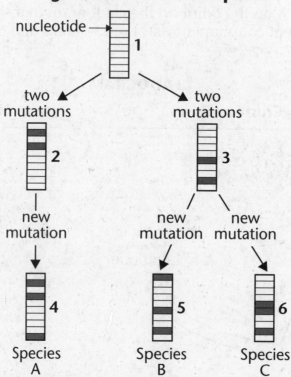

Use the diagram to answer the questions.

1. Which species is most closely related to Species B? Circle the correct answer.   Species A   Species C

2. Explain how you used the DNA sequences to answer question 1.

   _____

   _____

   _____

3. How can you tell that Species C developed from the organism with gene 3?

   _____

   _____

© Pearson Education, Inc., publishing as Pearson Prentice Hall.

Three Domains

All organisms belong to one of three domains, depending on their characteristics. A domain is the most inclusive taxonomic category. A single domain can contain one or more kingdoms.

Write each of the following domain names in the correct place in the table: Bacteria, Archaea, *and* Eukarya.

Three Domains		
Domain	**Organism Characteristics**	**Kingdoms Included in Domain**
	Prokaryotes with cell walls made up of peptidoglycan	Eubacteria
	Eukaryotes	Protista, Fungi, Plantae, Animalia
	Prokaryotes whose cell walls do not contain peptidoglycan and whose cell membranes contain unusual lipids	Archaebacteria

Answer the questions.

1. Which domains are composed of unicellular organisms only?

_____

2. To which domain do organisms whose cells contain nuclei belong?

_____

3. To which domain does the kingdom Eubacteria belong?

_____

Identifying Kingdoms

The domain Eukarya is made up of four kingdoms: *Animalia, Fungi, Plantae,* and *Protista.*

Fill in the table with the correct kingdom.

Kingdom	Cell Structures	Number of Cells	Mode of Nutrition
	Cell walls of cellulose in some; some have chloroplasts	Most unicellular; some colonial; some multicellular	Autotroph or heterotroph
	Cell walls of chitin	Most multicellular; some unicellular	Heterotroph
	Cell walls of cellulose; chloroplasts	Multicellular	Autotroph
	No cell walls or chloroplasts	Multicellular	Heterotroph

Use the table to answer the questions.

1. Which kingdoms contain autotrophs?

_____

2. Which kingdoms contain unicellular organisms?

_____

3. To which kingdom do grizzly bears belong?

_____

4. What do fungi and plants have in common?

_____

© Pearson Education, Inc., publishing as Pearson Prentice Hall.

Chapter 18   Classification

Vocabulary Review

Completion   *Use the words below to fill in the blanks with terms from the chapter.*

cladogram	Eubacteria
domain	family

1. The kingdom _____ makes up the domain Bacteria.

2. The newest and largest classification category is the

   _____.

3. A group of genera that share many characteristics is called

   a(an) _____.

4. A diagram that shows evolutionary relationships among a

   group of organisms is a(an) _____.

Completion   *Use the words below to fill in the blanks with terms from the chapter.*

binomial nomenclature	kingdom	taxonomy
genus	phylogeny	

5. The largest and most inclusive taxon in Linnaeus's system is

   the _____.

6. A group of closely related species is a _____.

7. The study of evolutionary relationships among organisms is

   called _____.

8. The science of classifying living things is _____.

9. A system of naming in which organisms are given names made

   up of two names is called _____.

© Pearson Education, Inc., publishing as Pearson Prentice Hall.

Chapter 19   Bacteria and Viruses

Summary

19–1 Bacteria

The smallest and most common microorganisms are prokaryotes. **Prokaryotes** are unicellular and lack a nucleus. There are two kingdoms of prokaryotes: eubacteria and archaebacteria.

- Eubacteria live almost everywhere. Most eubacteria have a cell wall that contains the carbohydrate peptidoglycan. Inside the cell wall is a cell membrane that surrounds the cytoplasm.
- Archaebacteria look like eubacteria, but they have some differences. **Archaebacteria do not have peptidoglycan in their cell walls. They have many different membrane lipids. Also, the DNA sequences of key archaebacterial genes are more like those of eukaryotes than those of eubacteria.** Archaebacteria may be the ancestors of eukaryotes.

Prokaryotes are identified by characteristics that include the following:

- **Shape**   Prokaryotes have three different shapes: rod-shaped (bacilli), sphere-shaped (cocci), or spiral-shaped (spirilla).
- **Chemical makeup of cell walls**   Prokaryotes have two types of cell walls. Gram staining is used to tell them apart. Gram-positive bacteria appear violet when stained. Gram-negative bacteria appear pink.
- **Means of movement**   Prokaryotes move in a variety of ways.
- **Means of getting energy**   Most prokaryotes are heterotrophs, organisms that get energy by consuming food. Other pro-karyotes are autotrophs, organisms that make their own food.

Prokaryotes get energy through cellular respiration and fermentation.

- **Obligate aerobes** need a constant oxygen supply in order to live.
- **Obligate anaerobes** do not need oxygen, and may be killed by it.
- **Facultative anaerobes** can survive with or without oxygen.

Bacteria reproduce asexually by **binary fission.** When a bacterium has grown to nearly double its size, it replicates its DNA and divides in half. Bacteria also reproduce by **conjugation.** During conjugation, genetic material is transferred from one bacterium to another. Many bacteria can form an **endospore** when conditions are bad. An endospore is a thick internal wall that surrounds the DNA and part of the cytoplasm of the bacterium. The spore can survive harsh conditions that would kill the bacterium in its active form.

© Pearson Education, Inc., publishing as Pearson Prentice Hall.

Bacteria are vital to the living world. Some are producers that carry out photosynthesis. Others are decomposers that break down dead matter. Some soil bacteria convert nitrogen gas into a form that plants can use through a process called nitrogen fixation. Humans use bacteria in industry, food production, and other ways.

19–2 Viruses

Viruses are particles of nucleic acid and protein. Some contain lipids, too. A typical virus is made of a core of DNA or RNA surrounded by a protein coat called a capsid.

To reproduce, a virus must invade, or infect, a living host cell. Viruses that infect bacteria are called bacteriophages. After a virus enters a host cell, one of two processes may occur.

- In a lytic infection, a virus attaches itself to a host cell. It injects its DNA into the cell. The host cell starts making messenger RNA from the viral DNA. The messenger RNA takes over the host cell. Copies of viral DNA and the viral protein coats are made and assembled into new viruses. Then, the host cell bursts and the new viruses infect other cells.

- In a lysogenic infection, the virus does not reproduce immediately after infecting the host cell. Instead, the nucleic acid of the virus is inserted into the DNA of the host cell. The viral DNA may stay within the host DNA for quite some time. However, eventually it may become active, remove itself from the host DNA, and begin the production of new viruses.

Some viruses, called retroviruses, contain RNA as their genetic information. They produce a DNA copy of their RNA genes when they infect a cell. AIDS is a disease caused by a retrovirus.

Viruses are parasites. They must infect a living cell in order to reproduce. Because viruses are not made up of cells and cannot live on their own, viruses are not considered to be living.

19–3 Diseases Caused by Bacteria and Viruses

Some bacteria and viruses can be pathogens. Pathogens are disease-causing agents.

Bacterial Disease
Bacteria can cause tuberculosis, strep throat, and tetanus. Bacteria cause disease in two general ways.

1. Bacteria break down cells for food.

2. Bacteria release toxins (poisons) that disrupt normal body functions in the host.

© Pearson Education, Inc., publishing as Pearson Prentice Hall.

To prevent some bacterial diseases, vaccines are used. A **vaccine** is a preparation of weakened or killed pathogens. A vaccine works by prompting the body to form immunity to a disease. **Immunity** is the body's natural way of killing pathogens.

When a bacterial infection occurs, antibiotics may help fight the disease. **Antibiotics** are compounds that block the growth and reproduction of bacteria.

Bacterial growth can be controlled. **Sterilization, disinfectants, and proper food storage and food processing can control bacteria.** Disinfectants include soaps and cleaning solutions. Food storage includes using a refrigerator.

Not all bacteria are pathogens. Some live in and on the human body and help it carry out needed functions. For example, bacteria that live in the intestines make vitamin K.

Viral Disease

Like bacteria, viruses cause disease by disrupting the body's normal equilibrium, or balance. In many viral infections, viruses attack and destroy certain body cells. This causes the symptoms of the disease. Viral diseases in humans include the common cold, influenza, AIDS, chickenpox, and measles. Some viral diseases can be prevented with vaccines. Viruses also cause diseases in animals and plants.

Two viruslike particles also can cause disease.

- **Viroids** are single-stranded RNA molecules that have no surrounding capsids. Viroids cause disease in plants.
- **Prions** are particles containing only protein—there is no DNA or RNA. Prions cause disease in animals, including humans.

© Pearson Education, Inc., publishing as Pearson Prentice Hall.

Prokaryote Structure

A prokaryote is a unicellular organism that lacks a nucleus. Most prokaryotes have a cell wall, a cell membrane, and cytoplasm. The bacterium below is one example of a prokaryote.

Follow the prompts to locate structures in a typical bacterium.
- Color the cell membrane yellow.
- Color the cell wall blue.
- Color the flagella red.
- Color the pili orange.
- Color the DNA green.

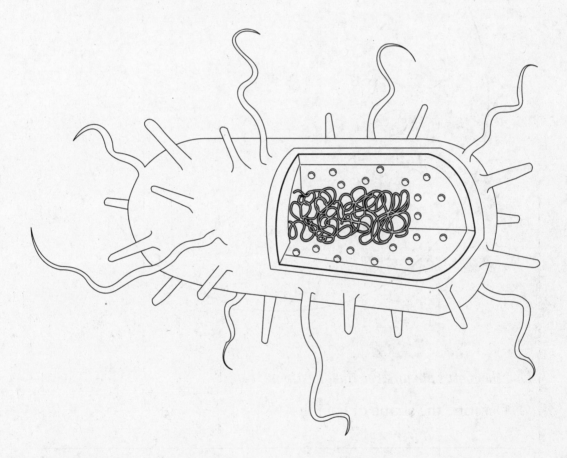

Use the diagram to answer the questions. Circle the correct answer.

1. What does the bacterium use to move?

pili   flagellum

2. What is the bacterium's genetic material called?

cell membrane   DNA

© Pearson Education, Inc., publishing as Pearson Prentice Hall.

Bacteria Shapes

The picture shows several kinds of bacteria. Color the bacilli *blue. Color the* cocci *red. Color the* spirilla *yellow.*

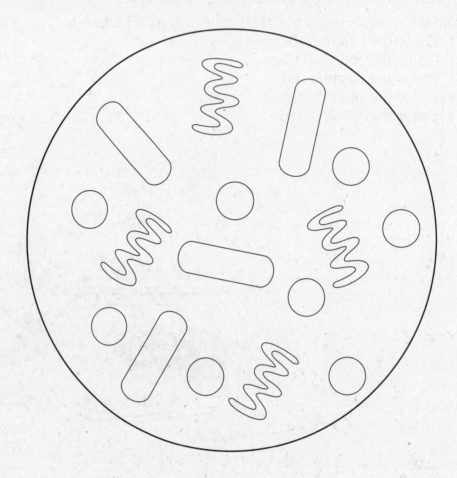

Use the picture to answer the questions.

1. Describe the shape of bacilli.

_____

2. Describe the shape of cocci.

_____

3. Describe the shape of spirilla.

_____

© Pearson Education, Inc., publishing as Pearson Prentice Hall.

What Makes Up a Virus?

Viruses are particles made up of protein, genetic material, and some-times lipids. The genetic material in a virus can be RNA or DNA. The protein coat that surrounds the genetic material is called the capsid.

The diagrams show three kinds of viruses. Circle the genetic material in each virus. Color the protein parts of each virus yellow.

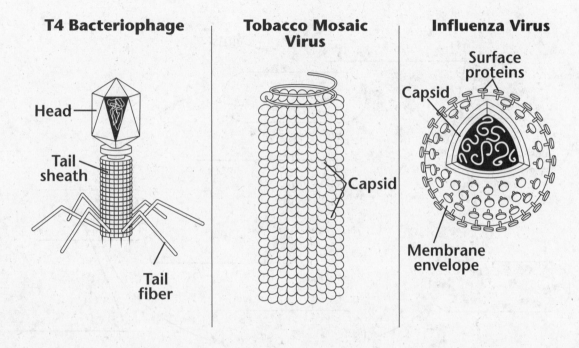

T4 Bacteriophage

Head

Tail sheath

Tail fiber

Tobacco Mosaic Virus

Capsid

Influenza Virus

Surface proteins

Capsid

Membrane envelope

Use the diagrams to answer the questions.

1. Where is the genetic material in a T4 bacteriophage located?

_____

_____

2. In general, is the genetic material in a virus inside or outside the protein parts?

_____

3. Which structure contains proteins that enable a virus to enter a host cell? Circle the correct answer.

capsid   RNA

© Pearson Education, Inc., publishing as Pearson Prentice Hall.

Lytic Infections

A bacteriophage is a virus that can infect bacteria. A lytic infection is one kind of viral infection. It results in lysis, or bursting of the host cell. The diagram shows how a bacteriophage causes a lytic infection in a bacterium.

Label the bacterial DNA, host bacterium, viral DNA, and virus. Then, circle the step that shows lysis of the host cell.

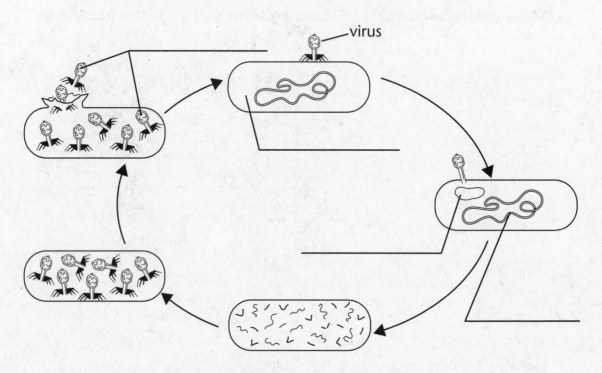

Use the diagram to answer the questions.

1. Summarize what happens in a lytic infection.

_____

_____

_____

2. What is one result of a lytic infection? Circle the correct answer.

lysis of the virus   lysis of the host cell

© Pearson Education, Inc., publishing as Pearson Prentice Hall.

Lysogenic Infections

A lysogenic infection occurs when viral DNA inserts itself into the DNA of the host cell. The viral DNA is replicated along with the host cell DNA. Eventually, the viral DNA will separate out of the host DNA and direct the construction of new virus particles. The diagram shows how a bacteriophage causes a lysogenic infection in a bacterium.

Circle the viral DNA in each diagram of the bacterium.

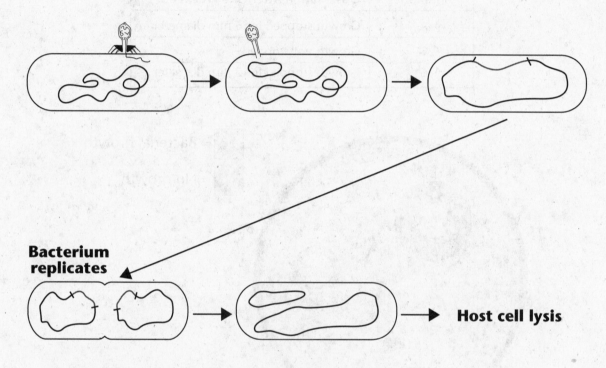

Bacterium replicates

Host cell lysis

Use the diagram to answer the questions.

1. What happens after the viral DNA is inserted into the bacterial DNA?

_____

_____

2. How does a lysogenic infection help a virus spread?

_____

_____

© Pearson Education, Inc., publishing as Pearson Prentice Hall.

Antibiotics

Antibiotics are compounds that block the growth and reproduction of bacteria. The picture shows a petri dish of bacteria with three antibiotic disks in it.

Use the picture and the table to label each disk with the letter of the antibiotic used on it.

Effects of Antibiotics	
Antibiotic	**Observation After One Week**
A	Growth stopped for 6 mm diameter
B	Growth not stopped
C	Growth stopped for 2 mm diameter

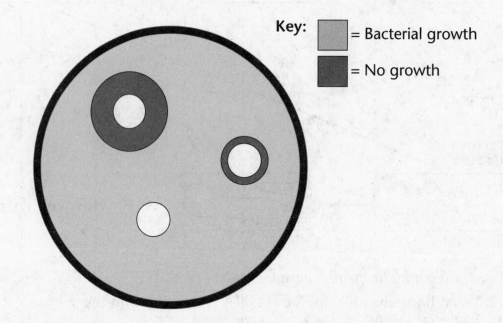

Key:

■ = Bacterial growth

■ = No growth

Use the picture and table to answer the questions.

1. Which antibiotic was most effective against the bacteria in the petri dish?

_____

2. Why did you choose that antibiotic?

_____

© Pearson Education, Inc., publishing as Pearson Prentice Hall.

Chapter 19 Bacteria and Viruses

Vocabulary Review

Matching *In the space provided, write the letter of the definition that best matches each term.*

_____ **1.** endospore

_____ **2.** virus

_____ **3.** coccus

_____ **4.** prokaryote

_____ **5.** bacillus

_____ **6.** vaccine

_____ **7.** spirillum

a. bacterium with a rod shape

b. bacterium with a corkscrew shape

c. particle of nucleic acid, protein, and possibly lipids that can reproduce only by infecting other cells

d. unicellular organism that lacks a nucleus

e. preparation of weakened or killed pathogen that, when injected, may prompt the body to develop an immunity to the disease

f. bacterium with a sphere shape

g. thick internal wall produced by a bacterium when growth conditions become unfavorable

Matching *In the space provided, write the letter of the definition that best matches each term.*

_____ **8.** bacteriophage

_____ **9.** retrovirus

_____ **10.** prion

_____ **11.** capsid

_____ **12.** lytic

_____ **13.** binary fission

_____ **14.** conjugation

a. exchange of genetic material in bacteria

b. infectious protein particle

c. type of viral infection that causes the cell to burst

d. protein coat of a virus

e. virus that infects bacteria

f. asexual form of reproduction carried out by bacteria

g. virus having RNA as its genetic material

© Pearson Education, Inc., publishing as Pearson Prentice Hall.

Chapter 20   Protists

Summary

20–1 The Kingdom Protista

The kingdom Protista is a diverse group. **Protists are eukaryotes that are not members of the kingdoms Plantae, Animalia, or Fungi.** Most protists are unicellular. Earth's first eukaryotes were protists. One way protists are classified is according to how they obtain nutrition. Thus, many protists that are heterotrophic are called animal-like protists. Protists that produce their own food by photosynthesis are called plantlike protists. Protists that obtain their food by external digestion are called funguslike protists.

20–2 Animal-like Protists: Protozoans

Animal-like protists are called protozoans. Protozoans are heterotrophs. There are four phyla of animal-like protists. They are classified according to how they move.

- **Protists that swim using flagella are classified in the phylum Zoomastigina.** They are called zooflagellates. Flagella are long, whiplike projections that allow a cell to move.
- **Members of the phylum Sarcodina move by using pseudopods. Sarcodines also use pseudopods for feeding. Pseudopods** are temporary projections of cytoplasm. Sarcodines called amoebas have thick pseudopods. An ameoba moves by first extending its psuedopod. The cell's cytoplasm flows into the pseudopod. The rest of the cell then follows. This type of movement is called **amoeboid movement.**
- **Members of the phylum Ciliophora, known as ciliates, use cilia for feeding and movement. Cilia** are short, hairlike projections similar to flagella. Some of the best-known ciliates belong to the genus *Paramecium.* The cilia of a paramecium are organized into evenly spaced rows and bundles. Just under the cell membrane, a paramecium has small defense structures called **trichocysts.** When a paramecium is in danger, the trichocysts release stiff projections that protect the cell.
- **Members of the phylum Sporozoa do not move on their own. They are parasites that reproduce by means of sporozoites.**

   Some animal-like protists cause serious diseases. For example, *Plasmodium* is a sporozoan that causes malaria. *Trypanosoma* is a zooflagellate. It causes African sleeping sickness.

   Some animal-like protists are helpful. *Trichonympha* lives in the digestive system of termites. This protist helps termites digest wood.

© Pearson Education, Inc., publishing as Pearson Prentice Hall.

20–3 Plantlike Protists: Unicellular Algae

Plantlike protists are called algae. One of the key traits used to classify algae is the photosynthetic **pigments** they contain. **Chlorophyll and accessory pigments allow algae to harvest and use the energy from sunlight.** Unicellular plantlike protists include four phyla.

- **Euglenophytes have two flagella and no cell wall.** Euglenophytes have chloroplasts, but in most other ways they are like zooflagellates. The phylum gets its name from the genus *Euglena.* To move, a euglena spins the longer of its two flagella. This pulls the euglena through the water.
- **Chrysophytes are a diverse group of plantlike protists that have gold-colored chloroplasts.**
- **Diatoms produce thin, delicate cell walls rich in silicon (Si).**
- Dinoflagellates generally have two flagella. **About half of the dinoflagellates are photosynthetic. The other half live as heterotrophs.**

Plantlike protists are ecologically important. They make up much of phytoplankton. Phytoplankton are small photosynthetic organisms that float near the ocean's surface.

Many protists grow quickly in places where sewage is dumped into water. When the amount of waste is excessive, algae grow into huge masses called algal blooms.

20–4 Plantlike Protists: Red, Brown, and Green Algae

Three phyla of plantlike protists include mostly multicellular organisms. They are grouped by their photosynthetic pigments.

- Red algae are members of phylum Rhodophyta. **These algae can live at great depths because of their ability to harvest light energy. They contain chlorophyll *a* and reddish accessory pigments called phycobilins.**
- Brown algae are members of the phylum Phaeophyta. **They contain chlorophyll *a* and *c* and a brown accessory pigment.** The largest alga is giant kelp, a brown alga that grows to more than 60 meters long.
- Green algae, which share many characteristics with plants, are members of the phylum Chlorophyta. **Both plants and green algae have the same photosynthetic pigments, chlorophyll *a* and *b*.** Scientists hypothesize that the ancestors of modern land plants looked like green algae. Several species of green algae live in multicellular colonies.

Many algae life cycles include both a diploid and a haploid stage. The process of switching back and forth between haploid and diploid stages in a life cycle is called **alternation of generations.**

Algae produce much of Earth's oxygen through photosynthesis. Algae are a major food source for animals and people. Industry uses algae in making plastics and other products.

20–5 Funguslike Protists

Like fungi, funguslike protists are heterotrophs that absorb food from dead or decaying organic matter. Unlike most fungi, though, funguslike protists have centrioles. They also lack the chitin cell walls of fungi.

Slime molds are funguslike protists that play key roles in recycling organic matter. At one stage of their life cycle, slime molds look like amoebas. At other stages, they form moldlike clumps that produce spores. There are two kinds of slime molds.
- In **cellular slime molds,** individual cells remain distinct during every phase of the life cycle. They spend most of their lives as free-living cells.
- In **acellular slime molds,** cells fuse to form large cells with many nuclei. These structures are known as plasmodia. **Fruiting bodies,** or sporangia, spring up from a plasmodium.

Water molds, or oomycetes, are members of the phylum Oomycota. **Oomycetes thrive on dead or decaying organic matter in water. Some oomycetes are plant parasites on land.**

Slime molds and water molds are important recyclers of organic material. Some funguslike protists can cause diseases in plants. An oomycete caused a disease in the Irish potato crop in 1845 and 1846, leading to mass starvation.

© Pearson Education, Inc., publishing as Pearson Prentice Hall.

Protist Characteristics

Animal-like protists are divided into four groups according to the way they move. Unicellular plantlike protists are divided into four groups according to various cellular characteristics.

Use the words below to complete the table. The first one in each table has been done for you.

chrysophytes	diatoms	sarcodines
ciliates	euglenophytes	zooflagellates

Animal-like Protists	How They Move
sporozoans	do not move; parasitic
	pseudopods
	flagella
	cilia

Plantlike Protists	Identifying Characteristics(s)
dinoflagellates	some photosynthetic, some heterotrophs; generally have flagella
	two flagella; no cell wall
	gold-colored chloroplasts
	cell walls rich in silicon

Use the tables to answer the following questions. Circle the correct answer.

1. A paramecium uses cilia to swim through the water. What type of protist is it?

sarcodine   ciliate

2. What cell structures do both zooflagellates and euglenophytes have?

chloroplasts   flagella

© Pearson Education, Inc., publishing as Pearson Prentice Hall.

Paramecium

A paramecium is an animal-like protist called a ciliate. It uses cilia for feeding and movement.

Label the cilia. *Then, color the structures of the paramecium.*
- Color the structures used for defense orange.
- Color the structures that contain genetic information yellow.
- Color the structures that eliminate waste materials, including excess water, green.

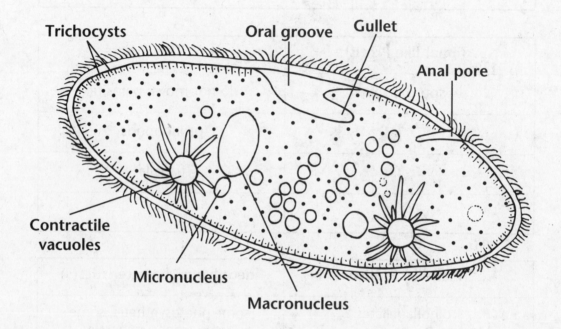

Answer the questions.

1. What is a trichocyst?

_____

_____

2. Which structure helps maintain homeostasis by removing excess water? Circle the correct answer.

contractile vacuole   gullet

© Pearson Education, Inc., publishing as Pearson Prentice Hall.

Protists as Parasites

Some animal-like protists are parasites that cause serious diseases in humans and other animals. The life cycle of the sporozoan *Plasmodium* is diagrammed below.

Follow the prompts.
- Circle the stage in which a mosquito becomes infected with the protist.
- Place an X on the stage in which a human becomes infected with the protist.

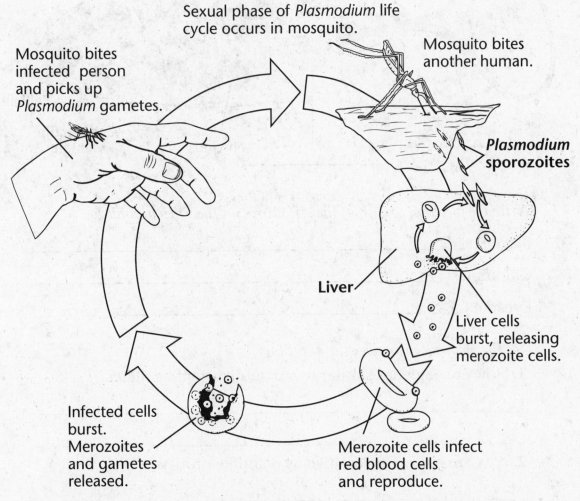

Sexual phase of *Plasmodium* life cycle occurs in mosquito.

Mosquito bites infected person and picks up *Plasmodium* gametes.

Mosquito bites another human.

Plasmodium sporozoites

Liver

Liver cells burst, releasing merozoite cells.

Infected cells burst. Merozoites and gametes released.

Merozoite cells infect red blood cells and reproduce.

Use the diagram to answer the questions.

1. Which type of human cell releases *Plasmodium* gametes when it bursts? Circle the correct answer.

liver cells   red blood cells

2. What disease does *Plasmodium* cause?

_____

© Pearson Education, Inc., publishing as Pearson Prentice Hall.

Euglena

The euglena is a plantlike protist. It has two flagella but no cell wall.
Label the flagella, chloroplast *and* eyespot *on the diagram.*

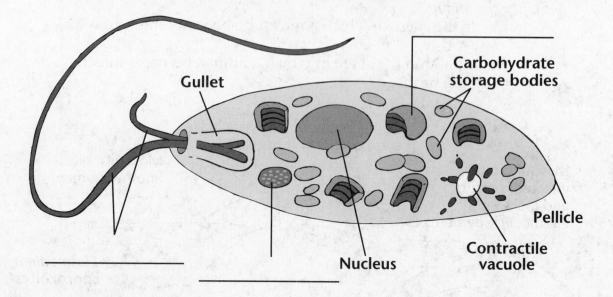

Write the function of each of the structures on the lines provided.

Flagella _____

Chloroplast _____

Eyespot _____

Use the diagram to answer the questions.

1. How are euglenas similar to animal-like zooflagellates?

_____

_____

2. Why are euglenas classified as plantlike protists?

_____

_____

Algae Life Cycle

Recall that a *haploid* cell contains only a single set of chromosomes. A *diploid* cell contains two sets of chromosomes. Many algae switch back and forth between haploid and diploid stages during their life cycles. This process is called alternation of generations.

Color the arrows representing haploid phases of the algae life cycle yellow. Color the arrows representing diploid phases blue.

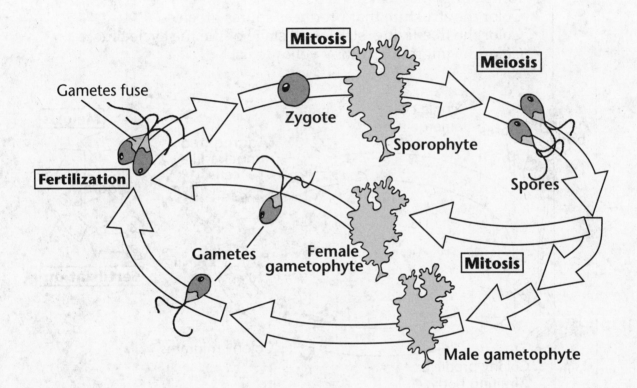

Use the diagram to answer the questions.

1. What does a sporophyte produce?

_____

2. What does a gametophyte produce?

_____

3. What forms when gametes fuse?

_____

© Pearson Education, Inc., publishing as Pearson Prentice Hall.

Cellular Slime Molds

Cellular slime molds spend most of their lives as single, free-living cells. When their food supply runs low, they aggregate, or come together. This aggregate of cells functions like a single organism. The life cycle of a cellular slime mold is diagrammed below.

Color the life cycle according to the prompts below.
- Color the stage that shows single cells coming together to form a migrating colony red.
- Color the structure that produces spores green.
- Color the free-living, single-cell stage of the life cycle blue.
- Color the migrating colony yellow.

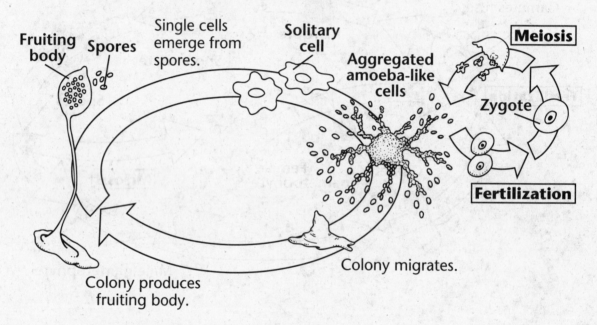

Answer the questions. Circle the correct answer.

1. What type of protists are cellular slime molds?

plantlike   funguslike

2. What does the fruiting body produce?

spores   zygotes

© Pearson Education, Inc., publishing as Pearson Prentice Hall.

Chapter 20   Protists

Vocabulary Review

Multiple Choice   *In the space provided, write the letter of the term that best completes each sentence.*

____ 1. Small photosynthetic organisms living near the ocean surface are called
    a. cilia.
    b. plasmodia.
    c. phytoplankton.

____ 2. The life cycle of many types of algae switches back and forth between a haploid and diploid stage through a process called
    a. amoeboid movement.
    b. conjugation.
    c. alternation of generations.

____ 3. The single structure with many nuclei that is formed by an acellular slime mold is a
    a. plasmodium.
    b. cilium.
    c. zoosporangium.

____ 4. Amoebas move and feed by using their
    a. pseudopods.
    b. oogonium.
    c. eyespots.

____ 5. An organism that is not a prokaryote, a plant, an animal, or a fungus is a
    a. phycobilin.
    b. protist.
    c. gullet.

____ 6. Some ciliates can exchange genetic material with other individuals through a reproductive process called
    a. amoeboid movement.
    b. conjugation.
    c. fruiting bodies.

____ 7. To help find sunlight, euglenas use their
    a. micronuclei.
    b. macronuclei.
    c. eyespots.

____ 8. The haploid reproductive cell made by *Ulva* that can grow into a new individual without fusing with another cell is a
    a. spore.
    b. trichocyst.
    c. sporophyte.

____ 9. A paramecium moves by using hairlike projections called
    a. gametophytes.
    b. contractile vacuoles.
    c. cilia.

© Pearson Education, Inc., publishing as Pearson Prentice Hall.

Chapter 21   Fungi

Summary

21–1 The Kingdom Fungi

Fungi are eukaryotic heterotrophs with cell walls made of chitin.
Chitin is a complex carbohydrate. Fungi do not ingest their food.
Instead, fungi digest food outside their bodies and then absorb it.

All fungi except for yeasts are multicellular. Multicellular fungi
are made up of thin filaments called **hyphae** (singular: hypha).
Each hypha is only one cell thick. **The bodies of multicellular
fungi are made of hyphae tangled together into a thick mass
called a mycelium.** The **mycelium** allows a large surface area to
come into contact with the food source through which the fungi
grow. The **fruiting body** of a fungus is a reproductive structure
growing from the mycelium in the soil beneath it. In a mushroom,
the fruiting body is the aboveground part of the mushroom.

Most fungi reproduce both asexually and sexually.

- Asexual reproduction can occur when cells or hyphae
  break off and begin to grow on their own. Some fungi
  also make spores. In some fungi, spores are formed in
  structures called **sporangia.** Sporangia are found at the tips
  of hyphae called **sporangiophores.**

- Sexual reproduction in fungi usually involves two different
  mating types. One type is called "+" (plus), and the other is
  called "−" (minus). When the hyphae of a "+" fungus meets
  the hyphae of a "−" fungus, they fuse together in the same
  cell. After a period of growth and development, the nuclei
  form a diploid zygote. The diploid zygote enters meiosis,
  and produces haploid spores.

Spores of fungi exist in almost every environment. Many fungi
produce dry, almost weightless spores that are easily scattered
by wind. For these spores to grow, they must land in a favorable
environment. Temperature, moisture, and food conditions must
be in the right combination. Most spores, therefore, do not grow
into mature organisms.

© Pearson Education, Inc., publishing as Pearson Prentice Hall.

21–2 Classification of Fungi

There are four main groups of fungi: common molds, sac fungi, club fungi, and imperfect fungi. Fungi are classified according to their methods of reproduction and their structure.

Common molds (phylum Zygomycota) grow on meat, cheese, and bread. **These fungi have a life cycle that includes a zygospore.** A **zygospore** is a resting spore that contains zygotes formed during the sexual phase of the mold's life cycle.

Common molds include the black bread mold. During the sexual phase in black bread mold, hyphae from different mating types fuse to form gamete-making structures called **gametangia.** Black bread mold has two kinds of hyphae.

- The rootlike hyphae that go through the bread's surface are rhizoids.
- The stemlike hyphae that run along the surface of bread are stolons.

Sac fungi (phylum Ascomycota) include the large cup fungi and the unicellular yeasts. **These fungi are named for the ascus, a reproductive structure that contains spores.** The life cycle of an ascomycete includes both sexual and asexual reproduction.

In sexual reproduction, haploid hyphae from two different mating types (+ and −) grow close together to make a fruiting body. An **ascus** forms within the fruiting body. Two nuclei of different mating types fuse within the ascus to form a diploid zygote. Asexual reproduction in cup fungi and yeast are different.

- In cup fungi, tiny spores called **conidia** form at the tips of specialized hyphae called conidiophores.
- Asexual reproduction in yeast occurs by cell division. This process is called **budding.**

Club fungi (phylum Basidiomycota) include mushrooms, shelf fungi, and puffballs. **These fungi have a reproductive structure that resembles a club.** The cap of the fruiting body of a basidiomycete is made up of tightly packed hyphae. The lower side of the cap has gills, thin blades of tissue lined with basidia. A **basidium** is a spore-bearing structure. Two nuclei in each basidium fuse to form a diploid zygote cell. The zygote cell undergoes meiosis, forming clusters of spores called **basidiospores.** A single mushroom can produce billions of basidiospores.

Imperfect fungi **(phylum Deuteromycota) include fungi that are not placed in other phyla because researchers have never been able to observe a sexual phase in their life cycles.** An example of an imperfect fungus is *Penicillium notatum*, a mold that grows on fruit. It is the source of the antibiotic penicillin.

© Pearson Education, Inc., publishing as Pearson Prentice Hall.

21–3 Ecology of Fungi

All fungi are heterotrophs. Some fungi are saprobes. **Saprobes are organisms that obtain food from decaying organic matter. Fungi play an essential role in maintaining balance in ecosystems. Fungi recycle nutrients as they break down the remains and wastes of other organisms.** Many fungi feed by releasing digestive enzymes that break down organic material into simple molecules. In breaking down this matter, fungi help recycle nutrients and essential chemicals. Without such decomposers, the energy-rich compounds that organisms accumulate would be lost forever.

Parasitic fungi cause plant and animal diseases. A few cause diseases in humans.

- Fungal diseases in plants include corn smut and wheat rust.
- Fungal diseases in humans include athlete's foot, ringworm, thrush, and yeast infections of the female reproductive tract.

Some fungi are symbiotes that form mutualistic relationships in which both partners benefit.

- **Lichens** are an association between a fungus and green alga, a cyanobacterium, or both. The alga or cyanobacterium provides the fungus with a source of energy by carrying out photosynthesis. The fungus provides the photosynthetic organism with water and minerals and shades it from intense sunlight.
- Mutualistic associations of plant roots and fungi are called **mycorrhizae.** The hyphae of fungi aid the plant in absorbing water and minerals. The fungi also release enzymes that free nutrients from the soil. The plant provides the fungi with the products of photosynthesis. The presence of mycorrhizae is needed for the growth of many plants.

© Pearson Education, Inc., publishing as Pearson Prentice Hall.

Hyphae Structure

Hyphae are thin filaments that make up multicellular fungi. Each hypha is one cell thick. Some hyphae have cross walls that divide each hypha into cells with one or two nuclei. Other hyphae lack cross walls and have many nuclei.

In each diagram, label the following structures: cell wall, cytoplasm, cross wall, nuclei. *Some structures appear in both diagrams.*

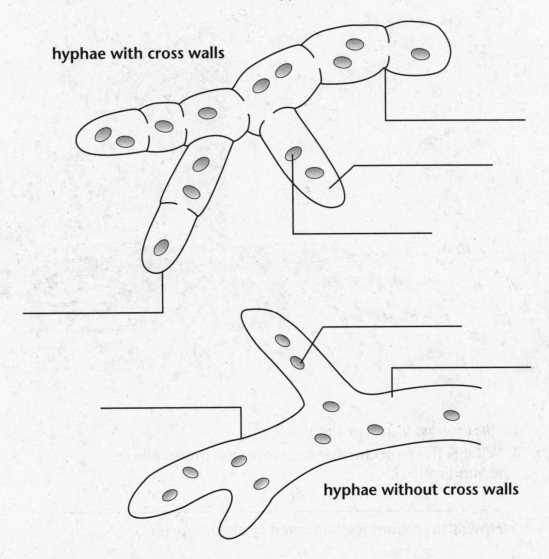

hyphae with cross walls

hyphae without cross walls

Circle the correct answer.

1. What makes up the cell walls of hyphae?

chitin   mycelium

2. What is the thick mass of tangled hyphae that makes up most fungi called?

mycelium   yeast

© Pearson Education, Inc., publishing as Pearson Prentice Hall.

Fungus Structure

A multicellular fungus is made up of many hyphae tangled together in a thick mass. This mass of hyphae is called the mycelium. The mycelium produces a reproductive structure called a fruiting body. One mycelium can produce many fruiting bodies.

Color the hyphae *red. Then label the* fruiting body *and the* mycelium.

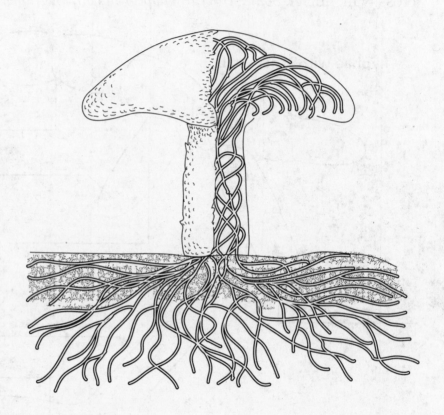

Use the diagram to answer the questions.

1. What is the reproductive structure that grows above ground called?

   _____

2. How is mycelium well-adapted to absorb food?

   _____

   _____

© Pearson Education, Inc., publishing as Pearson Prentice Hall.

Bread Mold Life Cycle

A bread mold can reproduce both sexually and asexually. In asexual reproduction, the mold directly produces spores. In sexual reproduction, a zygospore forms that contains zygotes. These zygotes can undergo meiosis and form spores.

Color the arrow that shows asexual reproduction red. Color the arrows that show sexual reproduction blue.

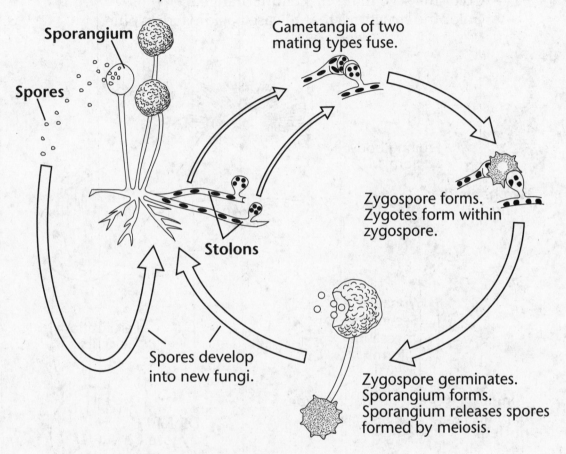

Use the diagram to answer the questions.

1. Which structure releases spores? Circle the correct answer.

   sporangium   gametangia

2. The zygospore can remain dormant for long periods before it germinates. Why might this be useful to a fungus?

   _____

   _____

   _____

© Pearson Education, Inc., publishing as Pearson Prentice Hall.

Club Fungi Life Cycle

Club fungi, or basidiomycetes, reproduce sexually through the fusion of nuclei found in structures called basidia.

Follow the prompts below to identify important stages in the life cycle of club fungi.
- Color the fruiting body red.
- Color the primary mycelium yellow.
- Color the secondary mycelium orange.
- Color the structures that release basidiospores blue.

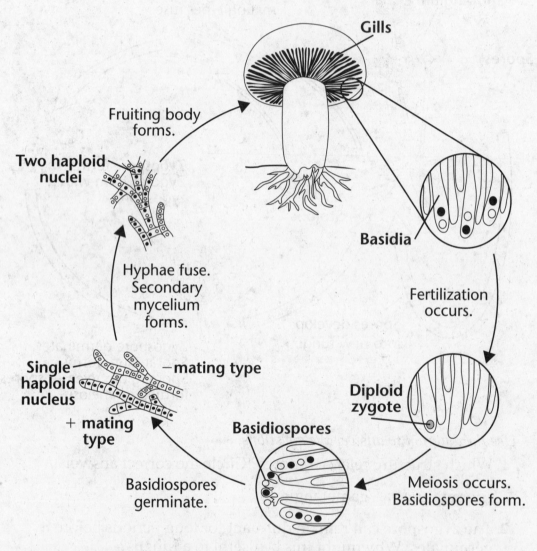

Use the diagram to answer the questions.

1. What do basidiospores grow into?

_____

2. What are the spore-bearing structures called? Circle the correct

answer.   basidia   primary mycelium

© Pearson Education, Inc., publishing as Pearson Prentice Hall.

Lichens

Lichens are formed by the symbiotic relationship of a fungus and a photosynthetic organism. The lichen shown below is composed of fungi and algae. It grows on rock.

Color the hyphae of the fungus brown. Color the algae green. Then label the algae *and* hyphae.

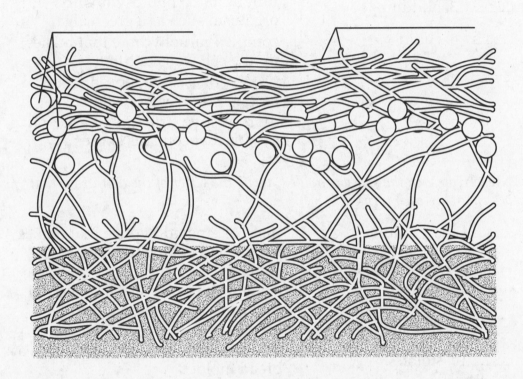

Answer the questions.

1. Which term best describes the relationship between the algae and the fungus in the diagram above? Circle the correct answer.

   parasitic   mutualistic

2. What do the algae provide for the fungus?

   _____

3. What does the fungus provide for the algae?

   _____

© Pearson Education, Inc., publishing as Pearson Prentice Hall.

Chapter 21   Fungi

Vocabulary Review

Matching   *In the space provided, write the letter of the definition that best matches each term.*

_____ **1.** ascus

_____ **2.** basidium

_____ **3.** budding

_____ **4.** chitin

_____ **5.** lichen

a. the spore-bearing structure of a club fungus

b. a symbiotic association between a fungus and a photosynthetic organism such as a green alga

c. complex carbohydrate that makes up the cell walls of fungi

d. process of asexual reproduction carried out by yeast cells

e. reproductive structure of a sac fungus that contains spores

Matching   *In the space provided, write the letter of the definition that best matches each term.*

_____ **6.** mycelium

_____ **7.** rhizoid

_____ **8.** saprobe

_____ **9.** sporangium

_____ **10.** stolon

a. mass of tangled hyphae that makes up the body of a multicellular fungus

b. a stemlike hypha on a bread mold that runs across the surface of bread

c. a structure that contains spores in a bread mold

d. an organism that obtains food from decaying organic matter

e. a rootlike hypha that anchors a bread mold to the bread

© Pearson Education, Inc., publishing as Pearson Prentice Hall.

Chapter 22   Plant Diversity

Summary

22–1 Introduction to Plants

Plants form the base of land food chains. They also provide shade, shelter, and oxygen for animals. **Plants are multicellular organisms with cell walls made of cellulose. They develop from multicellular embryos. They make their own food through photosynthesis using green pigments called chlorophyll *a* and *b*.**

Plant life cycles have two phases. A diploid (2N) phase alternates with a haploid (N) phase. This is known as alternation of generations.

The diploid phase is known as the **sporophyte,** or spore-producing plant. The haploid phase is known as the **gametophyte,** or gamete-producing plant. The sporophyte forms haploid spores. The spores grow into haploid gametophytes. The gametophyte forms male and female reproductive cells, called gametes. Male and female gametes fuse during fertilization to produce a new sporophyte.

In order to survive, plants need sunlight, water, minerals, gas exchange, and a transport system. Plants have evolved many different adaptations to meet these needs in dry, land environments. For example, seeds help plants reproduce successfully without water.

Early land plants evolved from an organism that was like today's multicellular green algae. As early land plants adapted to a dry habitat, several plant groups evolved. Today, scientists divide the plant kingdom into four basic groups: mosses and their relatives, ferns and their relatives, cone-bearing plants, and flowering plants. These groups are based upon three important adaptations: water-conducting tissue, seeds, and flowers.

22–2 Bryophytes

Unlike all other plants, bryophytes do not have vascular tissue or specialized tissues to conduct water and nutrients. **Bryophytes have life cycles that depend on water for reproduction. Bryophytes include mosses, liverworts, and hornworts.**

Bryophytes do not have true leaves, stems, or roots. They grow in wet habitats and where soil quality is poor. Instead of roots, **rhizoids** anchor mosses to the ground.

Bryophyte life cycles have alternation of generations. **In bryophytes, the gametophyte is the dominant stage of the life cycle.** Bryophytes have sperm cells that must swim through water to fertilize eggs. Thus, bryophytes must live in moist habitats.

© Pearson Education, Inc., publishing as Pearson Prentice Hall.

Bryophytes reproduce both sexually and asexually. They have several structures that produce reproductive cells. One structure, **antheridia** makes sperm cells. Another structure, **archegonia** makes egg cells.

- After fertilization, the diploid zygote grows into a sporophyte. The sporophyte produces spores. When the sporophyte matures, it releases the spores which are carried off by wind and water.
- When a spore lands in a moist place, it grows into the green, haploid gametophyte plant we think of as moss.

22–3 Seedless Vascular Plants

Seedless vascular plants are the first true land plants. They have a very important adaptation: special tissues that carry water and food throughout a plant. These tissues are called **vascular tissue.** There are two types of vascular tissue, xylem and phloem. **Xylem** moves water from the roots to all parts of the plant. **Phloem** carries nutrients and food from place to place within the plant.

Seedless vascular plants have roots, leaves, and stems. **Roots** absorb water and minerals. **Leaves** make food by photosynthesis. **Stems** support the plant and connect leaves and roots.

Seedless vascular plants include club mosses, horsetails, and ferns. Ferns are the most common. Ferns have strong roots, creeping or underground stems called **rhizomes,** and large leaves called **fronds.**

Ferns and other vascular plants have a life cycle in which the diploid sporophyte is the main stage. Fern sporophytes make haploid spores on the underside of the fronds in structures called sporangia. When spores are ripe, they burst from sporangia and are carried by wind and water. In the right conditions, they will grow to form haploid gametophytes. On the underside of the gametophyte are the antheridia and archegonia. When mature, sperm from the antheridia swim to the archegonia to fertilize the eggs. The diploid zygotes begin to grow into new sporophyte plants.

22–4 Seed Plants

Seed plants are divided into two groups, gymnosperms and angiosperms. **Gymnosperms,** or cone-bearing plants, produce seeds directly on the surface of cones. **Angiosperms,** or flowering plants, produce seeds inside a tissue that protects them.

Gymnosperms are the oldest surviving seed plants. Gymnosperms make seeds that are protected by a seed coat. **Gymnosperms include gnetophytes, cycads, ginkgoes, and conifers.**

© Pearson Education, Inc., publishing as Pearson Prentice Hall.

Like other plants, seed plants have alternation of generations. Seed plants do not require water for reproduction. This adaptation allows seed plants to live just about anywhere. **Adaptations that allow seed plants to reproduce without water include flowers or cones, the transfer of sperm by pollination, and the protection of embryos in seeds.**

- The gametophytes of seed plants are made up of only a few cells. They grow and mature within **flowers** and **cones.**
- The entire male gametophyte fits in a tiny **pollen grain.** Pollen can be carried to the female gametophyte by wind, water, and animals. This process is called **pollination.**
- **Seeds** protect the zygote of seed plants. After fertilization, the zygote grows into a tiny plant. This plant is an embryo. When conditions are right, the embryo grows. It uses a stored food supply inside the seed when it starts growing. A **seed coat** surrounds the embryo, keeping it from drying out.

22–5 Angiosperms—Flowering Plants

Angiosperms are the most common of all land plants. **Angiosperms have reproductive organs called flowers.** Flowers attract animals, which carry pollen from flower to flower. This is a more efficient way of pollination than the wind pollination of most gymnosperms. **Flowers contain ovaries, which surround and protect the seeds.** The structure that protects the seeds develops into a **fruit.**

The two groups of angiosperms are monocots and dicots. **Monocots and dicots are named for the number of seed leaves, or cotyledons, in the plant embryo. Monocots have one seed leaf. Dicots have two.** Other differences between monocots and dicots include the following:

- Arrangement of veins in leaves
- Number of flower petals
- Structure of roots
- Arrangement of vascular tissue in the stem

Flowering plants can also be grouped by their life spans. **There are three categories of plant life spans.**

- **Annuals** complete their life cycle within one growing season.
- **Biennials** complete their life cycle in two years. They produce seeds and die in the second growing season.
- **Perennials** live through many years. Some die back each winter and regrow in spring. Others have woody stems.

Plant Life Cycle

All plants have life cycles with alternation of generations. This means that they have a haploid phase and a diploid phase. The diploid phase is called the sporophyte. The haploid phase is called the gametophyte.

Color the arrows showing haploid stages of the plant life cycle red. Color the arrows showing diploid stages blue. Then label the sporophyte plant *and* gametophyte plant *stages of the life cycle.*

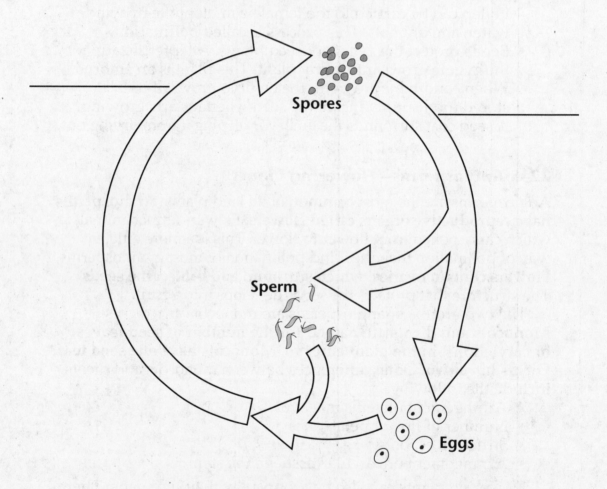

Use the diagram to answer the questions. Circle the correct answer.

1. Which of the following produces spores?

   sporophyte plant   gametophyte plant

2. Which best describes eggs and sperm?

   haploid   diploid

© Pearson Education, Inc., publishing as Pearson Prentice Hall.

Important Events in Plant Evolution

The cladogram shows plant evolution. The circles represent important adaptations in plant evolution.

Follow the prompts.
- Circle the plants that have vascular tissue.
- Mark an X on plants that have seeds.

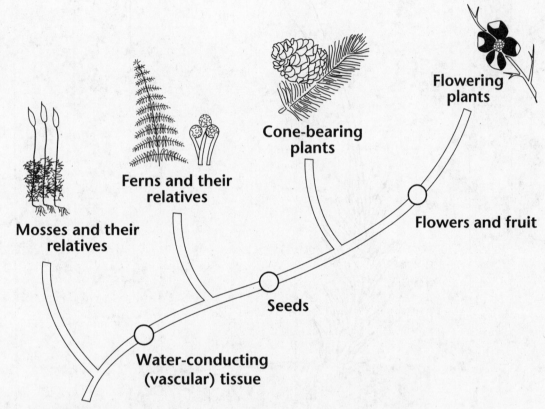

Green algae ancestor

Use the cladogram to answer the questions.

1. Which plants have flowers and fruit?

_____

2. Which of these evolved earlier? Circle the correct answer.

seeds   flowers

3. What plants do not have vascular tissue?

_____

Bryophyte Structure

This diagram shows the gametophyte of a bryophyte plant.
The sporophyte grows out of the gametophyte.

Color the gametophyte portion of the plant red. Color the sporophyte portion of the plant blue.

Use the diagram to answer the questions.

1. Where is the sporophyte found?

_____

_____

2. What is the role of the sporophyte?

_____

_____

© Pearson Education, Inc., publishing as Pearson Prentice Hall.

Fern Life Cycle

Ferns, like all other plants, have haploid and diploid stages of development. The diagram shows the life cycle of a fern.

Follow the prompts.
- Color the arrow that shows a haploid stage of development blue.
- Color the arrow that shows a diploid stage of development red.

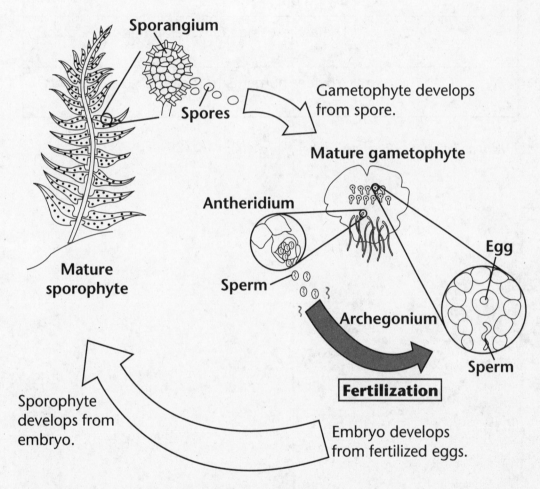

Use the diagram to answer the questions. Circle the correct answer.

1. Which structure produces eggs?

archegonium   sporangium

2. Which structure produces sperm?

antheridium   sporophyte

© Pearson Education, Inc., publishing as Pearson Prentice Hall.

Seed Structure

A seed has three parts: the *embryo,* the *seed coat,* and a *stored food supply.*

Use what you know about the parts of a seed to complete the table.

Seed Part	Function
	Protects the embryo and keeps the seed from drying out
	The earliest stage of development for a plant
	Provides nutrients to the embryo as it grows

Draw a sketch of a seed and label the parts.

Use the table to answer the questions.

1. Which part of the seed grows and develops? Circle the correct answer.

   seed coat   embryo

2. Why is the seed an important plant adaptation?

   _____

   _____

   _____

© Pearson Education, Inc., publishing as Pearson Prentice Hall.

Types of Plants

Use what you know about plants to fill in the missing information in the table. One row has been completed for you.

	Bryophytes	Ferns	Gymnosperms	Angiosperms
Vascular tissue	no	yes	yes	yes
Produce seeds		no		
Require water for fertilization			no	
Produce pollen				yes
Produce cones			yes	
Produce flowers and fruit		no		

Use the table to answer the questions.

1. Give an example of a seedless vascular plant.

_____

2. What characteristic do only angiosperms have?

_____

3. What characteristic do only gymnosperms have?

_____

4. What types of plants require water for fertilization?

_____

5. A pine tree has vascular tissue and produces cones. What type of plant is a pine tree?

_____

© Pearson Education, Inc., publishing as Pearson Prentice Hall.

Chapter 22   Plant Diversity

Vocabulary Review

Matching   *In the space provided, write the letter of the definition that best matches each term.*

_____ 1. angiosperm

_____ 2. bryophyte

_____ 3. cotyledon

_____ 4. dicot

_____ 5. gymnosperm

a. plant that bears its seeds on cones

b. nonvascular plant

c. any flowering plant

d. seed leaf

e. angiosperm having two seed leaves

Completion   *Use the words below to fill in the blanks with terms from the chapter.*

monocot	pollination	stem
phloem	sporophyte	xylem

6. In seed plants, the transfer of sperm from male reproductive structures to female reproductive structures is called

_____.

7. An angiosperm having only one seed leaf is a

_____.

8. The supporting structure in plants that connects roots and leaves is the _____.

9. A diploid, spore-producing plant is a _____.

10. Vascular tissue that transports solutions of nutrients is

_____.

11. Vascular tissue that carries water upward from roots is

_____.

© Pearson Education, Inc., publishing as Pearson Prentice Hall.

Chapter 23   Roots, Stems, and Leaves

Summary

23–1 Specialized Tissues in Plants

The cells of seed plants are organized into tissues and organs. **The three main plant organs are roots, stems, and leaves.**

- Roots absorb water and dissolved nutrients and anchor plants in the ground.
- Stems support the plant body and transport materials throughout the plant.
- Leaves are the main organs of photosynthesis. They also function in gas exchange.

Within the roots, stems, and leaves are specialized tissue systems. **The three main tissue systems:**

- **Dermal tissue** is like the "skin" of a plant. It protects the plant and prevents water loss. Dermal tissue is made up of **epidermal cells** having different shapes and functions.
- **Vascular tissue** consists of xylem and phloem.
  - Xylem tissue is made up of tracheids and vessel elements. Xylem moves water throughout the plant.
  - Phloem tissue is made of sieve tube elements and companion cells. Phloem moves sugars and other materials from the leaves to other parts of the plant.
- **Ground tissue** is made up of all of the cells that lie between dermal and vascular tissues. It is made up of three kinds of cells.
  - **Parenchyma cells** have thin cell walls. They function in photosynthesis and storage.
  - **Collenchyma cells** have strong, flexible cell walls that help support larger plants.
  - **Sclerenchyma cells** have thick, rigid cell walls that make ground tissue tough and strong.

A fourth kind of tissue, **meristematic tissue,** is responsible for plant growth. It produces new cells that later differentiate to perform specialized functions. **Meristematic tissue is the only plant tissue that produces new cells by mitosis.** The tips of stems and roots are made of meristematic tissue.

© Pearson Education, Inc., publishing as Pearson Prentice Hall.

23–2 Roots

As soon as a seedling begins to grow, it sends out a primary root. Secondary roots branch from the primary root. **The two main types of roots are taproots and fibrous roots.** In some plants, the primary root grows long and thick. Secondary roots stay small. This kind of primary root is called a **taproot.** In other plants, secondary roots grow and branch. These roots are called **fibrous roots.**

    Roots have two main functions.
- **to anchor a plant in the ground**
- **to absorb water and dissolved nutrients from the soil**

Roots are made up of cells from the four tissue systems. **A mature root has an outside layer of dermal tissue called the epidermis. It also has a central cylinder of vascular tissue called the vascular cylinder. Ground tissue, called the cortex, lies between these two tissues.** A thin layer of cells called the **endodermis** separates the vascular cylinder from the cortex.

    Once absorbed by the root hairs, water and nutrients move inward through the cortex. After passing through the endodermis into the vascular cylinder, the water cannot leave. This causes pressure, called root pressure, to build up. Root pressure forces water up through the xylem toward the stem.

23–3 Stems

Stems have three important functions:
- **to produce leaves, branches, and flowers**
- **to hold leaves up to the sunlight**
- **to carry water and nutrients between roots and leaves**

The arrangement of tissues in a stem differs among seed plants. **In monocots, vascular bundles are scattered throughout the stem. In dicots and most gymnosperms, vascular bundles are arranged in a ring.** Vascular bundles contain xylem and phloem tissue.

    Plant stems can grow in two ways. **Primary growth of stems is produced by cell divisions in the apical meristem. Such growth takes place in all seed plants.** Stems grow longer as meristematic tissue at the ends of the stems produces new cells. In **secondary growth,** a stem grows wider as meristematic tissue on its sides forms new cells. This growth produces wood and bark. Only plants with woody stems have secondary growth. **In conifers and dicots, secondary growth takes place in the vascular cambium and cork cambium. Vascular cambium** produces vascular tissue and increases the thickness of stems over time. **Cork cambium** produces the outer covering of stems.

© Pearson Education, Inc., publishing as Pearson Prentice Hall.

23–4 Leaves

The leaves of a plant are its main organs of photosynthesis. In photosynthesis, plants make food. Sugars, starches, and oils made by plants provide food for all land animals.

The structure of leaves lets them absorb light and make food. Most leaves have thin, flattened sections called **blades** to collect sunlight. Most leaves also are made up of a specialized ground tissue called **mesophyll.** Mesophyll cells have many chloroplasts. It is in these cells that photosynthesis occurs.

Xylem and phloem tissues in leaves are gathered in bundles called veins. These veins are connected to the xylem and phloem in the stem.

Plants can lose water as they exchange gases with the air. Leaves have an adaptation to help prevent water loss. They allow air in and out of their waterproof covering only through small openings called **stomata. Plants keep their stomata open just enough to allow photosynthesis to take place but not so much that they lose an excessive amount of water.**

23–5 Transport in Plants

Xylem tissue forms tubes that stretch from roots through stems and out into leaves. Root pressure forces water and nutrients into the xylem. Other forces pull water and nutrients through the plant. **The combination of root pressure, capillary action, and transpiration provides enough force to move water through the xylem tissue of even the tallest plant.**

- Water can be pulled up through xylem because a force called cohesion pulls its molecules together. Water molecules are also attracted to other molecules. This force is called **adhesion.** Together, cohesion and adhesion cause water to move upward through a plant. This movement is called **capillary action.**
- In large plants, a force called transpirational pull moves water up to the leaves. Transpirational pull happens because water moves from areas of high concentration to areas of low concentration. When water evaporates from leaves, water is drawn upward from the roots to replace it.

Phloem transports the sugars made in photosynthesis throughout the plant. The food is either used or stored. When nutrients are pumped into or removed from the phloem system, the change in concentration causes a movement of fluid in that same direction. As a result, phloem is able to move nutrients in either direction to meet the nutritional needs of the plant.

© Pearson Education, Inc., publishing as Pearson Prentice Hall.

Plant Tissue Types

Plants have four primary types of tissue: dermal tissue, ground tissue, meristematic tissue, and vascular tissue.

Identify each type of tissue listed in the table.

Tissue	Cells	Function
	epidermal cells, root hair cells, guard cells	protects plant, aids water absorption in roots, regulates water loss and gas exchange in leaves
	xylem: tracheids and, in angiosperms, vessel elements; phloem: sieve tube elements, companion cells	conducts water and other materials through the plant
	parenchyma, collenchyma, and sclerenchyma cells	site of most photosynthesis; helps support plants
	undifferentiated cells	produces new cells

Use the table to answer the questions.

1. Xylem and phloem are the principal subsystems in which type of tissue? Circle the correct answer.

   meristematic tissue   vascular tissue

2. In most plants, what type of cell makes up most ground tissue? Circle the correct answer.

   parenchyma   epidermal

3. Where in plants is meristematic tissue found?

   _____

© Pearson Education, Inc., publishing as Pearson Prentice Hall.

Vascular Tissue

Xylem and phloem are the two main subsystems of vascular tissue in plants. Xylem conducts water, while phloem conducts food and other materials. Xylem is made up of specialized cells called tracheids and vessel elements. Phloem is made up of sieve tube elements and companion cells.

In the diagram of xylem, color the tracheids *green. Color the* vessel elements *blue. In the diagram of phloem, color the* companion cells *yellow. Color the* sieve tube elements *orange.*

Xylem

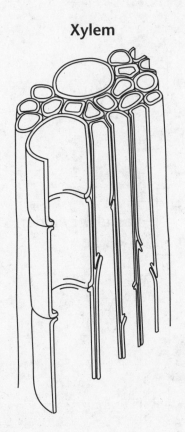

Phloem

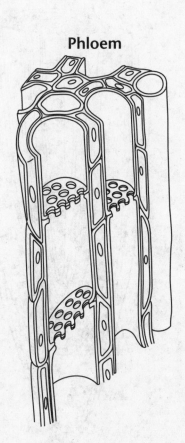

Use the diagrams to answer the questions. Circle the correct answer.

1. Which cells are mainly responsible for transporting carbo-hydrates and other materials through the plant?

sieve tube elements   tracheids

2. In what type of plants are vessel elements found?

angiosperms   mosses

© Pearson Education, Inc., publishing as Pearson Prentice Hall.

Root Structure

Plant roots are made up of a vascular cylinder surrounded by ground tissue and the epidermis. The epidermis protects the root and absorbs water. The spongy layer of ground tissue just inside the epidermis is called the cortex. The vascular cylinder includes xylem and phloem.

Color the epidermis blue. Color the vascular cylinder red. Color the cortex brown.

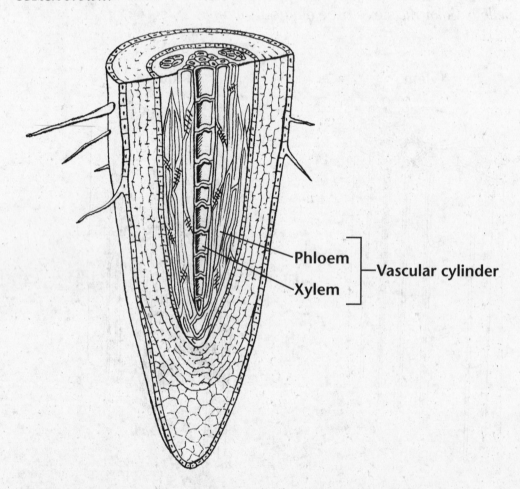

Phloem

Xylem

Vascular cylinder

Use the diagram to answer the questions. Circle the correct answer.

1. What type of tissue makes up the epidermis?

dermal   vascular

2. What type of tissue is located at the tip of the root?

vascular   meristematic

© Pearson Education, Inc., publishing as Pearson Prentice Hall.

Monocot and Dicot Stems

Both monocot and dicot stems have vascular bundles. The distribution of vascular bundles differs in dicots and monocots.

Label the dicot *stem and the* monocot *stem.*

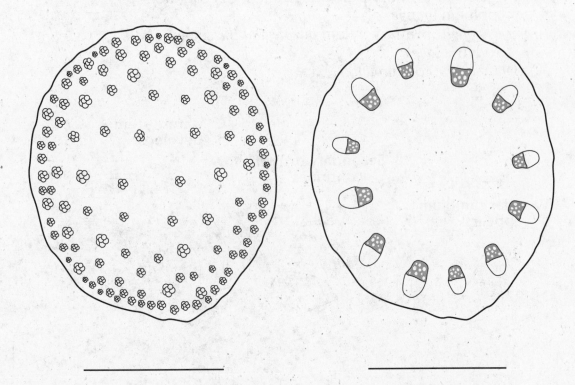

_____   _____

Use the diagram to answer the questions.

1. How is the arrangement of vascular bundles in a monocot different from that in a dicot?

_____

_____

2. What is the role of the vascular bundles?

_____

_____

© Pearson Education, Inc., publishing as Pearson Prentice Hall.

Dicot Stem Growth

As dicot plants grow larger, their stems get wider as well as longer. This increase in width is called secondary growth.

Follow the prompts to color the diagrams of secondary growth.
- *Color the* primary phloem *red and the* secondary phloem *orange.*
- *Color the* primary xylem *purple and the* secondary xylem *blue.*
- *Color the* cork *brown.*

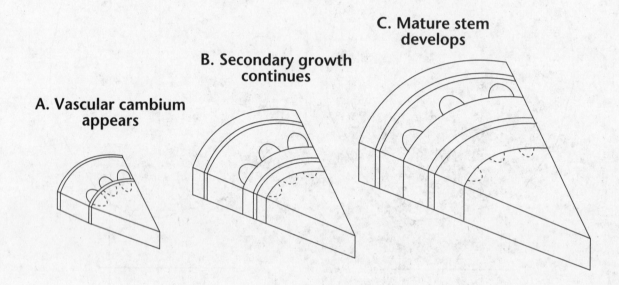

A. Vascular cambium appears

B. Secondary growth continues

C. Mature stem develops

Use the diagram to answer the questions.

1. In a mature dicot stem, which tissues make up bark?

_____

_____

2. Where does vascular cambium form?

_____

3. What type of tissue is vascular cambium? Circle the correct answer.

dermal   meristematic

© Pearson Education, Inc., publishing as Pearson Prentice Hall.

Leaf Structure

Most leaves are made primarily of mesophyll. Palisade mesophyll absorbs light. Spongy mesophyll cells are loosely packed and allow gases to pass in and out. Leaves also have vascular tissue, an epidermis, and a cuticle.

Color the leaf structures according to the prompts.
- *Color the* epidermis *blue.*
- *Color the* spongy mesophyll *green.*
- *Color the* palisade mesophyll *yellow.*
- *Color the* vascular tissue *orange.*
- *Color the* cuticle *purple.*

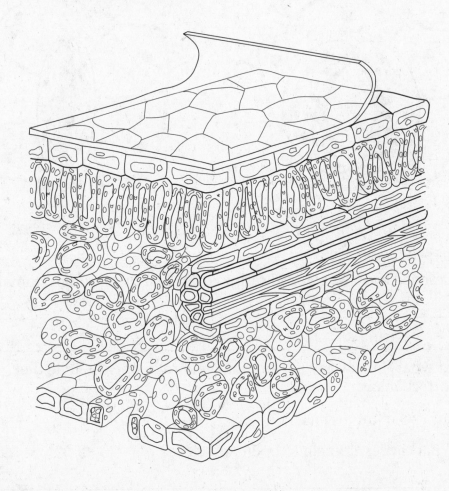

Answer the question. Circle the correct answer.

1. In which layer are stomata and guard cells located?

epidermis   palisade mesophyll

© Pearson Education, Inc., publishing as Pearson Prentice Hall.

Stomata

The stomata of a plant open and close to control the flow of gases to and from the leaves. Specialized cells in the epidermis, called guard cells, control whether a stoma is open or closed.

Label each diagram as an open *or closed* stoma. *Draw a blue arrow showing the movement of carbon dioxide through the open stoma. Draw a yellow arrow showing the movement of oxygen through the open stoma.*

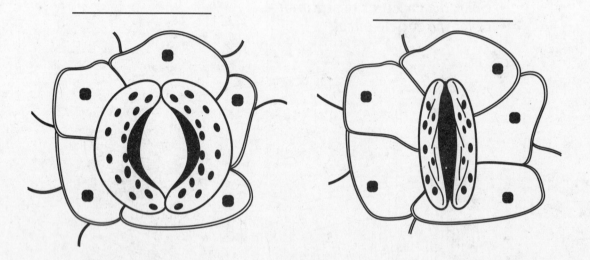

_____   _____

Answer the questions.

1. Describe how oxygen and carbon dioxide move through stomata.

_____

_____

2. At what time of day are stomata generally open? Circle the correct answer.

   day   night

3. What causes stomata to open and close?

_____

4. Why are stomata important to a plant?

_____

_____

© Pearson Education, Inc., publishing as Pearson Prentice Hall.

Sugar Movement–Source to Sink

Sugar moves through phloem in plants. It moves from a source cell, where sugar is made through photosynthesis, to a sink cell, where the sugar is used.

Draw arrows to show how sugar moves through the phloem. Arrows that represent the movement of water have already been drawn for you.

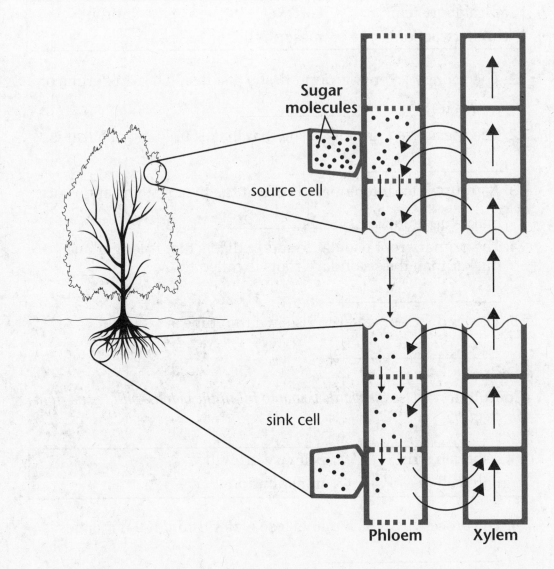

Use the diagram to answer the question. Circle the correct answer.

1. This diagram illustrates which hypothesis for phloem transport?

sink-to-source hypothesis   pressure-flow hypothesis

Chapter 23   Roots, Stems, and Leaves

Vocabulary Review

Completion   *Use the words below to fill in the blanks with terms from the chapter.*

apical meristem	cortex	taproot
capillary action	mesophyll	

1. The spongy layer of ground tissue just inside the epidermis of a

   root is the _____.

2. The specialized ground tissue that makes up most of a leaf is

   _____.

3. A group of undifferentiated cells at the tips of stems and roots

   makes up a(an) _____.

4. The primary root usually found in dicots that is longer and thicker than the secondary roots is called the

   _____.

5. The tendency of water to rise in a thin tube is

   _____.

Completion   *Use the words below to fill in the blanks with terms from the chapter.*

Casparian strip	primary growth
guard cell	transpiration

6. The process by which plants lose water through their leaves is

   _____.

7. A(An) _____ is a specialized cell in the epidermis of a leaf that controls the opening and closing of stomata.

8. The type of growth in plants that occurs only at the ends of the

   plants is called _____.

9. The structure that makes cells of the endodermis waterproof is

   the _____.

© Pearson Education, Inc., publishing as Pearson Prentice Hall.

Chapter 24   Reproduction of Seed Plants

Summary

24–1 Reproduction With Cones and Flowers

Seed plants are adapted to life on land especially in how they reproduce. The gametes of seed plants do not need water for reproduction. The way in which seed plants reproduce has allowed them to survive the dry conditions on land. In the seed plant life cycle, the sporophyte (spore-producing) generation alternates with the gametophyte (gamete-producing) generation. The familiar form of the plant is the sporophyte. The gametophyte is hidden within cones or flowers.

Reproduction in gymnosperms takes place in cones, which are produced by a mature sporophyte plant. Pollen cones form the male gametophytes—pollen grains. **Seed cones** form the female gametophytes—eggs. **Most gymnosperms are wind pollinated.** When a pollen grain lands near an ovule, it grows a **pollen tube** into the ovule. A sperm from the pollen tube fertilizes the egg. A zygote forms and develops into an embryo enclosed in a seed.

Angiosperms, or flowering plants, reproduce with flowers. **Flowers are reproductive organs with four kinds of leaves arranged in circles.** Sepals and petals are sterile leaves. Stamens and carpels are fertile leaves.

- **Sepals** are the outermost floral parts and are often green. They protect the flower bud.
- Colorful **petals** within the sepals attract insects and other pollinators to the flower.
- **Stamens** form the first inner circle of leaves. Each stamen has a long filament that supports an **anther,** which makes male gametophytes. In the anthers, cells undergo meiosis, forming four haploid pollen grains.
- One or more **carpels,** also called pistils, form the innermost circle. Carpels contain both an ovary and a style. The broad base is the **ovary.** Female gametophytes form in ovules inside the ovary. A single cell goes through meiosis to form four haploid cells. One of these cells goes through mitosis, producing the embryo sac, or the female gametophyte. Within the embryo sac is the egg cell. The carpel's stalk is a **style,** which is topped by the sticky **stigma.** Pollen is transferred from the anther to the stigma during pollination.

Most angiosperms are pollinated by animals. Some animals have evolved body shapes that let them reach nectar deep inside the flowers. **Some angiosperms are wind pollinated.**

© Pearson Education, Inc., publishing as Pearson Prentice Hall.

When a pollen grain lands on a stigma, it grows a pollen tube to the ovary. Two sperm nuclei enter the embryo sac, where two distinct fertilizations take place. This is known as **double fertilization.**

- First, one sperm nucleus fuses with the egg to form a diploid zygote. The zygote will grow into the plant embryo.
- The second sperm nucleus fuses with two other nuclei in the embryo sac to form the **endosperm.** The endosperm provides food for the embryo.

Reproduction in angiosperms takes place within the flower. Following pollination and fertilization, the seeds develop inside protective structures.

24–2 Seed Development and Germination

Seeds help make angiosperms successful on land. Seeds nourish and protect embryos. **As angiosperm seeds mature, the ovary walls thicken to form a fruit that encloses the seed.** Some fruits are fleshy, like grapes. Others are tough, like pea pods.

Angiosperm seeds can be dispersed, or spread away from the parent plant, in several different ways. The structure of the seeds often reflects the way they are dispersed.

- **Seeds dispersed by animals are typically contained in fleshy, nutritious fruits.** The animals eat the fruits, and disperse the seeds in their feces.
- **Seeds that are spread by wind and water are usually lightweight.** They float easily in the air or on water. For example, a coconut is light enough to float in sea water. Ash and maple tree seeds are encased in winglike structures. These structures help them glide away from the parent tree.

Many seeds enter a period of **dormancy.** Dormancy gives seeds time to spread to new areas or wait for better growing conditions. **The right temperature and moisture can end dormancy and cause germination.**

Germination is the stage of early growth of a plant embryo. When seeds germinate, they absorb water, swell, and open. The root emerges and begins to grow.

- In most monocots, a shoot emerges, protected by a sheath. The cotyledon stays underground.
- In some dicots, the cotyledons emerge above the ground. They protect the stem and the first leaves. In other dicots, the cotyledons stay underground to supply food for the seedling.

© Pearson Education, Inc., publishing as Pearson Prentice Hall.

24–3 Plant Propagation and Agriculture

Seeds and fruits form by sexual reproduction. Many plants also reproduce asexually by **vegetative reproduction**. Vegetative reproduction results in genetically identical offspring. **Vegetative reproduction includes the production of new plants from horizontal stems, from plantlets, and from underground roots.**

- Some plants send out horizontal stems that form roots or new shoots. For example, strawberry plants send out long stems that produce roots when they touch the ground.
- Other plants form tiny plantlets that detach and grow into new plants. Spider plants produce plantlets at the tips of long stems. If these plantlets fall to the ground, they can take root and grow into new plants.
- Some plants produce a new plant from a leaf that drops to the ground and grows roots.

Plant growers use plant propagation to make exact copies of a plant. **In plant propagation, horticulturists use cuttings, grafting, or budding to make many identical copies of a plant or to produce offspring from seedless plants.**

- One way to do this is by making a cutting of a stem that has meristematic tissue. The stem is treated with a special rooting mixture and partially buried in soil.
- Grafting and budding are other methods. A piece called a scion is cut from the parent plant. It is attached to a plant with strong roots, called the stock. In **grafting**, stems are the scions. In **budding**, buds are the scions.

Agriculture is the basis of human society. Farmers in North America grow enough food to feed millions of people worldwide. **Most people depend on the seeds of only a few crops—wheat, rice, and corn—for the bulk of their food supply.** Over time, farmers have increased the amount of crops they can harvest from an acre of land. Selective breeding and improved farming methods have made crop production more efficient.

© Pearson Education, Inc., publishing as Pearson Prentice Hall.

Gymnosperm Life Cycle

Follow the prompts to complete the diagram of the gymnosperm life cycle.
- Color the structure that produces female gametophytes red.
- Color the structure that produces male gametophytes blue.

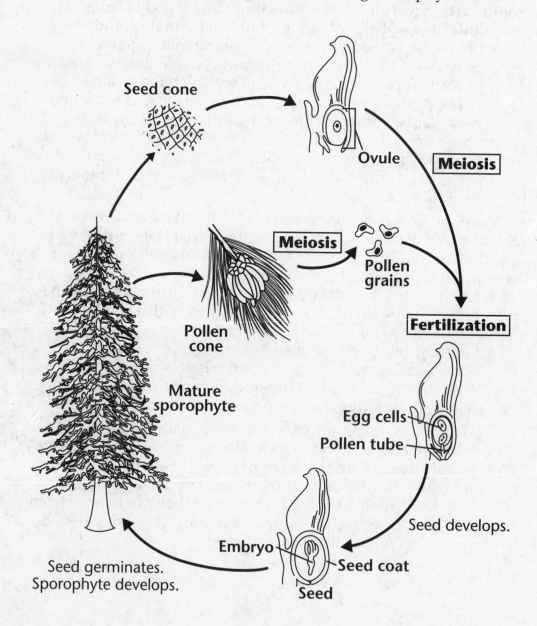

Use the diagram to answer the question.

1. Which structure produces male gametophytes? Circle the
correct answer.

seed cone   pollen cone

© Pearson Education, Inc., publishing as Pearson Prentice Hall.

Parts of a Flower

Flowers are angiosperm reproductive structures. They are made up of four types of specialized leaves: sepals, petals, stamens, and carpels.

Use the words below to label the parts of the flower. Then color the carpels yellow and the stamens red.

| anther | filament | ovary | stigma |

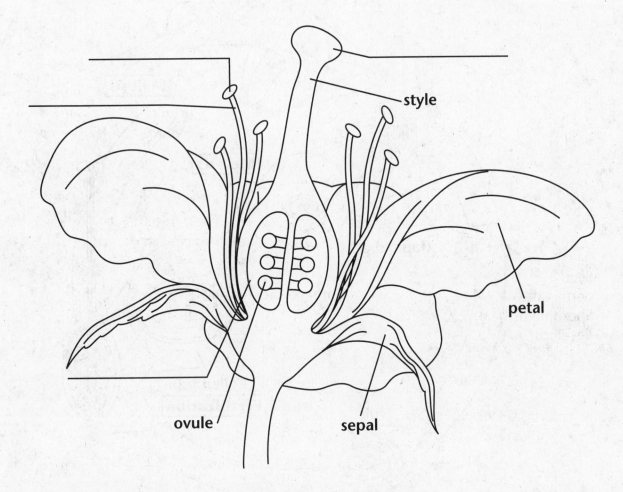

style

petal

ovule

sepal

Use the diagram to answer the questions.

1. What parts of the flower make up a stamen?

_____

2. What parts of the flower make up the carpel?

_____

© Pearson Education, Inc., publishing as Pearson Prentice Hall.

Angiosperm Life Cycle

Follow the prompts to complete the diagram of the angiosperm life cycle.
- Color the arrows showing haploid stages of the life cycle yellow.
- Color the arrows showing diploid stages of the life cycle blue.

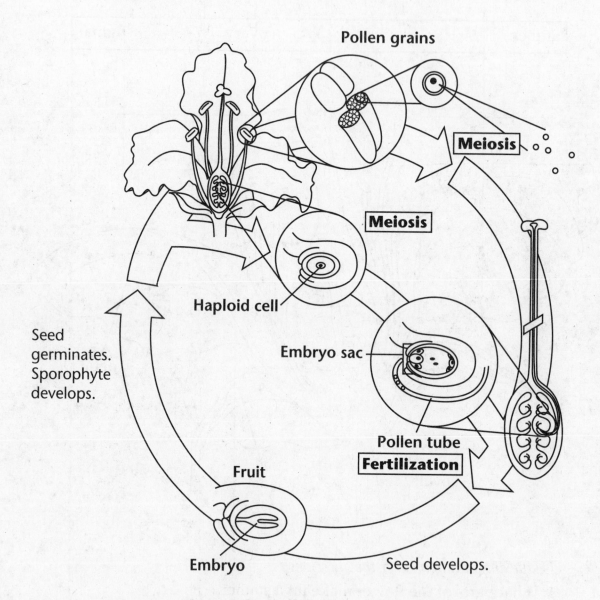

Pollen grains

Meiosis

Meiosis

Haploid cell

Embryo sac

Seed germinates. Sporophyte develops.

Pollen tube
Fertilization

Fruit

Embryo

Seed develops.

Use the diagram to answer the question.

1. What structure produces female gametophytes?

_____

© Pearson Education, Inc., publishing as Pearson Prentice Hall.

Seed Dispersal

Seed dispersal is the process by which seeds are dispersed, or moved away from, the parent plant.

Color the seed or seeds in each diagram.
- If the seeds are spread by wind, color them yellow.
- If they are spread by animals, color them red.
- If they are spread by water, color them blue.

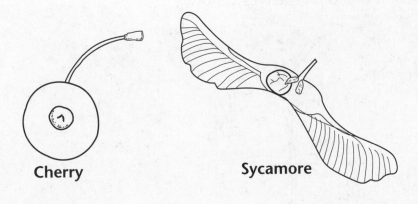

Cherry   **Sycamore**

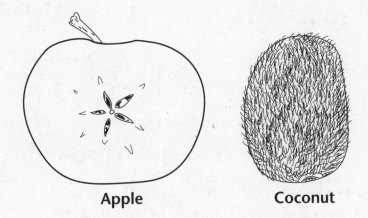

Apple   **Coconut**

Use the diagrams to answer the questions.

1. How can you tell how sycamore seeds are spread?

_____

2. How are seeds inside fleshy fruits usually spread?

_____

© Pearson Education, Inc., publishing as Pearson Prentice Hall.

Monocot and Dicot Germination

Cotyledons are the first leaves produced by seed plants. Monocot plants have one cotyledon. Dicot plants have two. The diagrams show how monocot and dicot plant seeds germinate, or sprout.

Follow the prompts to fill in both diagrams.
- Color the germinating seeds blue.
- Color the primary roots brown.
- Color the bean cotyledons green.
- Color the foliage leaves yellow.

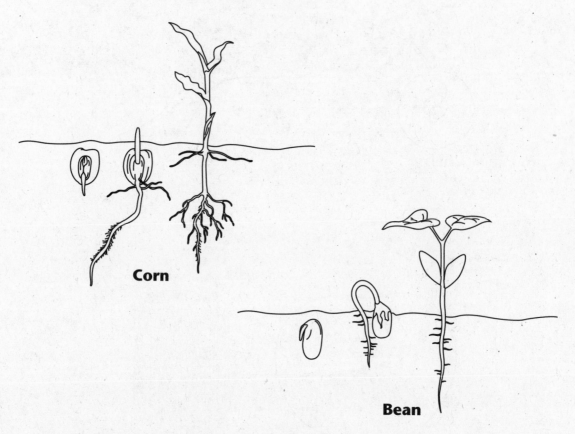

Corn

Bean

Use the diagrams to answer the question.

1. Which plant is a monocot, and which is a dicot?

_____

2. What happens first when a seed germinates? Circle the correct answer.

primary root emerges   seed absorbs water

3. After germination, what happens to the cotyledon in monocots? Circle the correct answer.

remains underground   emerges aboveground

© Pearson Education, Inc., publishing as Pearson Prentice Hall.

Chapter 24   Reproduction of Seed Plants

Vocabulary Review

Completion   *Use the words below to fill in the blanks with terms from the chapter.*

endosperm	germination	ovule
filament	grafting	

1. The use of a stem as a scion is called _____.

2. The part of a seed that nourishes the embryo is the

   _____.

3. The long, thin stalk of a flower that supports the anther is the

   _____.

4. In gymnosperms, the structure in which a female

   gametophyte develops is the _____.

5. _____ is the name given to the early growth

   stage of a plant embryo.

Completion   *Use the words below to fill in the blanks with terms from the chapter.*

petals	stamen
pollen tube	stigma

6. The colored parts of a flower found just inside the sepals

   are the _____.

7. In a gymnosperm, the structure that grows when a pollen

   grain lands near an ovule is the _____.

8. The sticky region at the top of a style is the

   _____.

9. The structure made up of the anther and filament is the

   _____.

© Pearson Education, Inc., publishing as Pearson Prentice Hall.

Chapter 25   Plant Responses and Adaptations

Summary

25–1 Hormones and Plant Growth

Plants grow in different patterns depending on the species of plant. Plant growth never stops. New cells are constantly made in meristems. Meristems are found at the tips of stems and roots. The new cells later develop into specialized tissues.

Plants grow in response to environmental factors such as light, moisture, gravity, and temperature. Hormones also control plant growth. A **hormone** is a substance made in one part of an organism that affects another part of the same organism. **Plant hormones are chemical substances that control a plant's patterns of growth and development and the plant's responses to environmental conditions.** The part of the organism affected by a hormone is the **target cell** or target tissue. Different kinds of target cells can respond to the same hormone. Thus, a single hormone may affect two types of tissues in different ways. There are several types of plant hormones.

- **Auxins are produced in the apical meristem and are transported downward into the rest of the plant. They stimulate cell elongation.** Auxins have different effects on different tissues. Auxins make stems grow toward light (**phototropism**) and away from the pull of gravity (**gravitropism**). Auxins also control plant branching by keeping the buds on the sides of the stem from growing.
- Growing roots and developing fruits and seeds make hormones called cytokinins. **Cytokinins stimulate cell division and the growth of lateral buds and cause dormant seeds to sprout.** Their effects are often the opposite of the effects of auxins.
- In the 1920s, Japanese scientists identified a substance produced by a fungus that stimulated plant growth. They named this substance **gibberellin.** Later, scientists learned that plants also make gibberellins. **Gibberellins cause great increases in size and rapid growth, particularly in stems and fruit.**
- **Plants release ethylene in response to auxins. Ethylene stimulates fruits to ripen.**

© Pearson Education, Inc., publishing as Pearson Prentice Hall.

25–2 Plant Responses

Plants respond to changes in their environment. They respond to gravity, light, and touch. These responses are called tropisms. There are three main tropisms.

- Gravitropism is the response of a plant to gravity.
- Phototropism is the response of a plant to light.
- A plant's response to touch is called **thigmotropism.**

Some plants have a rapid response to touch that does not involve growth. This kind of response is caused by changes in the osmotic pressure of some cells. These pressure changes cause leaves to fold up or snap shut. This response lets a Venus' flytrap trap an insect.

Many plants respond to periods of light and darkness. This is called **photoperiodism.** Changes in the length of periods of light and darkness affect plant pigments called **phytochromes. Photoperiodism in plants is responsible for the timing of seasonal activities such as flowering and growth.** Some plants, known as **short-day plants,** flower when days are short. Others, known as **long-day plants,** flower when the days are long.

Some plants lose their leaves and become dormant during the winter. **Dormancy** is the period during which an organism's growth and activity decrease or stop. Auxins and other hormones work together to control dormancy. **As cold weather approaches, deciduous plants turn off photosynthetic pathways, transport materials from leaves to roots, and seal leaves off from the rest of the plant.**

- Changes in the length of light and dark periods cause a change in the chemistry of phytochrome. This change in phytochrome causes auxin production to drop. The production of ethylene increases.
- The leaves stop making chlorophyll. Other pigments in the leaves become visible as the green coloring disappears.
- The cells that join a leaf to the stem become weak, and an **abscission layer** forms. The abscission layer seals the leaf off from the rest of the plant. The leaves fall from the tree.
- Thick, waxy bud scales form. They cover the buds at the ends of the branches. The bud scales protect the buds from winter cold.

© Pearson Education, Inc., publishing as Pearson Prentice Hall.

25–3 Plant Adaptations

Flowering plants live in many different environments. Through natural selection, plants have evolved different adaptations to live successfully in each environment.

- Aquatic plants often live in mud that has little oxygen. **To get enough oxygen, many aquatic plants have air-filled spaces in their tissues. Oxygen diffuses through these spaces from the leaves to the roots.** For example, waterlilies transport oxygen from the air to their roots through large spaces in their petioles.
- Some plants can grow in salt water or in very salty air near the ocean. Many salt-tolerant plants have cells that pump salt out of the plant tissues and onto the leaf surface. Rain then washes away the salt.
- **Xerophytes** are plants that live in the desert. These plants must tolerate high daytime heat, sandy soil, strong winds, and little rain. **Often, these plants have extensive roots, reduced leaves, and thick stems that store water.** Seeds of many desert plants can remain dormant for years. The seeds germinate only when enough moisture allows a chance of survival. Cacti are xerophytes. They have extensive root systems and their leaves have become reduced to sharp spines. They also have thick stems that can store water.
- Some plants grow in soil with few nutrients. **Carnivorous plants and parasites have adapted to living in environments with poor soil.** Carnivorous plants trap and digest insects to get nitrogen. Pitcher plants are one type of carnivorous plant. They have pitcher-shaped leaves that hold water and digestive enzymes. Pitcher plants drown their prey and digest them in these leaves. Parasites get water and nutrients directly from a host plant. Like all parasites, these plants harm their host plants. Mistletoe is a parasite that grows on many plants.
- **Epiphytes** are plants that are not rooted in soil. They grow directly on the bodies of other plants. Epiphytes are not parasites. They gather their own moisture, generally from rainfall. They also make their own food. Most epiphytes live in rain forests. Over half the species of orchids are epiphytes.
- **Many plants defend themselves against insect attack by manufacturing compounds that have powerful effects on animals.** Some are toxic to the animals that eat them. For example, milkweed plants are toxic to most animals. Others interrupt normal growth and development.

© Pearson Education, Inc., publishing as Pearson Prentice Hall.

Auxins and Stem Cells

Auxins are important plant hormones. They affect plant growth in many ways, including how plants respond to light. The picture shows how a growing plant stem responds to sunlight.

Shade in the cells that have the highest concentration of auxins.

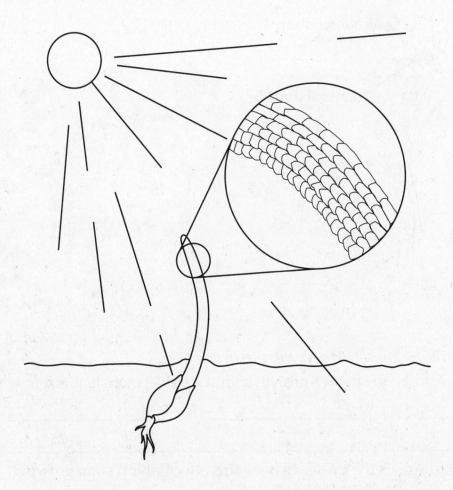

Use the picture to answer the questions.

1. Where is the concentration of auxins highest?

_____

_____

2. What is the result of the distribution of auxins?

_____

_____

© Pearson Education, Inc., publishing as Pearson Prentice Hall.

Apical Dominance

The apical meristem of a stem is located at its very tip. It produces auxins. Removing the apical meristem can affect how a plant grows.

Draw how the plant will grow after the apical meristem is removed.

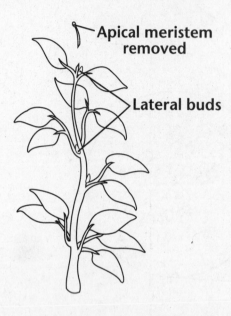

Apical meristem removed

Lateral buds

Use the pictures to answer the question.

1. Describe the plant's growth after the apical meristem is removed.

_____

_____

2. How does the presence of auxins affect lateral stem growth? Circle the correct answer.

inhibits   stimulates

3. Describe apical dominance.

_____

_____

_____

_____

© Pearson Education, Inc., publishing as Pearson Prentice Hall.

Hormone Functions

Auxins, cytokinins, ethylene, and gibberellins are four major types of plant hormones. Each affects plant growth in a different way.

Write auxins, cytokinins, ethylene, *or* gibberellins *to complete the first column.*

Hormone	Functions
	Stimulate cell elongation in stems; inhibit cell growth and elongation in roots; phototropism; gravitropism
	Stimulate cell division and the growth of lateral buds; cause dormant seeds to sprout
	Produce dramatic increases in size
	Stimulate fruit to ripen

Answer the question.

1. What is a hormone?

_____

_____

_____

© Pearson Education, Inc., publishing as Pearson Prentice Hall.

Tropisms

A tropism is a plant's response to external stimuli. Three important plant tropisms are gravitropism, phototropism, and thigmotropism.

For each tropism, identify whether the plant reacts to touch, gravity, *or* light.

Tropism	What Plant Reacts To	Description
gravitropism		Auxins build up on the lower side of roots and stems, causing cell elongation in stems and inhibiting it in roots.
phototropism		A higher concentration of auxins builds up in the shaded side of a plant, causing cell elongation.
thigmotropism		A plant that is touched may be stunted. Vines and climbing plants have shoots that wrap around objects.

Use the table to answer the question.

1. What hormones cause gravitropism and phototropism?

_____

2. In the space below, draw an example of thigmotropism.

© Pearson Education, Inc., publishing as Pearson Prentice Hall.

Photoperiodism

In photoperiodism, the amount of darkness a plant receives during a day affects whether the plant blooms.

Use what you know to identify whether a long-day plant *or a* short-day plant *would bloom when exposed to the described light conditions.*

		Discription of light conditions	Type of plant blooming
Long Day	Midnight Noon	Short peroid of darkness	
Short Day	Midnight Noon	Long period of darkness	
Interrrupted Night	Midnight Noon	Long period of darkness interrupted by short period of light	

Use the table to answer the questions.

1. Under what light conditions will a short-day plant bloom?

_____

_____

2. Under what light conditions will a long-day plant bloom?

_____

_____

© Pearson Education, Inc., publishing as Pearson Prentice Hall.

Plant Adaptations

Plants are found in many environments. In each environment, plants have adaptations that help them survive.

Use the words below to fill in the table. One row has been completed for you.

aquatic	epiphyte
carnivorous	salt-tolerant

Plant Type	Environment	Adaptations
xerophyte	desert	extensive roots, reduced leaves, thick stems
	ponds, lakes, mud	air-filled spaces in tissues
	salt water	leaves that pump salt out of plant tissues, roots that can tolerate high salt concentrations
	wet, acidic bogs with little nitrogen	specialized leaves to trap and digest insects
	moist biomes	ability to grow on bodies of other plants

Use the table to answer the questions. Circle the correct answer.

1. Spanish moss grows directly on the bodies of other plants. What type of plant is it?

   carnivorous   epiphyte

2. Cactus plants typically have thick stems that can store water and extensive root systems. What type of plant are cacti?

   parasites   xerophytes

© Pearson Education, Inc., publishing as Pearson Prentice Hall.

Chapter 25   Plant Responses and Adaptations

Vocabulary Review

Completion   *Use the words below to fill in the blanks with terms from the chapter.*

auxin	gibberellins	phototropism
ethylene	gravitropism	target cell

1. A(An) _____ is the portion of a plant that is affected by a hormone.

2. Fruit is stimulated to ripen by _____.

3. Dramatic increase in the size of stems and fruit are the result of

   _____.

4. The tendency of roots to grow down into soil and stems to

   grow up away from gravity is _____.

5. _____ is the substance produced in the apical meristem that stimulates cell elongation.

6. The tendency of a plant to grow toward light is

   _____.

Completion   *Use the words below to fill in the blanks with terms from the chapter.*

abscission layer	lateral bud	thigmotropism
epiphyte	photoperiodism	

7. The response of plants to touch is _____.

8. A plant's response to periods of light and darkness is

   _____.

9. The layer of cells at the petiole that seals off a leaf from the

   vascular system is the _____.

10. A plant that grows directly on the body of another plant is

    a(an) _____.

11. The area on the side of the stem that gives rise to side branches

    is called a(an) _____.

© Pearson Education, Inc., publishing as Pearson Prentice Hall.

Chapter 26   Sponges and Cnidarians

Summary

26–1 Introduction to the Animal Kingdom

All members of the animal kingdom share certain characteristics. **All animals are multicellular, eukaryotic heterotrophs whose cells lack walls.**

More than 95 percent of all animal species are grouped in one informal category: invertebrates. **Invertebrates** are animals that have no backbone, or vertebral column. The other 5 percent of animals are vertebrates. **Vertebrates** are animals with a backbone.

An animal's structure, or anatomy, allows it to carry out body functions. Many body functions help animals maintain homeostasis. Homeostasis is the process by which organisms keep internal conditions stable. Often this involves use of internal feedback mechanisms. For example, **feedback inhibition** occurs when the product of a process stops or limits the process itself.

Animals carry out the following essential functions:

- **Feeding** Animals must feed, or eat food. Herbivores eat plants, carnivores eat animals, and parasites live and feed on other organisms.
- **Respiration** All animals respire, or take in oxygen and give off carbon dioxide.
- **Circulation** Most animals have a system that circulates materials within their bodies.
- **Excretion** Most animals have an excretory system that helps eliminate wastes from the body.
- **Response** Animals respond to their environment using nerve cells.
- **Movement** Most animals move from place to place using muscles and some type of skeletal system.
- **Reproduction** Most animals reproduce sexually by producing haploid gametes. Sexual reproduction helps create and maintain genetic diversity in populations. Many invertebrates can reproduce asexually as well. Asexual reproduction produces offspring that are genetically identical to the parent.

Complex animals tend to have high levels of cell specialization and internal body organization. They also tend to have bilateral body symmetry, a front end or head with sense organs, and a body cavity.

© Pearson Education, Inc., publishing as Pearson Prentice Hall.

- **Early Development** Animals that reproduce sexually start life as a fertilized egg, or zygote. The zygote divides several times to form a **blastula,** a hollow ball of cells. The blastula then folds in on itself to form a single opening called a blastopore. The blastopore leads to a central tube that becomes the digestive tract. In time, the blastopore forms either a mouth or an anus. The anus is the opening through which wastes leave the digestive tract. If the blastopore forms a mouth, the animal is a **protostome.** If the blastopore forms an anus, the animal is a **deuterstome.**

The cells of most animal embryos differentiate into three germ layers. The **endoderm** is the innermost germ layer. The middle layer is the **mesoderm.** The **ectoderm** is the outermost germ layer.

- **Body cavity formation** Most animals have a body cavity. A *body cavity* is a fluid-filled space that lies between the digestive tract and the body wall.
- **Body symmetry and cephalization** All animals, except sponges, show some type of body symmetry. In **radial symmetry,** any number of imaginary planes can be drawn through the center of the animal to divide it into equal halves. In **bilateral symmetry,** only one imaginary plane can divide the body into two equal halves. Animals with bilateral symmetry typically have cephalization. **Cephalization** is a concentration of sense organs and nerve cells at the front of the body. More complex animals have bilateral symmetry.

26–2 Sponges

Sponges make up the phylum Porifera. **Like all animals, sponges are multicellular and heterotrophic. They have no cell walls and have only a few specialized cells.** Sponges live their entire adult lives attached to a surface.

Sponges sift microscopic food particles from water moving through them. Specialized cells called **choanocytes** move a current of water through the sponge body. This water enters through pores in the body wall. It leaves through the **osculum,** a large hole at the top of the central cavity. Digestion is intracellular; it takes place inside cells. **The movement of water through a sponge also supplies a sponge with everything it needs for respiration, circulation, and excretion.**

Sponges reproduce both sexually and asexually. In sexual reproduction, eggs are fertilized internally. The zygote then develops into a larva. A **larva** is an immature stage of an organism that looks different from the adult form. The larva are motile. They are carried by ocean currents until they settle to the sea floor and grow into a mature sponge. Sponges reproduce asexually by budding.

© Pearson Education, Inc., publishing as Pearson Prentice Hall.

26–3 Cnidarians

The phylum Cnidaria includes hydras, jellyfishes, sea anemones, and corals. **Cnidarians are soft-bodied carnivores that have stinging tentacles arranged in circles around their mouths. They are the simplest animals having body symmetry and specialized tissues.** Cnidarians exhibit radial symmetry. They have a central mouth surrounded by numerous tentacles. Cnidarians get their name from the cnidocytes, or stinging cells, on their tentacles.

Most cnidarians have a life cycle with two very different stages: a polyp and a medusa.

- A **polyp** has a cylindrical body with armlike tentacles and usually does not move. A polyp lives attached to a surface with its mouth pointing upward.
- A **medusa** has a bell-shaped body with a mouth at the bottom. Medusas are free-swimming.

A cnidarian has a **gastrovascular cavity**—a digestive chamber with one opening. Food and wastes enter and leave through this opening. Digestion is extracellular, meaning it takes place outside cells.

After digestion, nutrients are transported throughout the body by diffusion. Cnidarians take in oxygen and release wastes by diffusion through their body walls.

Cnidarians gather information from their environment using specialized sensory cells. Both polyps and medusas have a nerve net. A **nerve net** is a network of nerve cells that together let cnidarians detect stimuli.

Some cnidarians have a **hydrostatic skeleton.** This skeleton consists of a layer of circular muscles and a layer of longitudinal muscles that, together with the water in the gastrovascular cavity, enable the cnidarian to move.

Cnidarians reproduce both sexually and asexually. Polyps reproduce asexually by budding. Sexual reproduction takes place with external fertilization in water.

There are three classes of cnidarians. They include jellyfishes, hydras and their relatives, and sea anemones and corals.

- Jellyfishes live mostly as medusas.
- Hydras and related animals grow in branching colonies. The Portuguese man-of-war is a colonial hydrozoan composed of many specialized polyps.
- Sea anemones and corals have only the polyp stage in their life cycles. Most corals are colonial. Their polyps grow together in large numbers. As the colonies grow, they secrete an underlying skeleton of calcium carbonate (limestone). Coral colonies form structures called coral reefs.

© Pearson Education, Inc., publishing as Pearson Prentice Hall.

Early Animal Development

During the early development of most animals, cells divide
to form a hollow ball called a blastula. An opening, called a
blastopore, forms. The blastopore of a protostome develops into
a mouth. The blastopore of a deuterostome develops into an anus.
Most early animal embryos differentiate into three layers of cells
called germ layers. These three layers, from innermost to outermost, are the *endoderm, mesoderm,* and *ectoderm.*

Color the endoderm *yellow and* ectoderm *blue. The mesoderm has
already been shaded for you.*

Protostome

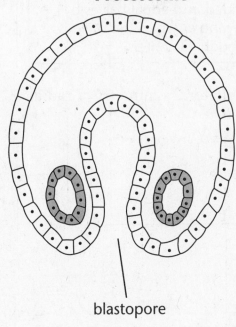

blastopore

Deuterostome

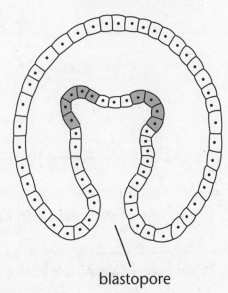

blastopore

Use the diagram to answer the questions.

1. Which germ layer develops into the lining of the digestive tract
   and the respiratory system?

   _____

2. Which germ layer develops into the outer layer of skin?

   _____

© Pearson Education, Inc., publishing as Pearson Prentice Hall.

Symmetry

Study the information in the table.

Bilateral Symmetry	Radial Symmetry

An object or organism with bilateral symmetry can be divided into two matching halves at only one point.	An object or organism with radial symmetry can be divided into equal halves by drawing any number of lines through its center.

Look carefully at each animal below. Write bilateral symmetry *or* radial symmetry *on the line beneath each illustration.*

_____   _____

_____   _____

Use your observations to answer the question.

1. What type of symmetry do humans have?

_____

2. What type of symmetry do cats have?

_____

© Pearson Education, Inc., publishing as Pearson Prentice Hall.

Sponges

A sponge moves water through its body in order to carry out basic life functions. It takes in water through its pores. Water leaves a sponge through a hole at its top called the osculum.

Look at the water flow arrow in the diagram on the right. Draw arrows to show the water flow into and out of the sponge in the left part of the illustration.

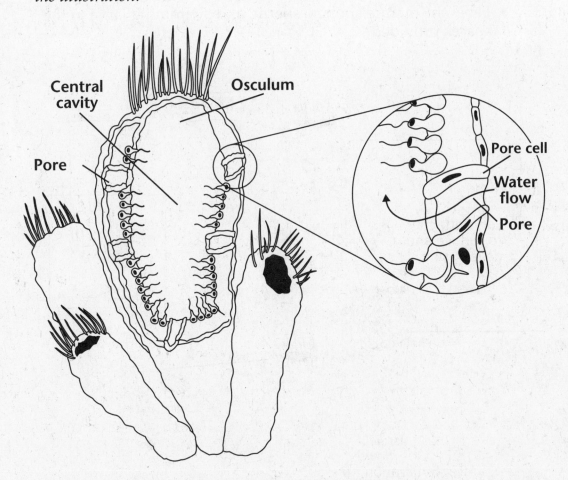

Name two basic life functions that sponges carry out by moving water through their bodies. One function has been identified for you.

1. circulation _____

2. _____

3. _____

Answer the question. Circle the correct answer.

1. What type of symmetry do sponges have?

   bilateral   radial   no symmetry

© Pearson Education, Inc., publishing as Pearson Prentice Hall.

Sponge Life Cycle

Sponges can reproduce both sexually and asexually. For sexual reproduction, most sponges produce both sperm and eggs, but at different times. The steps involved in the sexual reproduction of sponges are diagrammed below.

Mark the life cycle of a sponge according to the statements below.
- Circle the part of the life cycle that shows internal fertilization.
- Label the mature sponge, sperm, and swimming larva in the spaces provided.

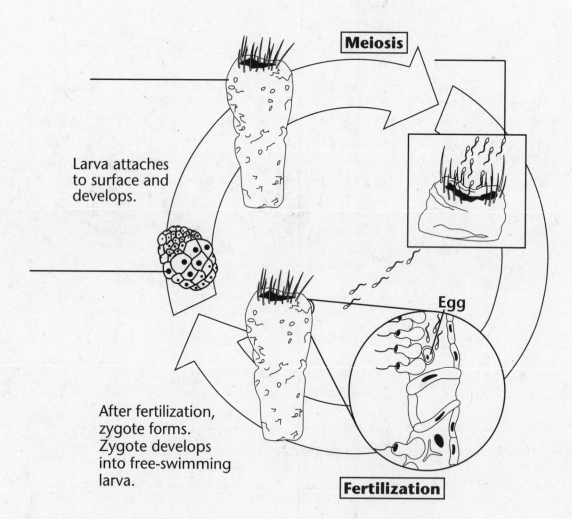

Meiosis

Larva attaches to surface and develops.

Egg

After fertilization, zygote forms. Zygote develops into free-swimming larva.

Fertilization

Answer the question.

1. What is a larva?

_____

_____

© Pearson Education, Inc., publishing as Pearson Prentice Hall.

Cnidarian Body Forms

Most cnidarians have both a polyp and a medusa form during their life cycles.

Label the polyp *and* medusa *forms of the cnidarian pictured below. Then, circle the tentacles on each diagram.*

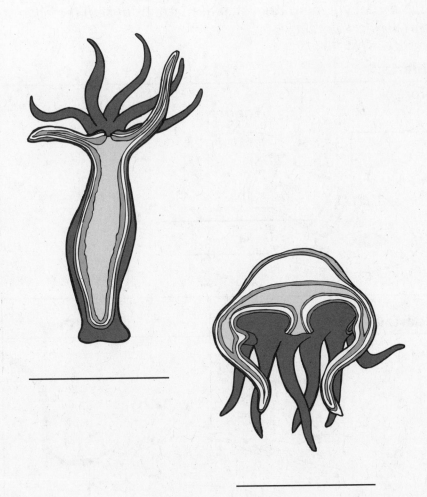

_____

_____

Use the illustrations to answer the questions.

1. What is the function of a cnidarian's tentacles?

_____

_____

2. Which body form shown above is motile?

_____

3. Which body form shown above is sessile?

_____

© Pearson Education, Inc., publishing as Pearson Prentice Hall.

Cnidocytes

Along their tentacles, cnidarians have stinging cells called cnidocytes. They use these cells for defense and to capture prey.
Cnidocytes contain poison-filled stinging structures called nema-
tocysts. The drawing below shows a cnidocyte before and after it
encounters prey.

*Label the cnidocyte, nematocyst, and filament in both the before and
after parts of the diagram.*

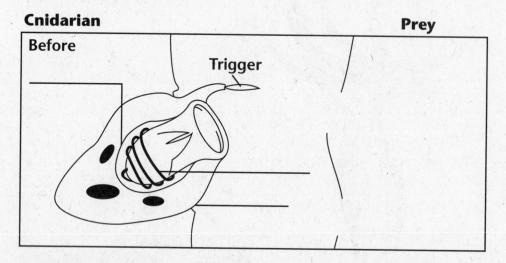

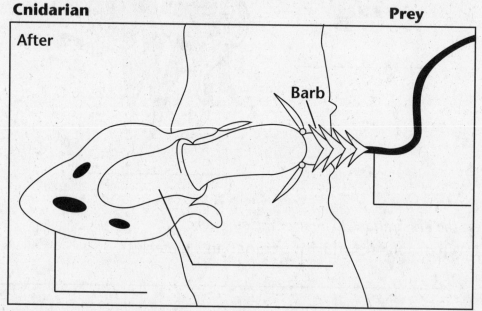

Use the drawing to answer the question.

1. What happens when prey comes in contact with the trigger?

_____

_____

© Pearson Education, Inc., publishing as Pearson Prentice Hall.

Cnidarian Life Cycle

Most cnidarians can reproduce both asexually and sexually. The life cycle of a jellyfish is diagramed below. It involves both haploid and diploid stages.

Color the arrows showing haploid stages of the life cycle orange. Color the arrows showing diploid stages purple.

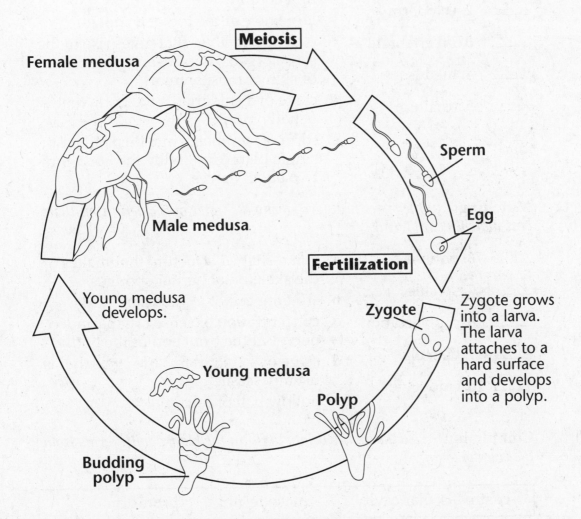

Use the drawing to answer the question. Circle the correct answer.

1. What forms as a result of meiosis?

egg   polyp

© Pearson Education, Inc., publishing as Pearson Prentice Hall.

Chapter 26   Sponges and Cnidarians

Vocabulary Review

Matching   *In the space provided, write the letter of the definition that best matches each term.*

_____ **1.** bilateral

_____ **2.** ectoderm

_____ **3.** invertebrate

_____ **4.** medusa

_____ **5.** osculum

a. animal that has no backbone or vertebral column

b. large hole at the top of a sponge

c. outer germ layer that gives rise to the sense organs, nerves, and outer layer of skin of most animals

d. stage of a cnidarian's life cycle that is usually motile

e. form of symmetry in which only a single plane can divide the body into two equal halves

Matching   *In the space provided, write the letter of the definition that best matches each term.*

_____ **6.** polyp

_____ **7.** spicule

_____ **8.** cephalization

_____ **9.** blastula

_____ **10.** cnidocyte

a. spike-shaped structure that makes up the skeleton of harder sponges

b. stinging cell of a cnidarian

c. concentration of sense organs and nerves at the front end of the body

d. stage of a cnidarian's life cycle that is usually sessile

e. hollow ball of cells

Completion   *Use the words below to fill in the blanks with terms from the chapter.*

gastrovascular cavity	mesoderm	protostome

11. An animal whose mouth is formed from the blastopore is a

_____.

12. The middle germ layer, or _____, gives rise to muscles and many organ systems.

13. The digestive chamber found in cnidarians is the

_____.

© Pearson Education, Inc., publishing as Pearson Prentice Hall.

Chapter 27   Worms and Mollusks

Summary

27–1 Flatworms

Flatworms make up the phylum Platyhelminthes. **Flatworms are soft, flattened worms with tissues and internal organ systems. They are the simplest animals having three germ layers, bilateral symmetry, and cephalization.** Flatworms are **acoelomates.** There is no coelom between the tissues of flatworms. A **coelom** is a fluid-filled body cavity that is lined with tissue formed by mesoderm.

All flatworms use diffusion for body functions. Some have specialized **flame cells** that remove excess water from the body. Flatworms have a digestive cavity with one opening—a mouth. Near the mouth is a muscular tube called a **pharynx,** which pumps food into the digestive cavity. The three main groups of flatworms are turbellarians, flukes, and tapeworms.

- **Turbellarians are free-living flatworms. Most live in marine or fresh water.** In free-living flatworms, several **ganglia,** or groups of nerve cells, control the nervous system. Many free-living flatworms have eyespots to detect changes in light. They reproduce both asexually (by fission) and sexually. Planarians are the most familiar species.
- **Flukes are parasitic flatworms. Most flukes infect the internal organs of their hosts.** Flukes reproduce sexually in the primary host and asexually in their intermediate host.
- **Tapeworms are long, flat, parasitic worms. They live in the intestines of their hosts.**

27–2 Roundworms

Roundworms make up the phylum Nematoda. **Roundworms are unsegmented worms that have pseudocoeloms. They also have digestive systems with two openings—a mouth and an anus.** A **pseudocoelom** is a body cavity that lies between the endoderm and mesoderm tissues. This cavity is only partly lined with mesoderm tissue.

Roundworms rely on diffusion for respiration, circulation, and excretion. The muscles and fluid in the pseudocoelom act as a hydrostatic skeleton. Roundworms reproduce sexually by internal fertilization.

Although most roundworms are free-living, some roundworms are parasitic. **Parasitic roundworms include trichinosis-causing worms, filarial worms, ascarid worms, and hookworms.**

© Pearson Education, Inc., publishing as Pearson Prentice Hall.

Trichinosis is a painful disease caused by the roundworm *Trichinella. Trichinella* are parasites of humans, pigs, and other mammals.

Filarial worms live in the blood and lymph of birds and mammals. The filarial worms are passed from host to host by biting insects, especially mosquitoes.

Ascarid worms are parasites of humans and other animals. They cause malnutrition by absorbing digested food from the host's small intestine. They are spread by eating vegetables and other foods that are not washed properly.

Hookworm eggs develop in soil. If they find an unprotected foot, they burrow into the skin and enter the bloodstream. They suck the host's blood causing weakness and poor growth.

27–3 Annelids

The phylum Annelida includes earthworms. **Annelids are worms with segmented bodies. They have a true coelom that is lined with tissue derived from mesoderm.**

Internal walls called **septa** separate the segments that divide the annelid body. Most segments are similar to one another. A few segments, like those with eyes or antennae, are modified for special jobs. Many annelids have bristles called **setae** attached to each segment.

Annelids have complex organ systems. Many annelids use a pharynx to get their food. In earthworms, food moves through the **crop,** where it is stored. Food then moves through the **gizzard,** an organ that grinds food into smaller pieces. Annelids typically have a **closed circulatory system** in which blood is contained in a network of vessels.

Aquatic annelids may breathe through gills. A **gill** is an organ specialized for the exchange of gases in water. Most annelids reproduce sexually. Some annelids, like earthworms, are hermaphroditic. A hermaphroditic organism has both male and female reproductive organs. When eggs are ready to be fertilized, a **clitellum**—a band of thickened segments—secretes a mucous ring in which fertilization takes place.

There are three classes of annelids.
- **The oligochaetes—class Oligochaeta—are annelids that have streamlined bodies with relatively few setae. Most, including earthworms, live in soil or fresh water.**
- The class Hirudinea includes leeches. **Most leeches are external parasites. They feed on the blood and body fluids of their hosts.**
- The polychaetes—class Polychaeta—are marine annelids. **They have paired, paddlelike appendages tipped with setae.**

© Pearson Education, Inc., publishing as Pearson Prentice Hall.

27–4 Mollusks

Mollusks—phylum Mollusca—are soft-bodied animals that often have an internal or external shell. Many aquatic mollusks have a free-swimming larval stage called a **trochophore.** Mollusks can be herbivores, carnivores, detritivores, or parasites. **The body plan of most mollusks has four parts.**

- The muscular **foot** is used for crawling, burrowing, or catching prey.
- The **mantle** is a thin layer of tissue that covers most of the mollusk's body.
- The **visceral mass,** made up of the internal organs, is just beneath the mantle.
- Most mollusks have a **shell.** Glands in the mantle secrete calcium carbonate (limestone) to form the shell.

Mollusks have either open or closed circulatory systems. In an **open circulatory system,** blood is pumped through vessels into large saclike spaces called sinuses. In a closed circulatory system, blood is contained in blood vessels throughout the body.

Mollusk nervous systems vary from very simple to complex. For example, the nervous systems of clams are made up of small ganglia, a few nerve cords, and simple sense organs. Octopi, however, have more complex nervous systems with well-developed brains.

There are three major classes of mollusks.

- The gastropods include pond snails, land slugs, and nudibranchs. **Gastropods are shell-less or single-shelled mollusks. They move by using a muscular foot on their ventral (lower) side.** Snails and slugs feed by using a flexible, tongue-shaped structure called a **radula.**
- The bivalves include clams, oysters, mussels, and scallops. **Bivalves have two shells held together by muscles.**
- Cephalopods include octopi, squids, cuttlefishes, and nautiluses. **Cephalopods are typically soft-bodied mollusks in which the head is attached to a single foot. The foot is divided into tentacles.** Most cephalopods have small internal shells or no shells at all. Cephalopods have many complex sense organs.

© Pearson Education, Inc., publishing as Pearson Prentice Hall.

Flatworm Development

Flatworms are the simplest animals whose embryos develop three layers of cells, called germ layers. These layers, from innermost to outermost, are the endoderm, mesoderm, and ectoderm. Different parts of a flatworm develop from each germ layer.

Color the endoderm layer of the flatworm red. Color the mesoderm layer yellow. Color the ectoderm layer blue.

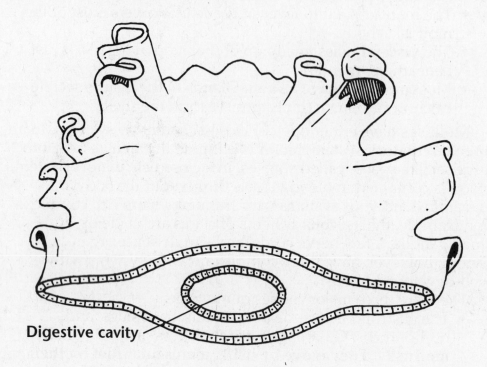

Digestive cavity

Use the diagram to answer the questions.

1. What type of tissue forms the digestive cavity?

_____

2. Which term describes a flatworm? Circle the correct answer.

   acoelomate   coelomate

3. What type of tissue forms the outermost layer of the flatworm?

_____

© Pearson Education, Inc., publishing as Pearson Prentice Hall.

Flatworm Anatomy

Like other animals, flatworms have body systems for waste removal (the excretory system) and response (the nervous system).

Color the excretory system blue. Color the nervous system yellow.

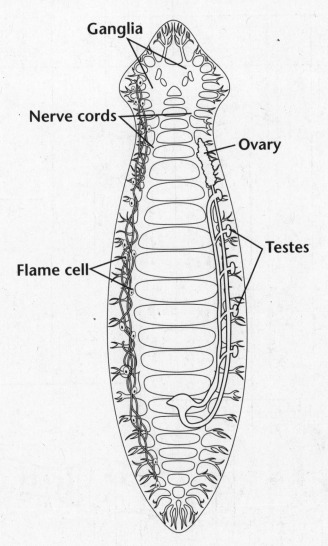

Ganglia

Nerve cords

Ovary

Testes

Flame cell

Use the diagram to answer the questions.

1. Which are parts of the nervous system? Circle the correct answer.

   ganglia   ovaries

2. What cells remove excess water and cell wastes from the flatworm?

   _____

© Pearson Education, Inc., publishing as Pearson Prentice Hall.

Annelid Anatomy

The earthworm shown is one example of the group of worms called annelids. Annelids are segmented worms with true coeloms.

Use the words below to label the diagram of an annelid.

body segments	crop	nephridia
clitellum	gizzard	setae

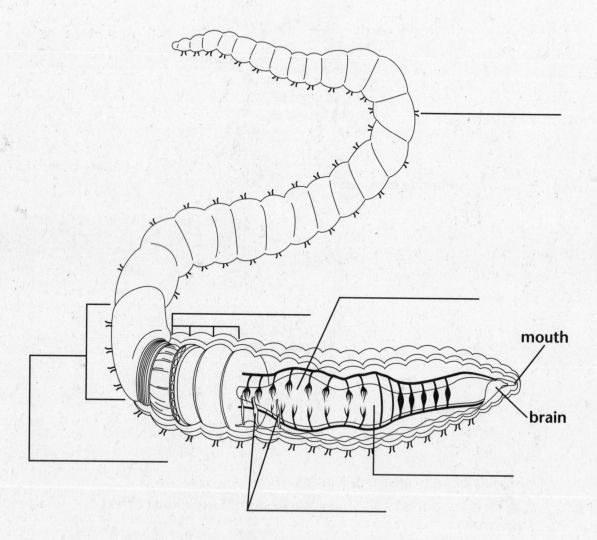

Use the diagram to answer the question.

1. Which of the structures on the diagram are part of the annelid's digestive system?

_____

© Pearson Education, Inc., publishing as Pearson Prentice Hall.

Types of Worms

There are three main groups of worms: *annelids*, *flatworms*, and *roundworms*. Each group has distinctive body structures and methods of movement.

Use what you know about worms to complete the table. Write the type of worm in the first column.

Worm Type	Body Shape and Structure	Movement
	very thin, with bilateral symmetry and cephalization	Cilia help glide through water; muscle cells allow twisting and turning.
	unsegmented tube-within-a-tube	Muscles along length of body and fluid in pseudocoelom enable movement.
	body segments (some may be specialized) divided by septa	Longitudinal and circular muscles contract alternately, and setae prevent slipping.

Use the table to answer the questions.

1. Which worms have a pseudocoelom?

_____

2. Which worms have a true coelom?

_____

© Pearson Education, Inc., publishing as Pearson Prentice Hall.

Mollusk Body Plans

Most mollusks have a mantle, a muscular foot, a visceral mass, and a shell. In some cases, the shell is internal. The mantle is a layer of tissue that covers most of the mollusk's body.

Choose one color for each item in the key. Fill out the key to show which colors you chose. Then color the parts of each mollusk to match your key.

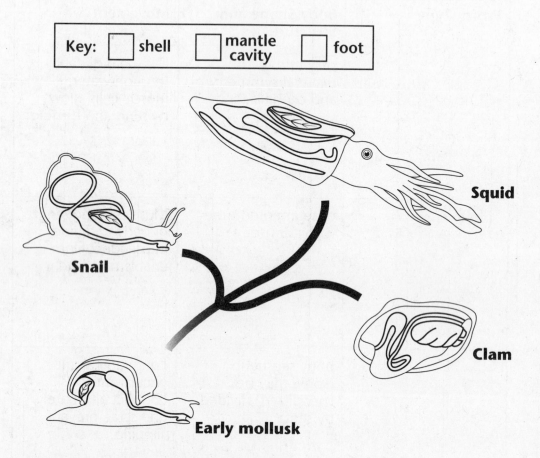

Use the diagrams to answer the questions.

1. Which mollusk does not have an external shell?

_____

2. What is located just beneath the mantle in mollusks?

_____

© Pearson Education, Inc., publishing as Pearson Prentice Hall.

Clam Anatomy

Use the words below to label the diagram of a clam.

excurrent siphon	gills	mantle cavity
foot	heart	shell

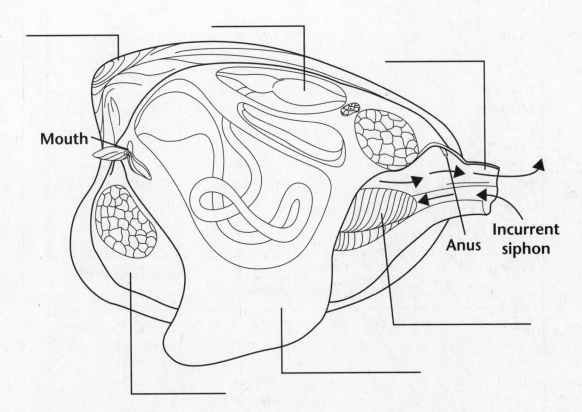

Mouth

Anus

Incurrent siphon

Use the diagram to answer the questions.

1. Which is part of the clam's respiratory system? Circle the correct answer.

   shell   gills

2. Explain how the clam uses its incurrent and excurrent siphons.

   _____

   _____

© Pearson Education, Inc., publishing as Pearson Prentice Hall.

Types of Mollusks

Use what you know to label each mollusk as a bivalve *or a* cephalopod.
The gastropods have been labeled for you.

Mollusk	Class	Shell	Movement
Nudibranch	gastropod	none	large, muscular foot
Clam		two external	little movement; burrows in mud or sand
Nautilus		one external	regulates depth with amount of air in shell
Octopus		none	draws water into its mantle and forces it out through a siphon
Scallop		two external	flapping shells
Snail	gastropod	one external	large, muscular foot
Squid		internal supporting rod	muscular foot

Use the table to answer the questions.

1. What do the bivalves listed have in common?

_____

2. What do the gastropods listed have in common?

_____

3. A newly discovered mollusk has two shells that it flaps to move. To what group does this mollusk likely belong? Circle the correct answer.

bivalve   cephalopod

© Pearson Education, Inc., publishing as Pearson Prentice Hall.

Chapter 27   Worms and Mollusks

Vocabulary Review

Completion   *Use the words below to fill in the blanks with terms from the chapter.*

coelom	mantle	pharynx
gizzard	nephridium	proglottid

1. The thin layer of tissue that covers most of a mollusk is the

   _____.

2. The _____ is the muscular tube near the mouth of a flatworm.

3. A single segment of a tapeworm's body is a

   _____.

4. The _____ is a structure in annelids that grinds food.

5. The fluid-filled body cavity lined with tissue and derived from

   mesoderm is the _____.

6. An organ of excretion in annelids is the _____.

Completion   *Use the words below to fill in the blanks with terms from the chapter.*

radula	trocophore
scolex	visceral mass

7. The head of an adult tapeworm is the _____.

8. The free-swimming larval stage of an aquatic mollusk is a

   _____.

9. Located below the mantle, the _____ is made up of a mollusk's internal organs.

10. The tongue-shaped feed structure of snails and slugs is the

   _____.

© Pearson Education, Inc., publishing as Pearson Prentice Hall.

Chapter 28 Arthropods and Echinoderms

Summary

28–1 Introduction to the Arthropods

Crabs, spiders, and insects are in the phylum Arthropoda. **Arthropods have a segmented body, a tough exoskeleton, and jointed appendages.** An **exoskeleton** is a tough outer body covering. The exoskeleton is made from protein and the carbohydrate **chitin.** When arthropods outgrow their exoskeletons, they molt. During **molting,** an arthropod sheds its exoskeleton and makes a larger one to take its place.

The evolution of arthropods has led to fewer body segments and highly specialized appendages for feeding, movement, and other functions. Most living arthropods have two or three body segments. All arthropods have appendages with joints (places that bend). **Appendages** are structures that extend from the body wall. Specialized appendages of living arthropods include antennae, walking legs, wings, and mouthparts. Other characteristics of arthropods are listed below.

- Arthropods can be herbivores, carnivores, or omnivores.
- Most land arthropods breathe through a network of branching **tracheal tubes** that run throughout the body. Air enters and leaves tracheal tubes through small openings on the arthropod's body called **spiracles.** Some arthropods use book lungs to breathe. **Book lungs** are organs that have layers of respiratory tissue stacked like the pages of a book. Most aquatic arthropods breathe by using gills.
- Arthropods have an open circulatory system.
- Arthropods dispose of nitrogen-containing wastes by using saclike organs called **Malpighian tubules.**
- Most arthropods have a well-developed nervous system.
- Land arthropods have internal fertilization. Aquatic arthropods can have internal or external fertilization.

28–2 Groups of Arthropods

Arthropods are classified according to the number and structure of their body segments and appendages—particularly their mouthparts.

Crabs, shrimps, lobsters, crayfishes, and barnacles are crustaceans. **Crustaceans typically have two pairs of antennae, two or three body sections, and chewing mouthparts called mandibles.** Crustaceans with three body sections have a head, a thorax, and an abdomen. The thorax lies just behind the head and holds most of the internal organs. In crustaceans with two sections, the head and thorax are fused into a **cephalothorax.**

© Pearson Education, Inc., publishing as Pearson Prentice Hall.

Chelicerates include horseshoe crabs, spiders, ticks, and scorpions. **Chelicerates have two body sections and mouthparts called *chelicerae*. Most have four pairs of walking legs.**
- Horseshoe crabs are the oldest type of living arthropods.
- Spiders, mites, ticks, and scorpions are arachnids. Spiders, the largest group of arachnids, spin strong webs by forcing liquid silk through organs that contain silk glands. Mites and ticks are often parasitic. They have specialized structures to suck fluid from their hosts. Scorpions have a stinger on their abdomen that can kill or paralyze prey.

Centipedes, millipedes, and insects are uniramians. **Uniramians have jaws, one pair of antennae, and unbranched appendages.**
- Centipedes have a few to more than 100 pairs of legs. Most body segments have one pair of legs. Centipedes are carnivores.
- Millipedes have two pairs of legs per body segment. Millipedes are detritivores.

28–3 Insects

Insects have a three-part body: a head, a thorax, and an abdomen. Three pairs of legs are attached to the thorax. A typical insect has a pair of antennae, a pair of compound eyes, and two pairs of wings. Compound eyes have many lenses that can detect small changes in color and movement. Insects use three pairs of appendages as mouthparts, including a pair of mandibles. Insect mouthparts have many shapes.

Insect growth and development usually involves metamorphosis, a process of changing shape and form.
- In **incomplete metamorphosis,** the immature insects, called **nymphs,** look much like adults. Grasshoppers go through incomplete metamorphosis.
- In **complete metamorphosis,** insects hatch into larvae that look and act nothing like adults. A larva changes into a **pupa,** the stage in which the larva changes into an adult. Bees, moths, and beetles go through complete metamorphosis.

Many insects are destructive. Termites destroy wood. Mosquitoes bite and spread disease. However, insects may also be helpful. Insects pollinate many crops.

Insects use sound, chemicals, and other signals to communicate. For example, insects can communicate using pheromones. **Pheromones** are chemical messengers that affect behavior or development in other members of the same species.

A **society** is a group of animals of the same species that work together to benefit the whole group. **Ants, bees, termites, and some of their relatives form complex societies.**

© Pearson Education, Inc., publishing as Pearson Prentice Hall.

28–4 Echinoderms

Sea stars, sea urchins, and sand dollars are echinoderms. Echinoderms are marine animals. **All have spiny skin, a water vascular system, and tube feet. They also have an endoskeleton, or internal skeleton. Most adult echinoderms show five-part radial symmetry.** Echinoderms are deuterostomes. This suggests that echinoderms and vertebrates are closely related. In most echinoderms, waste is released as feces through the anus. Echinoderms reproduce by external fertilization.

Echinoderms have a system of internal tubes called a **water vascular system. The water vascular system is filled with fluid. It carries out vital body functions, including respiration, circulation, and movement.** This system opens to the outside through a structure called a **madreporite.** In sea stars, the madreporite connects to a ring canal. From the ring canal, five radial canals extend along body segments. Attached to each are hundreds of **tube feet.** A tube foot works much like a suction cup. Most echinoderms move by using their tube feet. Tube feet provide the main surface for respiration in many species of echinoderms. The water vascular system also functions to circulate materials through the echinoderm. Oxygen, food, and wastes are carried by the water vascular system.

Echinoderms have several feeding methods. For example, some use their water vascular system to capture floating plankton. Others feed on organisms such as clams and mussels. In most echinoderms, waste is released as feces through the anus. The nervous systems of echinoderms are simple. Most are made up of a nerve ring, radial nerves, and sensory cells. Echinoderms reproduce by external fertilization.

Classes of echinoderms include: sea urchins and sand dollars, brittle stars, sea cucumbers, sea stars, and sea lilies and feather stars.

© Pearson Education, Inc., publishing as Pearson Prentice Hall.

Arthropod Anatomy

The grasshopper shown is one example of an arthropod. The organs and body structures shown are common to many arthropods.

Use the words below to label the diagram. Some structures have been labeled for you.

brain	Malpighian tubules	tracheal tubes
compound eye	spiracles	

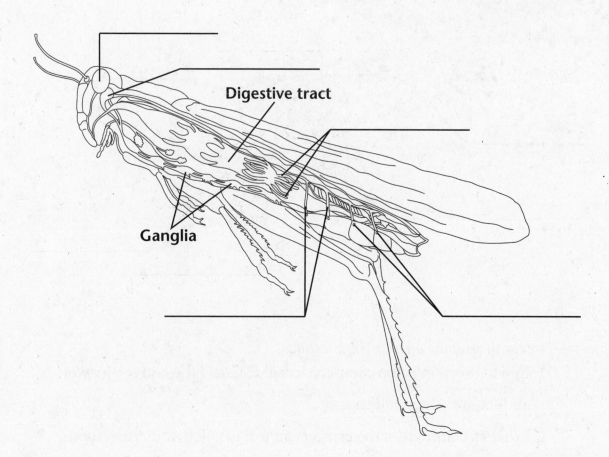

Digestive tract

Ganglia

Use the diagram to answer the questions.

1. Which is part of the excretory system? Circle the correct answer.

    compound eye   Malpighian tubules

2. Which structures shown are part of the respiratory system?

_____

© Pearson Education, Inc., publishing as Pearson Prentice Hall.

Crustacean Anatomy

The crayfish shown is one example of a crustacean. Most crustaceans have similar body organization and body structures.

Color the tail section red. Color the abdomen blue. Color the cephalothorax yellow. Then use the words below to label the diagram.

carapace	cheliped	mandible	swimmerets

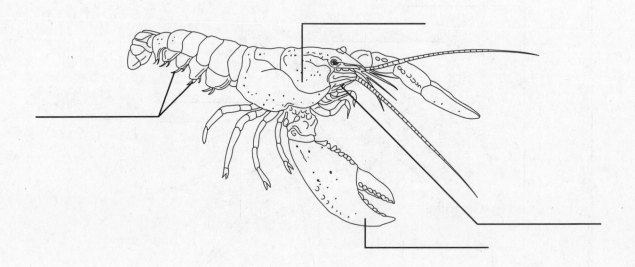

Use the diagram to answer the questions.

1. In what section is the carapace located? Circle the correct answer.

   abdomen   cephalothorax

2. What structure does the crustacean use to catch and crush food?

   _____

3. For what does the crustacean shown use its swimmerets?

   _____

4. What does the crustacean shown use to bite and grind food? Circle the correct answer.

   mandible   abdomen

© Pearson Education, Inc., publishing as Pearson Prentice Hall.

Spider Anatomy

Follow the prompts to identify the spider's body systems. The circulatory system is shaded for you.

- Color the structures in the digestive system green.
- Color the structures in the respiratory system blue.
- Color the structures in the reproductive system red.

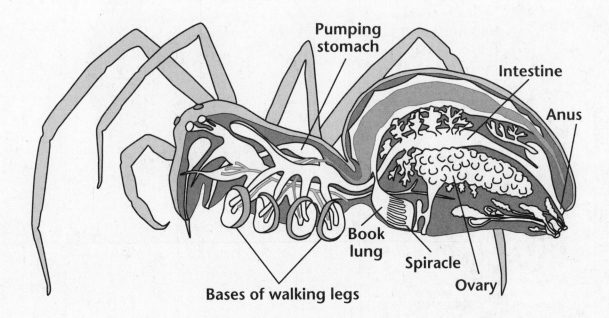

Use the diagram to answer the questions.

1. Which organ is part of the respiratory system? Circle the correct answer.

    spinneret   spiracle

2. What does a spider use its chelicerae for?

    _____

3. What labeled organs does a spider use for digestion?

    _____

4. Can spiders chew their prey? Explain.

    _____

    _____

© Pearson Education, Inc., publishing as Pearson Prentice Hall.

Most Animals Are Insects

Ninety-six percent of all animal species living today are invertebrates. Most of these animals are insects.

Use the circle graph to make a bar graph showing the percentage of all living animal species that are members of each group.

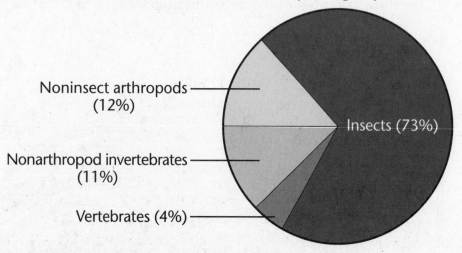

Noninsect arthropods (12%)

Nonarthropod invertebrates (11%)

Vertebrates (4%)

Insects (73%)

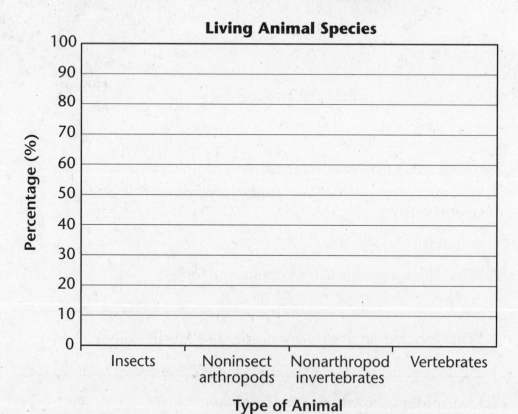

Living Animal Species

Use the graphs to answer the question.

1. Which group contains the largest percentage of all living animal species?

_____

© Pearson Education, Inc., publishing as Pearson Prentice Hall.

Insects

Insects have three body sections: the abdomen, the head, and the thorax.

Color the insect's abdomen yellow. Color the head red. Color the thorax blue.

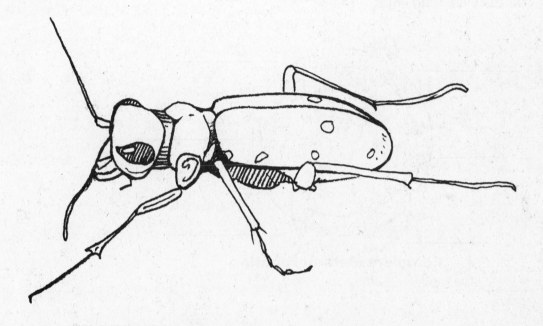

Use the diagram to answer the questions.

1. How many legs does an insect have? _____

2. In which section are the insect's antennae located? Circle the correct answer.

head   thorax

3. Where are an insect's wings typically located? Circle the correct answer.

abdomen   thorax

4. Where are an insect's legs attached? Circle the correct answer.

thorax   abdomen

© Pearson Education, Inc., publishing as Pearson Prentice Hall.

Complete and Incomplete Metamorphosis

As insects develop, they usually go through either complete or incomplete metamorphosis. Metamorphosis is the process of changing shape and form.

Label each stage as adult, eggs, larva, nymph, *or* pupa. *You may use labels more than once.*

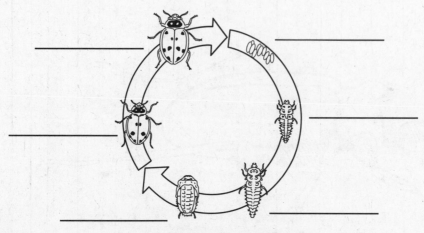

Complete Metamorphosis

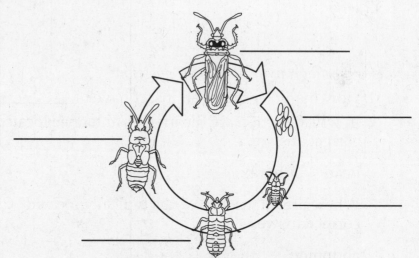

Incomplete Metamorphosis

Use the diagrams to answer the question.

1. What is the difference between complete and incomplete metamorphosis?

_____

_____

_____

© Pearson Education, Inc., publishing as Pearson Prentice Hall.

Types of Arthropods

The table lists characteristics of the three types of arthropods. Use what you know about the groups of arthropods to fill in the column headings. Identify each group as crustaceans, chelicerates, *or* uniramians.

Arthropod Type			
Example	crayfish, lobster, crab	spider, tick	grasshopper, ladybug
Antennae	two pairs	none	one pair
Mouthparts	mandibles	chelicerae and pedipalps	jaws
Number of Body Sections	two or three	two	varied; insects have three

1. A scorpion has chelicerae and pedipalps. To which group does it belong?

_____

2. In a crustacean with two body sections, what are the two sections called?

_____

© Pearson Education, Inc., publishing as Pearson Prentice Hall.

Echinoderm Anatomy

The sea star shown here is one example of an echinoderm. Its body structures are common to many echinoderms.

Use the words below to label the diagram.

eyespot	radial canal	stomach
madreporite	ring canal	tube foot

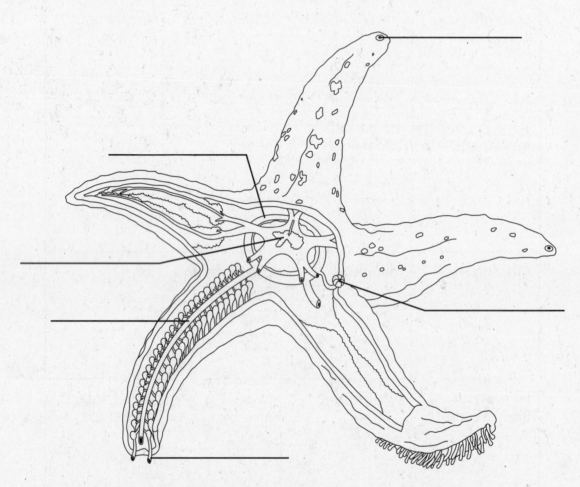

Use the diagram to answer the questions.

1. Which structures are part of the water vascular system?

_____

_____

2. What kind of skeleton do echinoderms have? Circle the correct answer.

external   internal

© Pearson Education, Inc., publishing as Pearson Prentice Hall.

Chapter 28   Arthropods and Echinoderms

Vocabulary Review

True or False   *If the statement is true, write* true. *If it is false, write* false.

_____ **1.** Arthropods have a tough outer covering called an endoskeleton.

_____ **2.** The body plan of a typical crustacean includes an abdomen and a water vascular system.

_____ **3.** During complete metamorphosis, the stage in which an insect changes from a larva to an adult is the nymph.

_____ **4.** Structures such as legs and antennae that extend from the body wall are appendages.

_____ **5.** A Malpighian tubule is an excretory structure of arthropods.

_____ **6.** A characteristic of echinoderms is a carapace.

_____ **7.** The water-vascular system of echinoderms is a system of internal tubes that carries out many vital functions.

_____ **8.** In arthropods, the abdomen is the posterior part of the body.

_____ **9.** The tube foot of the sea star works much like a suction cup and helps the sea star move.

_____ **10.** A mouthpart adapted for biting and grinding food in arthropods is a cheliped.

_____ **11.** During metamorphosis, arthropods shed their entire exoskeleton and make a larger one to take its place.

© Pearson Education, Inc., publishing as Pearson Prentice Hall.

Chapter 29   Comparing Invertebrates

Summary

29–1 Invertebrate Evolution

Paleontologists have identified microscopic fossils from 570 to 610 million years ago. They identified trace fossils from the same time period. Trace fossils are tracks and burrows made by soft-bodied animals.

Fossils of some primitive animals were discovered in the Ediacara Hills of Australia. The Ediacaran animals lived 543 to 575 million years ago. They were flat and plate-shaped. They lived on shallow sea bottoms and had soft, segmented bodies and bilateral symmetry. The animals appear to have lacked cell specialization or a front and a back end.

The Cambrian Period began 544 million years ago. It is marked by many kinds of fossils. The Burgess Shale of Canada is one of the best-known sites of Cambrian fossils. These animals evolved complex body plans. Because of its great growth in animal diversity, events of the early Cambrian Period are called the Cambrian Explosion. The Burgess Shale animals typically had body symmetry, segmentation, some type of skeleton, a front and a back end, and appendages having many functions.

The appearance of each animal phylum in the fossil record shows the evolution of a successful and unique body plan. Modern sponges and cnidarians have little internal specialization. As larger and more complex animals evolved, specialized cells formed tissues, organs, and organ systems.

All invertebrates except sponges have some type of body symmetry.

- Cnidarians and echinoderms have radial symmetry. **Radial symmetry** is a body plan in which the body parts repeat around the center of the body.
- Worms, mollusks, and arthropods have bilateral symmetry. **Bilateral symmetry** is a body plan in which only a single, imaginary line can divide the body into two equal halves.

A trend toward cephalization occurred with the evolution of bilateral symmetry. **Cephalization** is the concentration of sense organs and nerve cells in the front of the body. **Cephalization lets animals respond to the environment in more sophisticated ways.**

© Pearson Education, Inc., publishing as Pearson Prentice Hall.

Most complex animals are coelomates. They have a true coelom. A coelom is a body cavity lined with tissue derived from mesoderm.

- Flatworms are *acoelomates*—they have no coelom.
- Roundworms are *pseudocoelomates*. Their coelom is only partially lined with mesoderm.
- Mollusks, annelids, arthropods, and echinoderms all have a true coelom.

The zygote of most invertebrates divides to form a blastula. An opening, called the blastopore, then forms in this blastula.

- In protostomes, the blastopore develops into a mouth. Worms, arthropods, and mollusks are protostomes.
- In deuterostomes, the blastopore develops into an anus. Echinoderms (and chordates) are deuterostomes.

29–2 Form and Function in Invertebrates

Biologists learn a great deal about the nature of life by comparing the body systems of the various living invertebrates. All animals perform the same essential tasks: feeding and digestion, respiration, circulation, excretion, response, movement and support, and reproduction.

<u>Feeding</u> **The simplest animals—sponges—break down food inside their cells. Mollusks, annelids, arthropods, and echinoderms use extracellular digestion.** Food is broken down outside the cells of a digestive tract. Food enters the body through the mouth, and wastes leave through the anus.

<u>Respiration</u> **All respiratory systems share two features.**

(1) Respiratory organs have a large surface area that is in contact with air or water.

(2) Respiratory surfaces must be moist for diffusion to occur.

Aquatic mollusks, arthropods, and many annelids exchange gases through gills. In land animals, surfaces are covered with water or mucus. Such covering prevents water loss from the body. It also moistens air moving through the respiratory system.

<u>Circulation</u> All cells need a constant supply of oxygen and nutrients. They also must remove wastes. The smallest and thinnest animals exchange materials with the environment by diffusion. **More complex animals use a system of pumps and tubes for transport.** There are two types of circulatory systems.

- In an open circulatory system, blood is only partly contained within blood vessels. The blood moves through the vessels into a system of sinuses, where the blood comes into direct contact with the tissues.
- In a closed circulatory system, blood moves throughout the body in vessels. The blood moves under force from a heart or heartlike organ.

© Pearson Education, Inc., publishing as Pearson Prentice Hall.

Excretion Multicellular animals must control the amount of water in their tissues. They also must get rid of ammonia, a toxic nitrogen waste formed during metabolism. **Most animals have an excretory system to rid the body of metabolic wastes. The excretory system also controls the amount of water in the tissues.** Aquatic organisms get rid of ammonia through diffusion. Many land animals convert ammonia into urea. This compound is then eliminated from the body in urine.

Response The more complex an animal's nervous system is, the more developed its sense organs are. **Invertebrates show three trends in the evolution of the nervous system: centralization, cephalization, and specialization.** Simple animals have nerve cells that are spread through the body, while more complex animals have centralized nerve cells. More complex animals also have more highly specialized sense organs.

Support and Movement **Invertebrates have one of three main kinds of skeletal systems.**

- Annelids and certain cnidarians have a **hydrostatic skeleton.** In this system, muscles surround a fluid-filled body cavity that supports the muscles. The muscles contract and push against the water.
- Arthropods have an **exoskeleton,** or external skeleton.
- Echinoderms have an **endoskeleton,** a structural support located inside the body.

Reproduction **Some invertebrates may reproduce asexually. However, most reproduce sexually at some part of their life cycle.** Asexual reproduction allows animals to reproduce rapidly. Sexual reproduction maintains genetic diversity in a population by creating individuals with new combinations of genes. Most animals have separate sexes that produce eggs or sperm.

- In **external fertilization,** eggs are fertilized outside the female's body.
- In **internal fertilization,** eggs are fertilized inside the female's body.

© Pearson Education, Inc., publishing as Pearson Prentice Hall.

Major Adaptations in Animal Evolution

The cladogram shows one theory of the evolution of animals. Each circle represents the evolution of an important adaptation in animal development.

Follow the prompts to interpret the cladogram.
- Color the organism(s) that have a pseudocoelom brown.
- Color the organism(s) that have radial symmetry blue.
- Color the organism(s) that are deuterostomes red.
- Circle the organism(s) that have a true coelom.

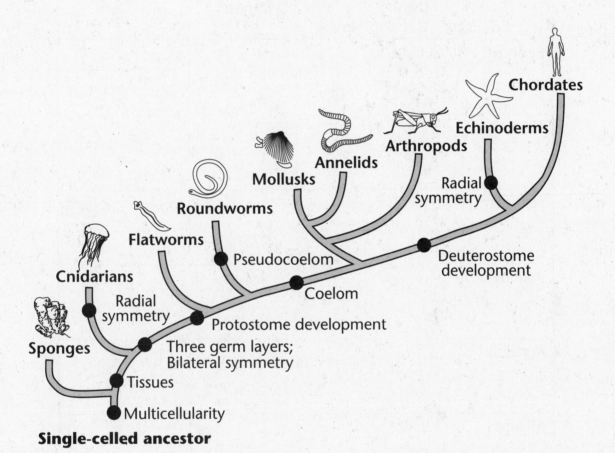

Use the cladogram to answer the question. Circle the correct answer.

1. Which evolved earlier?

coelom   bilateral symmetry

© Pearson Education, Inc., publishing as Pearson Prentice Hall.

Comparing Invertebrates

Invertebrates have a variety of body plans. During development, two or three germ layers may develop. Some invertebrates do not have any germ layers. They can have no body symmetry, radial symmetry, or bilateral symmetry. Some show cephalization, and others do not.

Complete the table. Some information has been filled in for you.

Organism	Germ Layers During Development	Body Symmetry	Cephalization
Sponges	none	none	no
Cnidarians	two		
Flatworms			yes
Roundworms		bilateral	
Annelids			yes
Mollusks	three		
Arthropods	three		
Adult Echinoderms		radial	

© Pearson Education, Inc., publishing as Pearson Prentice Hall.

Coelom Evolution

The embryos of most animals develop three layers of cells, called germ layers: the ectoderm, endoderm, and mesoderm. These layers develop into different structures in different animals. Some animals develop a coelom, or fluid-filled cavity lined with mesoderm.

Color the ectoderm in each diagram red. Color the mesoderm blue. Color the endoderm yellow.

Acoelomate

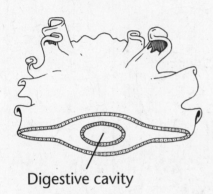

Digestive cavity

Pseudocoelomate

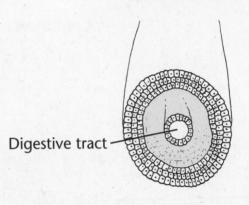

Digestive tract

Coelomate

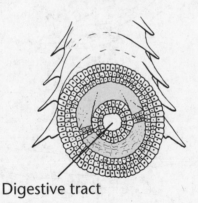

Digestive tract

Use the diagrams to answer the questions.

1. Which type of organism does not have a digestive tract?

_____

2. Which term describes a flatworm? Circle the correct answer.

acoelomate   pseudocoelomate   coelomate

© Pearson Education, Inc., publishing as Pearson Prentice Hall.

Invertebrate Digestive Systems

Most invertebrates have a mouth through which they consume food and an anus through which wastes are removed. In some animals, the same structure serves as both mouth and anus. These structures are part of the digestive system.

Color the digestive system in each organism blue. Then label the mouth *and* anus *on each diagram.*

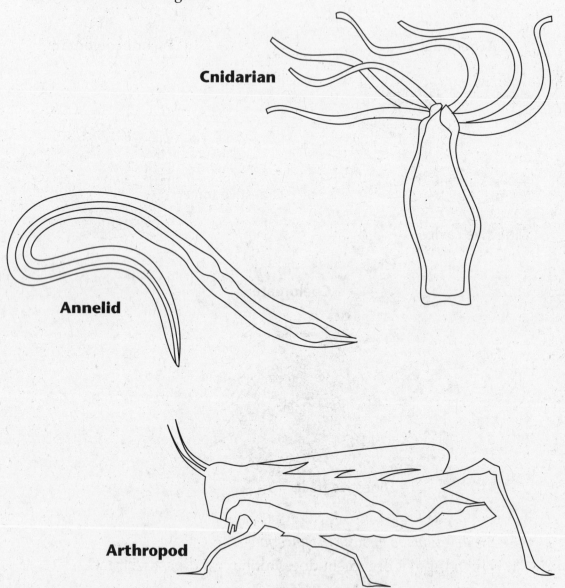

Cnidarian

Annelid

Arthropod

Use the diagrams to answer the question.

1. Which organism has a digestive system with only one opening?

_____

© Pearson Education, Inc., publishing as Pearson Prentice Hall.

Invertebrate Respiratory Systems

Invertebrates have a variety of respiratory systems. Aquatic invertebrates may have gills to obtain oxygen from water. Land invertebrates may use structures including book lungs and tracheal tubes to obtain oxygen from the air.

Color the respiratory system in each organism red. Then use the words below to label the structures in each organism.

book lung	gill	tracheal tubes	spiracles

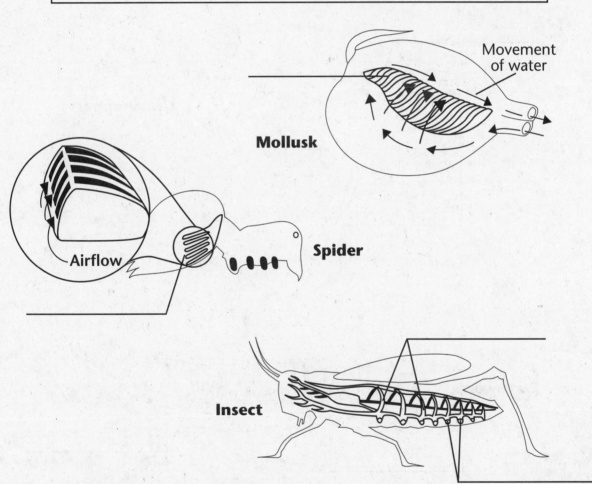

Mollusk

Movement of water

Airflow

Spider

Insect

Answer the questions.

1. What can you conclude about a mollusk that uses gills for respiration?

_____

2. What are spiracles?

_____

_____

© Pearson Education, Inc., publishing as Pearson Prentice Hall.

Invertebrate Circulatory Systems

In an open circulatory system, the hearts or heartlike organs pump blood into cavities called sinuses. The blood contacts tissues directly and eventually returns to the heart. In a closed circulatory system, the hearts or heartlike organs pump blood through vessels.

Color the circulatory system in each organism red. Label the hearts *and* blood vessels *in the grasshopper and the* heartlike structures *and* blood vessels *in the earthworm.*

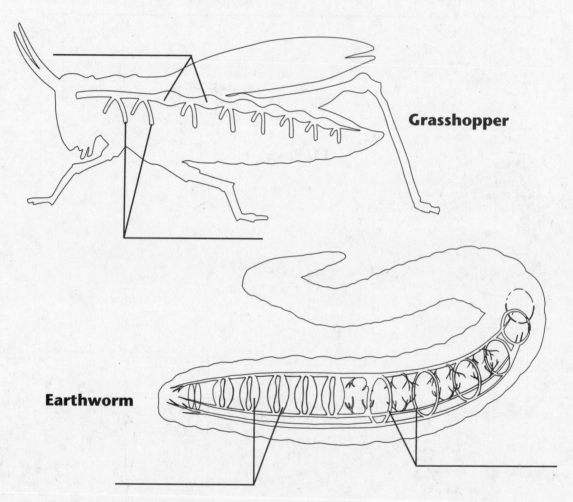

Grasshopper

Earthworm

Use the diagrams to answer the questions. Circle the correct answer.

1. What kind of circulatory system does the grasshopper have?

closed   open

2. What kind of circulatory system does the earthworm have?

closed   open

© Pearson Education, Inc., publishing as Pearson Prentice Hall.

Invertebrate Excretory Systems

The excretory system in animals removes wastes from the body. Invertebrates have evolved different structures, such as flame cells, Malpighian tubules, and nephridia, to accomplish this task.

Color the excretory structures in each organism blue. Then label the flame cells, Malpighian tubules, *and* nephridia.

Flatworm

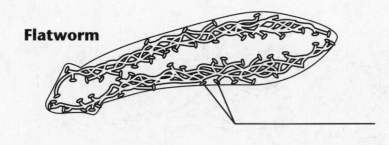

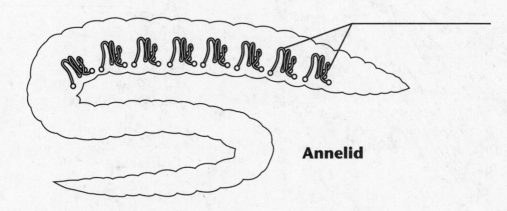

Annelid

Digestive tract

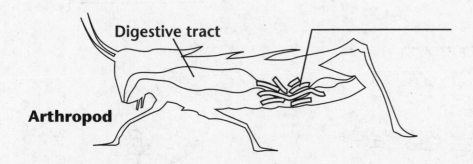

Arthropod

Use the diagrams to answer the questions.

1. Which organism uses nephridia to remove wastes?

_____

2. Explain how flame cells are used.

_____

© Pearson Education, Inc., publishing as Pearson Prentice Hall.

Invertebrate Nervous Systems

The nervous system controls an animal's response to its environment. Many animals have a brain or groups of nerve cells called *ganglia* that control the nervous system.

Label the nervous system structures in the following invertebrates. Choose from the following labels: nerve cells, brain, *and* ganglia. *Some words may be used more than once.*

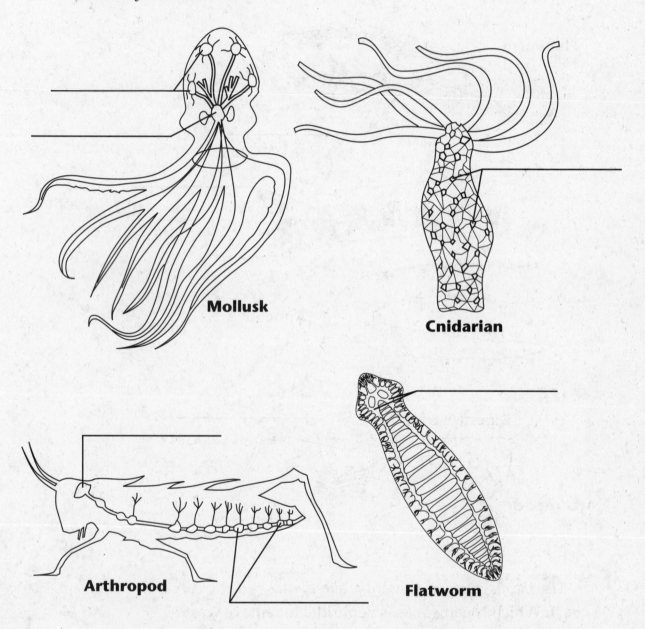

Mollusk

Cnidarian

Arthropod

Flatworm

Use the diagrams to answer the question.

1. Which organism shows cephalization? Circle the correct answer.

mollusk   cnidarian

© Pearson Education, Inc., publishing as Pearson Prentice Hall.

Chapter 29 Comparing Invertebrates

Vocabulary Review

Completion *Use the words below to fill in the blanks with terms from the chapter.*

bilateral	coelom	radial
cephalization	open	

1. Echinoderms and cnidarians have _____ symmetry—body parts that extend from the center part of the body.

2. Many invertebrates show _____, a concentration of nerve cells and sense organs in the front of the body.

3. The bodies of worms, mollusks, and arthropods show

_____ symmetry, right and left sides that are mirror images of each other.

4. Most complex animals have a true _____ that is lined completely with mesoderm.

5. In a(an) _____ circulatory system, blood is only partially contained within a system of blood vessels.

Completion *Use the words below to fill in the blanks with terms from the chapter.*

closed	exoskeleton	intracellular digestion
endoskeleton	hydrostatic skeletons	

6. A(An) _____ is a structural support located inside the body.

7. Annelids and some cnidarians have _____, or fluid-filled body cavities that support their muscles.

8. An external skeleton is called a(an) _____.

9. In a(an) _____ circulatory system, a heart or heartlike organ pumps blood through a system of enclosed blood vessels.

10. The simplest animals digest their food inside cells in a process

known as _____.

© Pearson Education, Inc., publishing as Pearson Prentice Hall.

Chapter 30   Nonvertebrate Chordates, Fishes, and Amphibians

Summary

30–1 The Chordates

A chordate is an animal with four features for at least some stage of its life:

- A **hollow nerve cord** runs along the back of the body. Nerves branch from it and connect to organs and muscles.
- A **notochord** is a support rod that runs just below the nerve cord.
- **Pharyngeal pouches** are paired structures in the throat. In some chordates, they become gills.
- A **tail** that extends beyond the anus is the fourth common feature.

Most chordates are vertebrates. **Vertebrates** have a backbone made up of vertebrae. The backbone replaces the notochord and supports and protects the spinal cord. It also gives muscles a place to attach. **Two groups of chordates do not have backbones.**

- **Tunicates** are ocean-living filter feeders. Adult tunicates have no notochord or tail. Larval tunicates have all chordate characteristics.
- **Lancelets** are small, fishlike animals. Adult lancelets have all four chordate characteristics. They also have a definite head region.

30–2 Fishes

Fishes are aquatic vertebrates; most fishes have paired fins, scales, and gills. Jaws and paired fins were important developments in fish evolution. Jaws improved defense and expanded food choices. Paired fins improved control of body movement.

Adaptations to aquatic life include various modes of feeding, specialized structures for gas exchange, and paired fins for locomotion.

- Feeding. Fishes feed in many ways. They may be herbivores, carnivores, parasites, filter feeders, or detritus feeders. One fish may feed in several ways, depending on the food available.
- Respiration. Most fishes breathe with gills. Gills have many tiny blood vessels that provide a large surface area for gas exchange. Fishes pull water in through the mouth. The water then moves over the gills and out of the body through openings in the sides of the pharynx.
- Circulation. Fishes have a closed circulatory system. It pumps blood in a loop from heart to gills to the body and back to the heart. The heart consists of two chambers: an atrium and a ventricle.

© Pearson Education, Inc., publishing as Pearson Prentice Hall.

- <u>Excretion</u>. Most fishes get rid of wastes as ammonia. Some wastes diffuse through the gills into the water. Others are removed from the blood by kidneys. Kidneys also help fishes control the amount of water in their bodies.
- <u>Response</u>. Fishes have well-developed nervous systems. The brain has several parts. Unlike other chordates, in fish the **cerebrum** is primarily involved in smell. The **cerebellum** coordinates body movements. The **medulla oblongata** controls the functioning of many internal organs. Most fishes also have a **lateral line system** that senses currents and vibrations in the water.
- <u>Movement</u>. Most fishes move by contracting muscles on either side of the backbone. Fins push the fish forward and help it steer. Many fishes have a gas-filled organ called a **swim bladder** that keeps them from sinking.
- <u>Reproduction</u>. Fishes reproduce in several ways. Eggs may be fertilized externally or internally, depending on the species.
  - **Oviparous** fishes lay eggs. The eggs develop and hatch outside the mother's body.
  - In **ovoviviparous** fishes, the fertilized eggs develop inside the female. The embryos are fed by yolk in the egg. The young are then "born alive" from the mother's body.
  - In **viviparous** fishes, embryos develop inside the mother. They get food from the mother's body, not from an egg. They are also born alive.

There are three classes of fishes.
- Lampreys and hagfishes are **jawless fishes.** Their bodies are supported by a notochord. They do not have true teeth or jaws. They are parasites and scavengers.
- The **cartilaginous fishes** include sharks, rays, and skates. These fishes have a skeleton made of cartilage. Most also have toothlike scales covering their skin.
- **Bony fishes** have skeletons made of bone. Most bony fishes are ray-finned fishes. Their fins have thin, bony spines that are joined by a thin layer of skin.

© Pearson Education, Inc., publishing as Pearson Prentice Hall.

30–3 Amphibians

An amphibian is a vertebrate that, with some exceptions, lives in water as a larva and on land as an adult. Amphibians breathe with lungs as adults, have moist skin that contains mucous glands, and lack scales and claws.

Early amphibians evolved several adaptations that helped them live at least part of their lives out of water. Bones in the limbs and limb girdles of amphibians became stronger, permitting more efficient movement. Lungs and breathing tubes enabled amphibians to breathe air. The sternum, or breastbone, formed a bony shield to support and protect internal organs, especially the lungs.

Other amphibian characteristics include:

- <u>Feeding</u>. Amphibian larvae are filter feeders or herbivores. They have long, coiled intestines that help them break down plant matter. Adults are carnivores and have a much shorter intestine.
- <u>Respiration</u>. In most larvae, gas exchange occurs through the skin as well as gills. Lungs usually replace gills as an amphibian becomes an adult. In adults, some gas exchange occurs through the skin and the lining of the mouth.
- <u>Circulation</u>. Amphibian hearts have three chambers: a left atrium, a right atrium, and a ventricle. The circulatory system of adult amphibians forms a double loop. The first loop carries oxygen-poor blood from the heart to the lungs and returns oxygen-rich blood to the heart. The second loop carries oxygen-rich blood from the heart to the body and returns oxygen-poor blood to the heart.
- <u>Excretion</u>. Kidneys remove wastes from blood. Urine passes through tubes called ureters into the cloaca. From there, it either passes directly to the outside or is stored in a small urinary bladder.
- <u>Reproduction</u>. Amphibian eggs lack shells. In most amphibians, the female usually lays eggs in water, where the male fertilizes them. The eggs hatch into larvae, often called tadpoles. Tadpoles change into adults.
- <u>Nervous system</u>. Amphibians have well-developed nervous systems and sense organs. Frogs have very good vision. Tympanic membranes, or eardrums, receive sound vibrations.

There are three amphibian groups: salamanders, frogs and toads, and caecilians.

- Salamanders have long bodies, four legs, and long tails.
- Frogs and toads do not have tails and can jump. Frogs live close to water, whereas toads often live in moist wooded areas.
- Caecilians do not have legs. Caecilians live in water or burrow in moist soil.

© Pearson Education, Inc., publishing as Pearson Prentice Hall.

Chordate Structure

At some stage in their lives, all chordates have four characteristics:
a hollow nerve cord, a notochord, pharyngeal pouches, and a
tail that extends beyond the anus. The nerve cord runs along the
animal's back. The notochord is a supporting rod. Most chordates
have a notochord only as embryos. Pharyngeal pouches are paired
structures in the throat region.

Color the notochord *yellow. Color the* hollow nerve cord *blue.*
Color the pharyngeal pouches *red.*

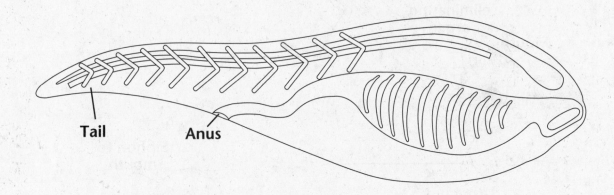

Use the diagram to answer the questions.

1. From which structure do nerves branch off? Circle the
   correct answer.

   nerve cord   pharyngeal pouches

2. In some chordates, slits connect the pharyngeal pouches to the
   outside of the body. In aquatic chordates, what may these slits
   develop into to use for gas exchange?

   _____

3. For what purpose do many aquatic chordates use their tails?

   _____

© Pearson Education, Inc., publishing as Pearson Prentice Hall.

Nonvertebrate Chordates

Tunicates are one of the two groups of chordates that do not have backbones. Larval tunicates have all four characteristics of chordates, although they lose many of them as adults.

Label the hollow nerve cord, notochord, pharynx with gill slits, *and* tail *on the diagrams. Remember that not all of the structures will appear in both diagrams.*

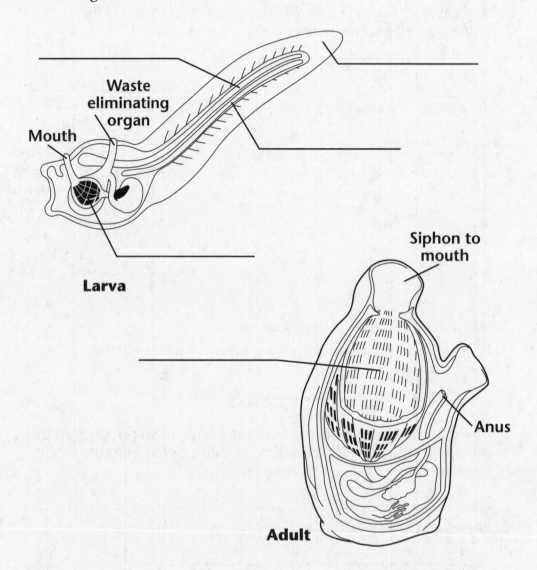

Larva

Adult

Use the diagrams to answer the question. Circle the correct answer.

1. Which structure common to chordates appears in both the larval and adult tunicates?

notochord   pharynx with gill slits

© Pearson Education, Inc., publishing as Pearson Prentice Hall.

Common Fish Structures

Although there are many kinds of fish, most of them have three features in common: paired fins, scales, and gills. The gills may be covered by an operculum, or gill cover. The diagram below shows one type of fish, called an African cichlid.

Label five fins, *the* scales, *and the* operculum *in the diagram.*

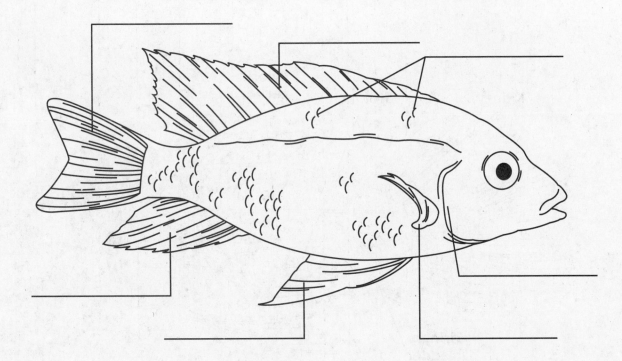

Use the diagram to answer the questions.

1. Which structures are used for movement? Circle the correct answer.

   fins   gills

2. Which structures are used for gas exchange? Circle the correct answer.

   gills   scales

3. What is the role of gills?

   _____

   _____

© Pearson Education, Inc., publishing as Pearson Prentice Hall.

Form and Function in Fishes

Fish have specialized body systems for digestion, excretion, and respiration.

Look at the labeled structures on the fish diagram below. Color these structures according to the prompts below.

- Color the parts of the digestive system blue.
- Color the parts of the excretory system yellow.
- Color the parts of the respiratory system orange.

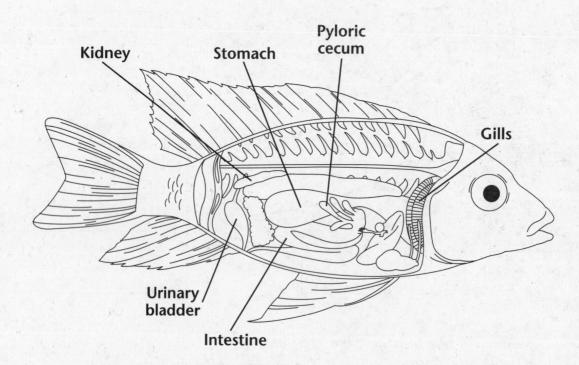

Use the diagram to answer the questions. Circle the correct answer.

1. Which structure is part of the digestive system?

    gills   pyloric cecum

2. Which structure is part of the excretory system?

    stomach   urinary bladder

3. What is one function of the kidney?

    filter wastes from blood   gas exchange

© Pearson Education, Inc., publishing as Pearson Prentice Hall.

Amphibian Land Adaptations

As amphibians evolved from lobe-finned fishes, they developed adaptations that helped them spend parts of their lives out of water. These included adaptations to their lungs, bones, and skin.

Use the words below to identify how each adaptation helps amphibians survive on land. The first one has been done for you.

> more efficient movement
> permits gas exchange
> protects internal organs

Body Part	Adaptation	How It Helps Survival
lungs	blood vessels, folds that increase surface area, breathing tubes	allows amphibians to breathe air
limb bones	stronger limb and pelvic bones	
chest bones	development of sternum, or breastbone	
skin	thin, richly supplied with blood vessels; watery mucus secreted by glands	

Answer the question. Circle the correct answer.

1. For how long does an amphibian live on land?

   its entire life   part of its life

© Pearson Education, Inc., publishing as Pearson Prentice Hall.

Frog Digestive System

Adult frogs are mostly carnivorous. Their digestive systems are specialized to digest other organisms.

Use the words below to label the structures in the frog's digestive system.

large intestine	pancreas	stomach
liver	small intestine	

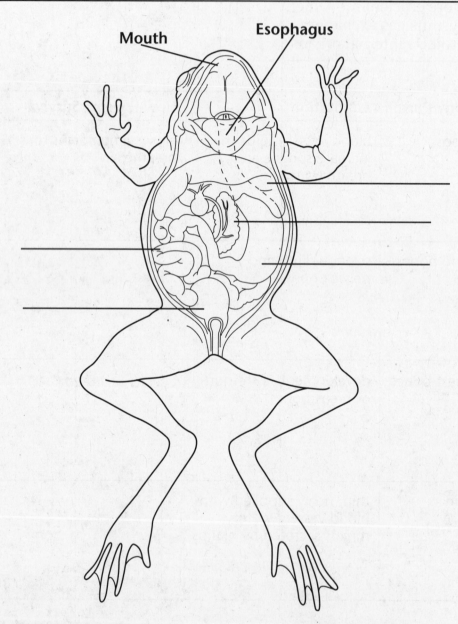

Mouth   **Esophagus**

Use the diagram to answer the question. Circle the correct answer.

1. Which is the first organ food passes through after it leaves the esophagus?

pancreas   stomach

© Pearson Education, Inc., publishing as Pearson Prentice Hall.

Fish and Amphibian Circulation

Complete the table to compare fish and adult amphibian circulatory systems. The first one has been done for you.

	Fish	Adult Amphibian
Structure of system	single loop	double loop
Organs that bring oxygen to blood	gills	
Number of atria in heart	one	
Do oxygen-poor and oxygen-rich blood mix in the heart?		yes

Answer the questions.

1. How many ventricles do the hearts of amphibians and fishes

   have? _____

2. Which describes the blood that passes through a fish's heart? Circle the correct answer.

   oxygen-rich   oxygen-poor

© **Pearson Education, Inc.**, publishing as Pearson Prentice Hall.

Frog Life Cycle

Like most other amphibians, frogs spend part of their life cycle living in water and part living on land. Frogs use gills for respiration when they live in the water, and lungs when they live on land.

Color the stages of the frog's life cycle that are lived on land brown. Color the stages that are lived in the water blue.

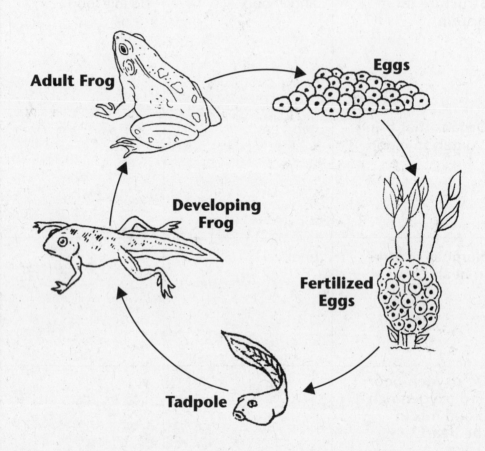

Use the diagram to answer the questions. Circle the correct answer.

1. Where do frog eggs hatch into tadpoles?

    in the water   on land

2. Which respiratory organs do adult frogs use?

    gills   lungs

© Pearson Education, Inc., publishing as Pearson Prentice Hall.

Chapter 30 Nonvertebrate Chordates, Fishes, and Amphibians

Vocabulary Review

Matching *In the space provided, write the letter of the definition that best matches each term.*

_____ **1.** cartilage

_____ **2.** cerebellum

_____ **3.** notochord

_____ **4.** ovoviviparous

_____ **5.** vertebra

a. a segment of the backbone

b. part of the brain that coordinates body movements

c. fishes whose eggs develop inside the mother's body and whose young are born alive

d. long, supporting rod that runs through the body just below the neve cord

e. strong tissue that supports the body and is more flexible than bone

Completion *Use the words below to fill in the blanks with terms from the chapter.*

atrium	chordates	tympanic membrane
cerebrum	cloaca	viviparous

6. Fishes, amphibians, reptiles, birds, and mammals are all

_____.

7. A large muscular chamber of the heart called a(an)

_____ serves as a one-way compartment.

8. Voluntary activities of the body are controlled by the

_____, a portion of the brain.

9. In _____ animals, the embryos stay in the mother's body after fertilization and obtain the nutrients they need from the mother's body.

10. The large muscular cavity at the end of an amphibian's large

intestine is the _____.

11. Another name for eardrum is_____.

© Pearson Education, Inc., publishing as Pearson Prentice Hall.

Chapter 31 Reptiles and Birds

Summary

31–1 Reptiles

At the end of the Carboniferous Period, the climate became drier. Amphibians began dying out. This led to new habitats for reptiles. The Mesozoic Era is called the Age of Reptiles because of the diversity and large numbers of reptiles that lived during that period. Dinosaurs were everywhere. The Age of Reptiles ended with a mass extinction at the end of the Cretaceous Period.

Reptiles are vertebrates adapted for life on land. They have several adaptations that make them better able to survive on land than amphibians. Reptiles have dry skin covered by protective scales. The scales help hold water in their bodies. **They have well-developed lungs. Reptiles also have eggs with a shell and several membranes.**

Most reptiles have adapted to a fully terrestrial life.

- Body Temperature Control. Reptiles are **ectotherms.** Their body temperature is controlled by behavior. To warm up, they bask in the sun. To cool down, they move into shade, burrow underground, or go for a swim.
- Feeding. Reptiles eat many foods and have many different ways of eating. Some reptiles are herbivores, others are carnivores.
- Respiration. The lungs of reptiles are better developed than those of amphibians. Reptile lungs have more gas-exchange area than those of amphibians. Muscles around a reptile's ribs allow the animal to expand its chest to inhale and collapse its chest to exhale. Although most reptiles have two lungs, some snakes have only one lung.
- Circulation. Reptiles have a double-loop circulatory system. One loop carries blood to and from the lungs. The other carries blood to and from the rest of the body. Most reptiles have a three-chambered heart. Crocodiles have two atria and two ventricles.
- Excretion. Reptiles get rid of liquid wastes as urine. In some reptiles, urine flows directly into a cloaca. In other reptiles, a urinary bladder stores urine. Reptiles that live mainly in water excrete ammonia. Those living on land convert ammonia to uric acid. Uric acid is less toxic than ammonia and less water is required to dilute it. By eliminating wastes that contain little water, a reptile can conserve water.
- Response. The cerebrum and cerebellum are larger in reptile brains than in amphibian brains. Reptiles have well-developed sense organs.

© Pearson Education, Inc., publishing as Pearson Prentice Hall.

- <u>Movement</u>. Reptiles have larger and stronger limbs than amphibians. In most reptiles, the legs are rotated under the body. This allows the legs to carry more body weight.
- <u>Reproduction</u>. Reptiles have internal fertilization. Most are oviparous, laying eggs that develop outside the mother's body. The embryos are covered with membranes and a protective shell. This type of egg, called an **amniotic egg** keeps the embryo from drying out. The amniotic egg is one of the most important adaptations to life on land. Some snakes and lizards are ovoviviparous—their young are born alive.

Four groups of reptiles survive today:
- **Lizards and snakes** Most lizards have legs, clawed toes, external ears, and movable eyelids. Snakes are legless.
- **Crocodilians** have long, broad snouts and a squat appearance. They are fierce carnivores that live only in tropical climates. Crocodilians include alligators, crocodiles, caimans, and gavials.
- **Turtles and tortoises** have backbones fused to a protective shell. Turtles usually live in water. Tortoises usually live on land. Instead of teeth, these reptiles have horny ridges on their jaws.
- The **tuatara** lives only on a few islands near New Zealand. They look somewhat like lizards, but lack external ears and have primitive scales. They also have a "third eye," which is part of a sense organ on the top of the brain.

31–2 Birds

Birds are reptilelike animals that maintain a constant internal body temperature. Birds have two legs covered with scales. Their front legs are modified into wings. Birds are covered with feathers. Feathers help most birds fly and stay warm.

Paleontologists agree that birds evolved from reptiles that are now extinct. Some think that birds evolved directly from dinosaurs. Others think that birds and dinosaurs evolved from an earlier common ancestor.

Birds have a number of adaptations that enable them to fly. These include highly efficient digestive, respiratory, and circulatory systems; aerodynamic feathers and wings; strong, lightweight bones; and strong chest muscles.
- <u>Body Temperature Control</u>. Birds have a high metabolic rate that produces heat. Animals that generate their own heat are called **endotherms.** A bird's feathers help conserve this heat. To maintain a high metabolic rate, birds need to eat large amounts of food. The beaks of birds are adapted to the type of food they eat.

© Pearson Education, Inc., publishing as Pearson Prentice Hall.

- Feeding. Some birds have digestive organs called a crop and a gizzard. The **crop,** located at the end of the esophagus, stores and moistens food. The **gizzard** is part of the stomach. It grinds and crushes food.
- Respiration. Birds have a very efficient respiratory system. Birds can remove oxygen from air both when they inhale and when they exhale. They can do this because their lungs are connected at the front and back to large air sacs. Air flows into the air sacs and out through the lungs in one direction. The lungs are always exposed to oxygen-rich air.
- Circulation. Birds have a four-chambered heart and two circulatory loops. A bird's heart has two separate ventricles. Oxygen-rich blood and oxygen-poor blood are completely separated.
- Excretion. Birds have an excretory system similar to that of reptiles. Nitrogen wastes are changed to uric acid and sent to the cloaca. The cloaca reabsorbs water from the wastes, which are then expelled.
- Response. Birds have a well-developed brain and sense organs. The cerebrum and cerebellum are large in relation to body size. These adaptations help birds respond quickly to stimuli and coordinate the movements for flight. Birds have well-developed sight and hearing, but do not smell or taste well.
- Movement. The bodies, wings, legs, and feet of birds are adapted to different habitats and lifestyles. Some of these adaptations, such as air spaces in bones, help birds fly. However, not all birds fly.
- Reproduction. Birds have internal fertilization. They lay amniotic eggs with hard shells. Most birds keep their eggs warm until they hatch. One or both parents may then care for the offspring.

© Pearson Education, Inc., publishing as Pearson Prentice Hall.

Reptilian Heart

The reptilian heart is made up of three chambers: two atria and one partially divided ventricle.

Color the blood vessels and chambers of the heart according to the prompts below.
- Color the areas that hold oxygen-rich blood red.
- Color the areas that hold oxygen-poor blood blue.

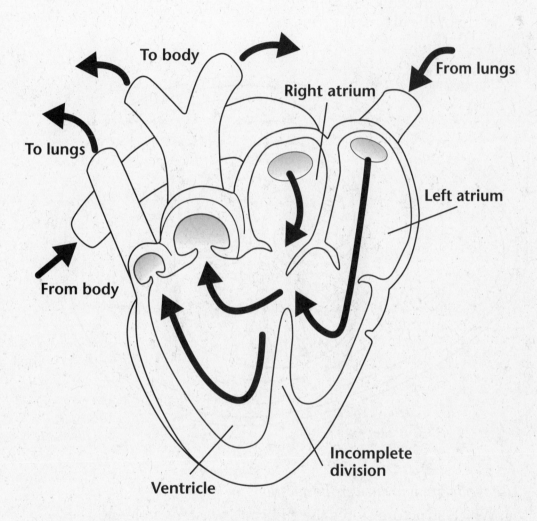

Use the diagram to answer the questions.

1. In which chamber do oxygen-rich blood and oxygen-poor blood mix?

_____

2. From where does the heart get oxygen-rich blood?

_____

© Pearson Education, Inc., publishing as Pearson Prentice Hall.

Amniotic Egg

The amniotic egg is an important adaptation for reptiles. It prevents the embryo from drying out. It allows reptiles to lay their eggs on land.

Color the diagram of an amniotic egg according to the prompts.
- Color the amnion orange.
- Color the chorion red.
- Color the yolk sac yellow.
- Color the allantois green.

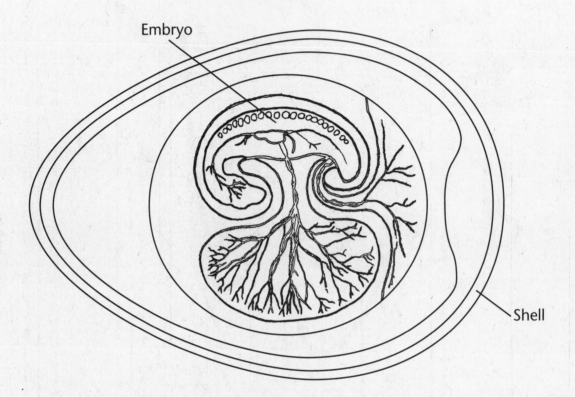

Embryo

Shell

Use the diagram to answer the questions.

1. Which structure stores the embryo's waste? Circle the correct answer.

   allantois   chorion

2. What is the function of the amnion?

   _____

   _____

Name_____ Class_____ Date_____

Types of Reptiles

Some characteristics of tuataras, crocodilians, snakes, lizards, *and* turtles and tortoises *are described below. Use what you know about reptiles to complete the table. One row has been done for you.*

Reptile	Typical Features	Where Found
lizards	legs, clawed toes; external ears; movable eyelids	many habitats
	legless; predators, some venomous	many habitats
	long and typically broad snout; carnivores	tropics and subtropics only; both freshwater and salt-water habitats
	shell built into skeleton; horny ridges instead of teeth; strong limbs	many habitats
	no external ears; primitive scales; "third eye" that senses sunlight	islands off New Zealand only

Use the table to answer the questions.

1. Which reptiles are legless?

_____

2. Which reptiles have a "third eye" that senses light?

_____

Feathers

Feathers make up the outer covering of birds. There are two main types of feathers: contour feathers and down feathers.

Circle the contour feather in red. Circle the down feather in blue.

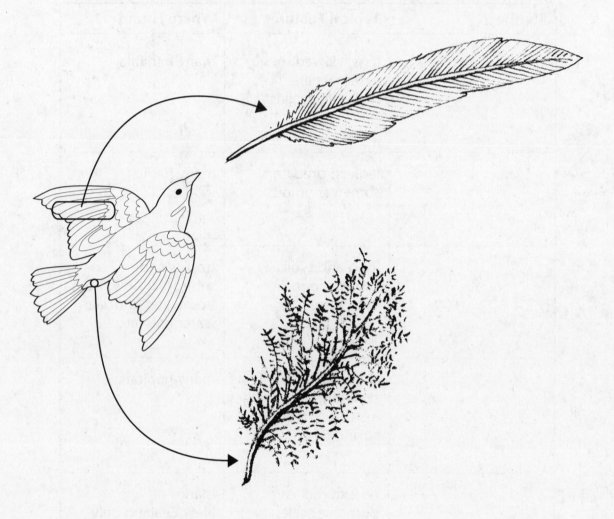

Answer the questions.

1. What is the function of contour feathers?

_____

2. What is the function of down feathers?

_____

© Pearson Education, Inc., publishing as Pearson Prentice Hall.

Bird Evolution

Modern scientists are not sure how birds evolved. The cladogram below shows two theories of bird evolution.

Color the path that shows birds evolving directly from dinosaurs blue. Color the path that shows birds and dinosaurs sharing an earlier common ancestor red.

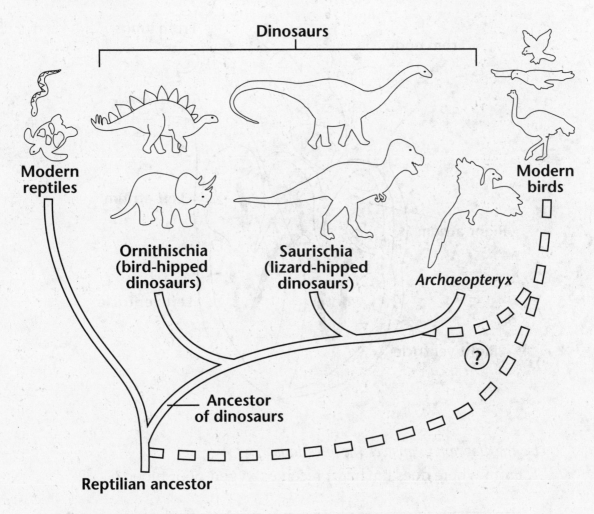

Answer the questions.

1. How does *Archaeopteryx* provide evidence to support the theory that birds evolved from dinosaurs?

_____

_____

_____

2. Which of the following characteristics do modern birds and living reptiles share? Circle the correct answer.

amniotic eggs   feathers

© Pearson Education, Inc., publishing as Pearson Prentice Hall.

Bird Heart

The bird heart is made up of four chambers: the right atrium, left atrium, right ventricle and left ventricle.

Color the blood vessels and areas of the heart that hold oxygen-rich blood red. Color the areas that hold oxygen-poor blood blue.

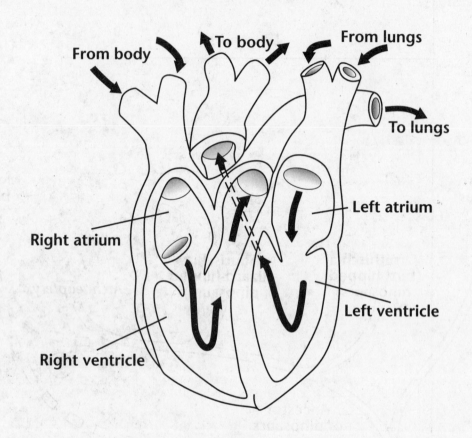

Use the diagram to answer the questions.

1. From where does the heart receive oxygen-poor blood?

_____

_____

2. How is a bird heart different from a reptile heart?

_____

_____

© Pearson Education, Inc., publishing as Pearson Prentice Hall.

Chapter 31   Reptiles and Birds

Vocabulary Review

Matching   *In the space provided, write the letter of the definition that best matches each term.*

_____ **1.** air sac

_____ **2.** amniotic egg

_____ **3.** carapace

_____ **4.** crop

_____ **5.** ectotherm

a. structure in birds that helps ensure that air flows one way through the lungs

b. structure in birds where food is stored and moistened

c. structure with a protective shell and membranes that allow an embryo to develop outside of water

d. animal that relies on interactions with the environment to control body temperature

e. dorsal part of a turtle shell

Matching   *In the space provided, write the letter of the definition that best matches each term.*

_____ **6.** endotherm

_____ **7.** feather

_____ **8.** gizzard

_____ **9.** plastron

a. muscular organ in birds that helps in the mechanical breakdown of food

b. ventral part of a turtle shell

c. structure in birds made mostly of protein that can aid in flight and temperature control

d. animal that generates its own body heat

© Pearson Education, Inc., publishing as Pearson Prentice Hall.

Summary

32–1 Introduction to Mammals

Mammals are animals with hair and mammary glands. In females, mammary glands produce milk to nourish the young. **All mammals breathe air, have four-chambered hearts, and are endotherms that generate their body heat internally.**

Mammals descended from ancient reptiles. **The first true mammals appeared during the late Triassic Period, about 220 million years ago.** These mammals were small and active only at night. When dinosaurs became extinct, mammals evolved to fill many niches.

Mammals have many adaptations that make them suitable to a wide range of habitats.

- Body Temperature Control. Mammals are endotherms. Their metabolism creates their body heat. Mammals have a layer of **subcutaneous fat** and fur or hair to prevent heat loss. Many mammals release heat through sweat glands. The ability of mammals to regulate their body heat from within is an example of homeostasis.
- Feeding. Mammals eat a great deal of food to maintain their high metabolic rate. Early mammals ate insects. **As mammals evolved, the form and function of their jaws and teeth became adapted to eat foods other than insects.** Mammals have specialized teeth, jaws, and digestive systems for eating plants, animals, or both.
- Respiration. All mammals breathe with lungs. Mammals share well-developed chest muscles, including a **diaphragm,** that separates the chest cavity from the abdomen. The diaphragm, along with other muscles in the chest, help pull air into the lungs and push air out.
- Circulation. Mammals have a double-loop circulatory system. They also have a four-chambered heart. Each side of the heart has an atrium and a ventricle. This arrangement separates oxygen-rich blood from oxygen-poor blood.
- Excretion. The kidneys of mammals are highly developed. This lets mammals live in many habitats. **The kidneys of mammals help maintain homeostasis by filtering urea from the blood, as well as by excreting excess water or retaining needed water.**

© Pearson Education, Inc., publishing as Pearson Prentice Hall.

- Response. Mammals have the most highly developed brain of any animal. Mammalian brains have a cerebrum, cerebellum, and medulla oblongata. The cerebrum has a well-developed outer layer called the **cerebral cortex.** It is the center of thinking and other complex behaviors. The cerebellum coordinates movements. The medulla oblongata regulates involuntary body functions such as breathing and heart rate.
- Movement. Mammals have adapted to living on land, in water, and in the air. Variations in limb bone structure allow mammals to run, walk, climb, burrow, hop, fly, and swim.
- Reproduction. Mammals have adaptations that help them reproduce successfully. All mammals reproduce by internal fertilization. Newborn mammals feed on milk from the mother. Most mammal parents care for their young after birth. The length of care varies among species.

32–2 Diversity of Mammals

Mammals are divided into three groups: monotremes, marsupials, and placentals. The three groups of mammals differ in their means of reproduction and development.

- **Monotremes lay eggs.** They also have a cloaca, similar to that of reptiles. When the soft-shelled eggs hatch, the young are nourished by their mother's milk. The duckbill platypus is an example of a monotreme.
- **Marsupials bear live young. The young are born at an early stage of development.** Soon after birth, the young crawl across the mother's fur and attach to a nipple inside the mother's pouch. The young continue nursing until they are able to live on their own. Marsupials include kangaroos and koalas.
- Most mammals are **placental mammals. In placental mammals, nutrients, oxygen, carbon dioxide, and wastes are exchanged efficiently between embryo and mother through the placenta.** After the birth of young, most placental mammals care for their offspring. Dogs, whales, and humans are examples of placental mammals.

There are twelve main orders of placental mammals. Two of these orders are adapted to life in the water. Sirenians are herbivores that live fully aquatic lives. Cetaceans are aquatic mammals that must come to the surface of the water to breathe. Chiropterans are the winged mammals, or bats. The land-based placental mammals include insectivores, rodents, perissodactyls, carnivores, artiodactyls, lagomorphs, xenarthrans, primates, and proboscideans.

© Pearson Education, Inc., publishing as Pearson Prentice Hall.

32–3 Primates and Human Origins

All primates share several key adaptations. They have binocular vision, a well-developed cerebrum, relatively long fingers and toes, and arms that rotate in broad circles around the shoulder joints.

Early in their evolutionary history, primates split into several groups. **Primates that evolved from two of the earliest branches look very little like typical monkeys and are called prosimians.** These animals are small, nocturnal primates. They have large eyes adapted for seeing in the dark.

Members of the more familiar primate group that includes monkeys, apes, and humans are called anthropoids. The anthropoids split into two major groups.

- New World monkeys. These monkeys now live in Central and South America. All New World monkeys have a **prehensile tail.** These tails can coil tightly enough around a branch to serve as a "fifth hand."

- Old World monkeys and the great apes. Old World monkeys do not have prehensile tails. Great apes are also called **hominoids.** This group includes gorillas, chimpanzees, and humans. The hominoid line gave rise to the branch that leads to modern humans. This group, called the **hominids,** evolved adaptations for upright walking. They have thumbs adapted for grasping as well as larger brains.

Recent fossil finds have changed the way paleontologists think about hominid evolution. **Researchers now believe that hominid evolution occurred in a series of adaptive radiations. This process led to several different species instead of one species that led directly to the next.**

Our genus, *Homo,* first appeared in Africa. Researchers do not agree when the first hominids began migrating from Africa. They are also unsure about when and where *Homo sapiens* arose. The multi-regional model suggests that modern humans evolved independently in several parts of the world. The out-of-Africa model proposes that modern humans arose in Africa and then migrated away.

About 100,000 years ago, two main groups of hominids existed: *Homo neanderthalensis* and *Homo sapiens.* Fossil evidence suggests that these hominids used stone tools and lived in similar ways.

About 50,000–40,000 years ago, *Homo sapiens* changed their way of life. These hominids made more sophisticated tools. They drew cave paintings. They also began burying their dead with elaborate rituals. In these ways, they began acting more like modern humans. The Neanderthals disappeared about 30,000 years ago. Since then, *Homo sapiens* has been the only hominid on Earth.

© Pearson Education, Inc., publishing as Pearson Prentice Hall.

Mammalian Teeth

Mammals have three kinds of teeth. Canines are pointed teeth that pierce, grip, and tear. Incisors are chisel-like teeth that cut and gnaw. Molars and premolars crush and grind food.

Color the incisors blue. Color the molars and premolars yellow. The canines have been shaded for you.

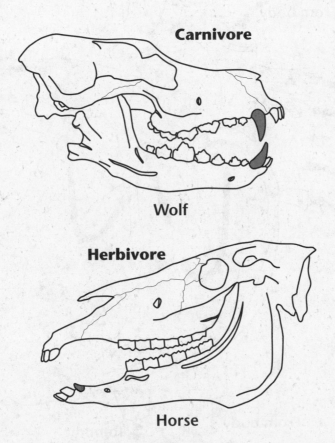

Carnivore

Wolf

Herbivore

Horse

Use the diagrams to answer the questions.

1. Which animal has larger canines? Circle the correct answer.

   wolf   horse

2. Think about your answer to question 1. Why does the animal you chose need larger canines?

   _____

   _____

3. For what purpose does a horse use its premolars and molars?

   _____

© Pearson Education, Inc., publishing as Pearson Prentice Hall.

Mammalian Heart

Color the parts of the heart that hold oxygen-rich blood red. Color the parts of the heart that hold oxygen-poor blood blue.

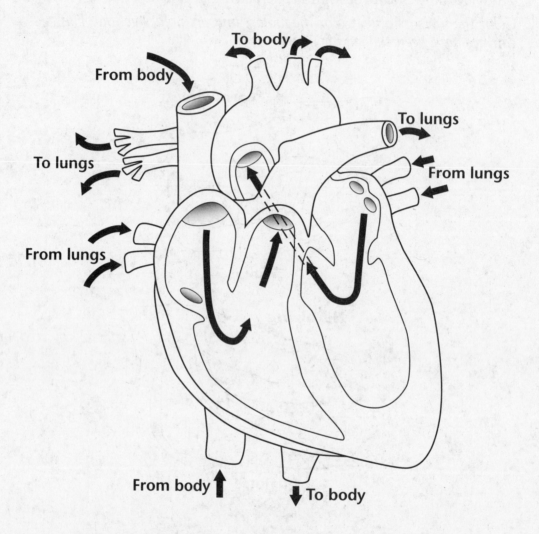

Use the diagram to answer the questions.

1. Oxygen-poor blood flows from the heart to the

_____.

2. Oxygen-rich blood flows from the lungs to the

_____.

3. Oxygen-rich blood flows from the heart to the

_____.

© Pearson Education, Inc., publishing as Pearson Prentice Hall.

Mammal Limbs, Fingers, and Toes

Homologous structures are those that develop from the same
embryonic tissue in different organisms. The structures may look
different when the organisms are mature. Look at the picture of
monkey and horse bones. The bones labeled with the same color
are homologous.

*Color the monkey and horse bones as marked. Then color the homologous
bones in the other three animals the same colors. (Hint: You may want to
look at pages 826–827 in your textbook for help.)*

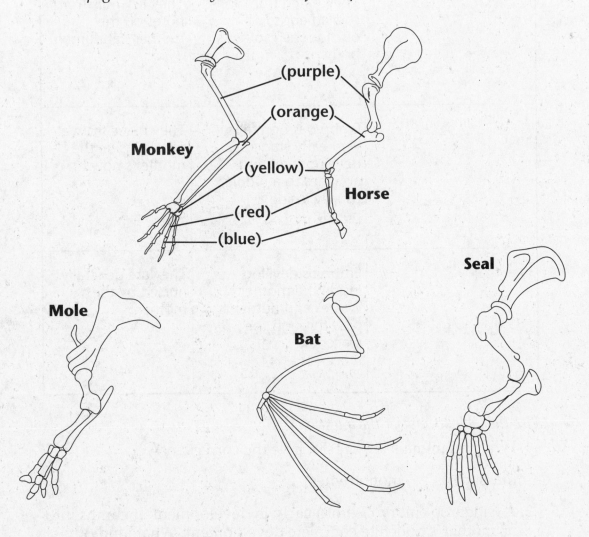

Use the diagrams to answer the question.

1. Which animal has adapted to fly?

_____

© Pearson Education, Inc., publishing as Pearson Prentice Hall.

Diversity of Mammals

There are three groups of living mammals: monotremes, marsupials, and placental mammals.

Write the name of each group in the correct place in the table.

Group	How Are Young Born?	How Are Young Fed?
	They hatch from soft-shelled eggs laid outside the mother's body.	They lick milk from pores on the mother's abdomen.
	Embryo is born at a very early stage of development and attaches to a nipple, usually inside a pouch.	They nurse from a nipple inside the mother's pouch.
	Embryos develop inside the mother. Wastes and nutrients pass through the placenta.	They are generally nursed by the mother.

Use the table to answer the questions.

1. Which mammals lay eggs? Circle the correct answer.

   marsupials   monotremes

2. A kangaroo embryo is born early in development. It climbs into its mother's pouch to complete development. What kind of mammal is a kangaroo?

   _____

3. Humans, sea lions, cats, dogs, and mice are all examples of what type of mammal? Circle the correct answer.

   placental   monotremes

© Pearson Education, Inc., publishing as Pearson Prentice Hall.

Primate Evolution

The cladogram shows how scientists believe modern primates are related to one another and to their common primate ancestor. The earliest two branches are called prosimians. The other primates are anthropoids. Anthropoids include New World monkeys, Old World monkeys, and the great apes, or hominoids.

Color the branches for prosimians red. Color the branches for anthropoids blue. Then, circle the hominoids.

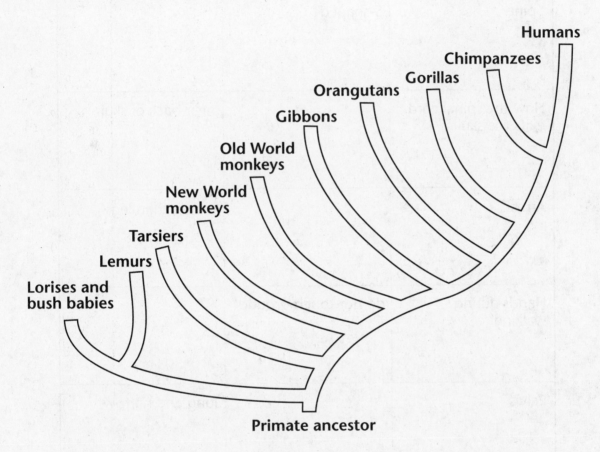

Use the cladogram to answer the questions. Circle the correct answer.

1. Which primate is a prosimian?

    gibbon   lemur

2. Which primate is a hominoid?

    Old World monkey   orangutan

© Pearson Education, Inc., publishing as Pearson Prentice Hall.

Human and Gorilla Skeletons

The skeleton of a modern human is adapted to walk upright on two legs. Gorillas use all four limbs.

Complete the table. Describe each feature in humans and gorillas. Some items have been completed for you

Feature	Human	Gorilla
Spine	S-shaped	
How the spinal cord exits the skull		near back of skull
Arms		longer than legs
Hands during walking	do not touch ground	
Pelvis		long and narrow
Angle of thigh bones	inward	

Use the table to answer the question.

1. Describe the spine of a gorilla.

_____

© Pearson Education, Inc., publishing as Pearson Prentice Hall.

Early Hominids

The timeline shows some fossil hominids that scientists have discovered. The bar shows the time ranges during which each species may have existed. Each species has a genus name and a species name.

Color the bars for all the species in the genus Homo *red. Color the bars for all the species in the genus* Australopithecus *blue. Color the bars for all the species in the genus* Paranthropus *yellow.*

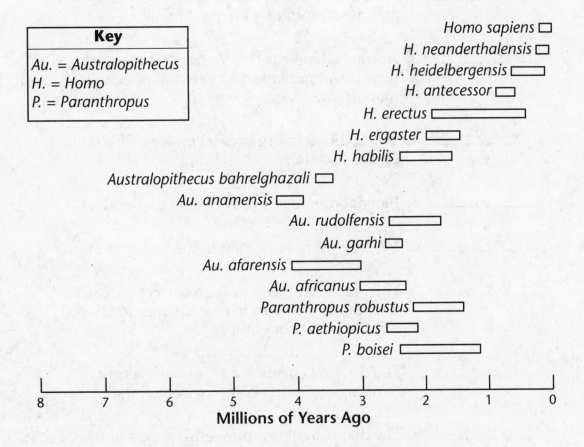

Key
Au. = Australopithecus
H. = Homo
P. = Paranthropus

Use the timeline to answer the questions. Circle the correct answer.

1. Which hominid probably existed earlier?

    Australopithecus africanus   *Homo neanderthalensis*

2. Is hominid evolution a simple straight-line transformation from one species to another? Explain.

_____

_____

© Pearson Education, Inc., publishing as Pearson Prentice Hall.

Chapter 32   Mammals

Vocabulary Review

True or False   *If the statement is true, write* true. *If it is false, write* false.

_____ 1. An opposable thumb enables hominids to grasp objects.

_____ 2. Humanlike primates, including humans, apes, and most monkeys, are prosimians.

_____ 3. Animals that bear live young that complete their development in an external pouch are monotremes.

_____ 4. The ability to merge visual images with both eyes is bipedal.

_____ 5. Bipedal organisms move about on two feet.

_____ 6. Modern humans belong to the hominid family.

_____ 7. The placenta allows nutrients, oxygen, carbon dioxide, and wastes to be exchanged between a mother and her embryo.

_____ 8. The cerebral cortex is a mammal's center of thinking and other complex behaviors.

_____ 9. The diaphragm is a powerful muscle at the base of the chest cavity that is used for breathing.

_____ 10. The great apes are also called prosimians.

Chapter 33   Comparing Chordates

Summary

33–1 Chordate Evolution

Embryo studies of living chordates help scientists learn about chordate evolution. In addition, evidence of early chordates was found in the fossilized remains of an organism called *Pikaia*. *Pikaia* had a notochord and paired muscles.

Chordates include vertebrates and nonvertebrates. **In the chordate family tree, vertebrates, tunicates, and lancelets share a common ancestor.** Modern amphibians, reptiles, birds, and mammals share more recent common ancestors.

Scientists infer how vertebrates evolved by studying fossils and the features of living chordates. **Over the course of evolution, the appearance of new adaptations—such as jaws and paired appendages—has launched adaptive radiations in chordate groups. Adaptive radiation** brings about new species with unlike adaptations. These species look different, but are related. The finches that Darwin studied are good examples of adaptive radiation. More than a dozen different finch species evolved from one species. Convergent evolution has also occurred many times during chordate evolution. **Convergent evolution** occurs when unrelated species adapt to similar environments. Convergent evolution results in unrelated species that look and behave alike. For example, convergent evolution has led to the development of birds and bats. Both can fly, but they are very different types of organisms.

33–2 Controlling Body Temperature

The control of body temperature is important for maintaining homeostasis in vertebrates. To control temperature, vertebrates need a source of body heat, a way to conserve heat, and a way to get rid of excess heat. In terms of how they generate heat, vertebrates can be classified into two groups: ectotherms and endotherms.

- Most reptiles, fishes, and amphibians are ectotherms. **Ectotherms are animals whose body temperatures are controlled primarily by taking heat from, or losing heat to, the environment.** Ectotherms have low metabolic rates. They also lack good insulation and easily lose heat to the environment.

- **Endotherms** make their own body heat. **Birds and mammals are endotherms, which means that they can generate and retain heat inside their bodies.** They have high metabolic rates. They have fat and outer coverings—such as feathers or hair—to keep heat within their bodies. They get rid of excess heat by sweating or panting.

© Pearson Education, Inc., publishing as Pearson Prentice Hall.

33–3 Form and Function in Chordates

Organ systems of different vertebrates are specialized to perform specific functions. These systems become more complex from fishes to mammals.

Digestion. Vertebrates have adaptations for eating a variety of foods. For example, the hummingbird's long bill and the honey possum's narrow snout are adaptations for feeding on nectar. Carnivores have sharp teeth that help them tear chunks of meat from their prey. **The digestive systems of vertebrates have organs that are well adapted for different feeding habits.** Herbivores have long digestive tracts. In addition, herbivores often have stomachs that house bacteria to help break down plant fibers.

Respiration. **Chordates have two basic respiratory plans: some use gills; others have lungs.**
- Water animals (tunicates, fishes, and amphibian larvae) use gills for respiration.
- Land animals (adult amphibians, reptiles, birds, and mammals) use lungs.

The efficiency of the lungs increases as you move from amphibians to reptiles to mammals. Birds have the most efficient respiratory system of all the vertebrates. Their air sacs and tubes ensure that oxygen-rich air is always in the lungs.

Circulation. **As chordates evolved, the heart developed chambers and partitions that helped to separate oxygen-rich blood from oxygen-poor blood.**
- Fish have two chambers: an atrium to receive blood from the body and a ventricle to pump blood.
- Amphibians have three chambers: two atria and one ventricle. Oxygen-rich and oxygen-poor blood mix in the ventricle.
- Most reptiles also have a three-chambered heart. However, the ventricle has a partial partition. This partition reduces the amount that oxygen-rich and oxygen-poor blood mix.
- Birds, mammals, and crocodiles have a four-chambered heart. Oxygen-rich blood is completely separated from oxygen-poor blood.

Vertebrates with gills have a single-loop circulatory system. Blood travels from the heart to the gills, to the rest of the body, and back to the heart. Vertebrates with lungs have a double-loop circulatory system. The first loop moves blood between the heart and the lungs. The second loop moves blood between the heart and the body.

© Pearson Education, Inc., publishing as Pearson Prentice Hall.

<u>Excretion</u>. The excretory system removes nitrogenous wastes from the body. It also controls the amount of water in the body.

- In nonvertebrate chordates and fishes, wastes in the form of ammonia diffuse out of the body through gills and gill slits.
- In most other vertebrates, kidneys filter wastes from the blood. Land vertebrates excrete wastes as urea or uric acid. This type of excretion helps these animals conserve water.

<u>Response</u>. **Nonvertebrate chordates have fairly simple nervous systems.** They do not have specialized sense organs. **Vertebrates have more complex brains.** Each region of the brain is distinct and has its own function. The sense organs and nerve cells in vertebrates are mostly at the front of the body. From fishes to mammals, the size and complexity of the cerebrum and cerebellum increase.

<u>Movement</u>. Vertebrates are more mobile than nonvertebrate chordates. All vertebrates, except jawless fishes, have an internal skeleton of bone, or in some fishes, cartilage. The bones are held together with tough, flexible tissues. These tissues allow movement and keep the bones in place. **The skeletal and muscular systems support a vertebrate's body and make it possible to control movement.** Amphibians have limbs that stick out sideways. Reptiles, birds, and mammals have limbs directly under the body. This placement supports more body weight.

<u>Reproduction</u>. Most chordates reproduce sexually. Fishes and amphibians have external fertilization. The eggs of reptiles, birds, and mammals are fertilized internally. Chordates may be oviparous, ovoviviparous, or viviparous.

- In oviparous species, eggs develop outside the mother's body. Most fishes, amphibians, reptiles, and all birds are oviparous.
- In ovoviviparous species like sharks, eggs develop inside the mother's body. The embryo gets nutrients from the egg yolk. The young are born alive.
- In viviparous species, which include most mammals, embryos get nutrients directly from the mother.

© Pearson Education, Inc., publishing as Pearson Prentice Hall.

Chordate Adaptations

The cladogram shows the relationships between modern chordates. Some important adaptations that have occurred during chordate evolution are indicated.

Follow the prompts to analyze the cladogram.
- Color the bar for chordates without vertebrae red.
- Color the bars for chordates that have jaws but no lungs blue.
- Color the bars for chordates that have lungs yellow.

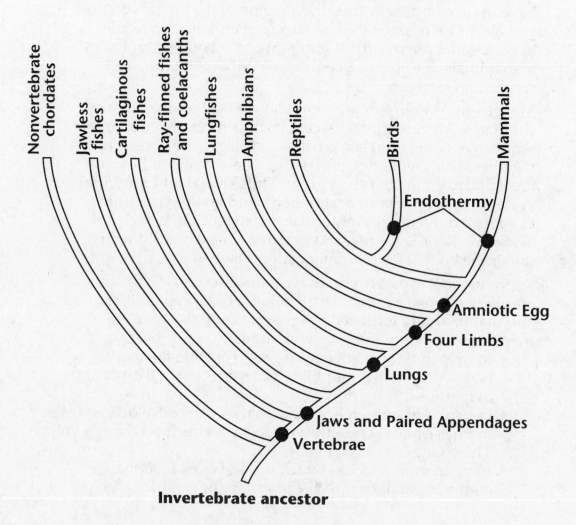

Invertebrate ancestor

Use the cladogram to answer the questions.

1. Which chordates are endotherms?

_____

2. Which chordates are most closely related to reptiles?

_____

© Pearson Education, Inc., publishing as Pearson Prentice Hall.

Ectotherms and Endotherms

Ectotherms are animals whose body temperature is mostly determined by the temperature of the environment. Endotherms are animals that can regulate their own body temperatures. Most reptiles, fishes, and amphibians are ectotherms. Birds and mammals are endotherms.

Use what you know about ectotherms and endotherms to complete the table. Write how the animal's body temperature will change in response to the environmental change. Write increase, decrease, *or* stay the same. *One row has been completed for you.*

Animal	Environmental Temperature Change	Body Temperature Change
turtle	increase	increase
salamander	decrease	
eagle	decrease	
alligator	increase	
rabbit	increase	
goldfish	decrease	

Use the table to answer the questions.

1. What happens to an endotherm's body temperature when the environmental temperature increases?

_____

2. What happens to an ectotherm's body temperature when the environmental temperature decreases?

_____

© Pearson Education, Inc., publishing as Pearson Prentice Hall.

Vertebrate Digestive Systems

Vertebrates have digestive systems adapted for the foods they eat. Most vertebrates, however, have some similar digestive organs.

Look at the diagram of the salamander. Find the esophagus, liver, stomach, *and* intestine. *Then color the other diagrams according to the prompts below.*

- Color the esophagus yellow.
- Color the liver orange.
- Color the intestine red.

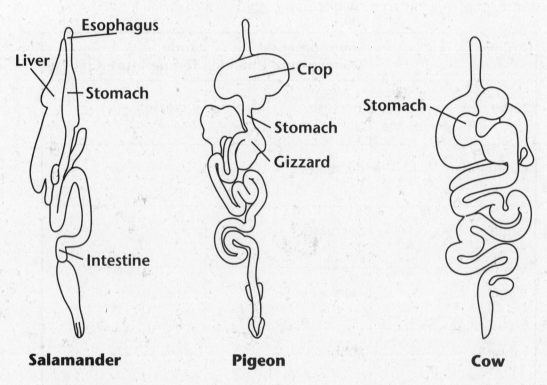

Salamander   **Pigeon**   **Cow**

Answer the questions.

1. Cows are herbivores. What might the bacteria in the intestines of cows do? Circle the correct answer.

   break down plant tissue   produce meat-digesting enzymes

2. How might the cow's intestines be different if a cow were a carnivore?

   _____

   _____

3. Why does the pigeon need a crop and gizzard?

   _____

   _____

© Pearson Education, Inc., publishing as Pearson Prentice Hall.

Respiratory Systems of Land Vertebrates

Land vertebrates use lungs to breathe. In most land vertebrates, air moves in and out through the same passageways, including the nostrils, mouth, throat, and trachea.

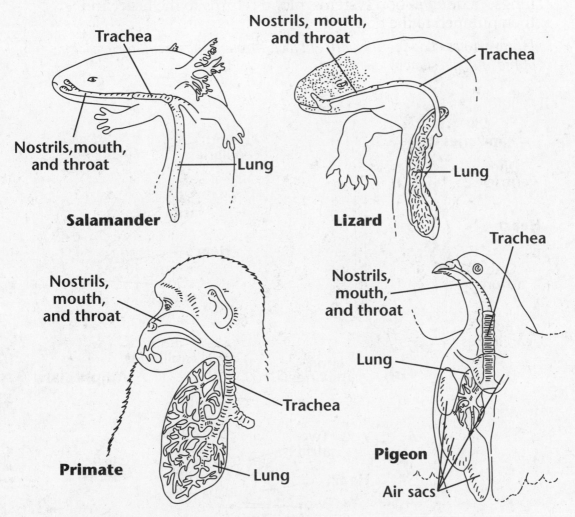

Use the diagrams to answer the questions.

1. How are salamander and lizard lungs different?

_____

_____

2. In mammalian lungs, gas exchange takes place in which structures? Circle the correct answer.

lungs   gills

3. What is the function of air sacs in the pigeon?

_____

_____

© Pearson Education, Inc., publishing as Pearson Prentice Hall.

Vertebrate Circulatory Systems

Vertebrates that use gills have single-loop circulatory systems.
Vertebrates that use lungs have double-loop circulatory systems.
In a single-loop system, the heart pumps blood to the gills or
lungs. In double-loop systems, blood returns to the heart and is
then pumped to the body.

*Draw arrows showing the path of blood through the circulatory systems
of the animals shown.*

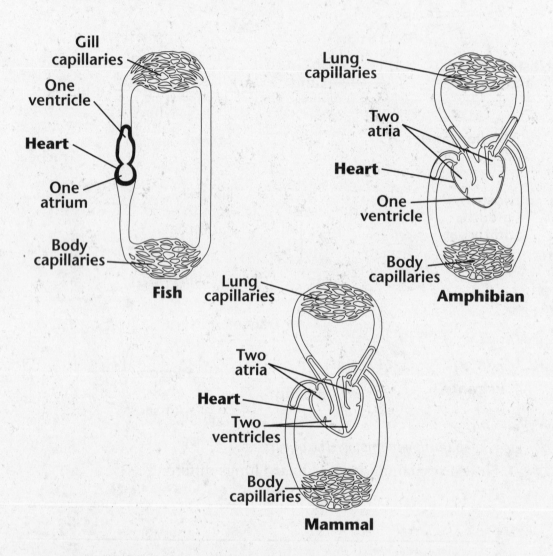

Use the diagrams to answer the question.

1. Which vertebrate shown has the simplest circulatory system?

_____

© Pearson Education, Inc., publishing as Pearson Prentice Hall.

Vertebrate Brains

Vertebrates have complex brains made up of several parts. Each part has a different function. For example, the medulla oblongata controls the functioning of many internal organs.

Look at the diagrams of the bony fish and amphibian brains. Then color the remaining diagrams according to the prompts below.

- Color the olfactory bulb purple.
- Color the optic lobe blue.
- Color the medulla oblongata yellow.
- Color the cerebellum red.
- Color the cerebrum orange.

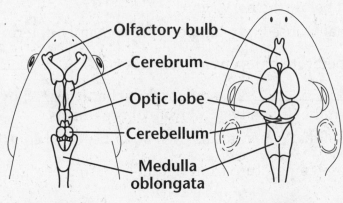

Bony Fish   **Amphibian**

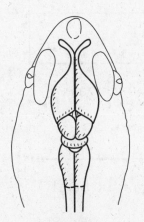   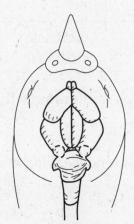   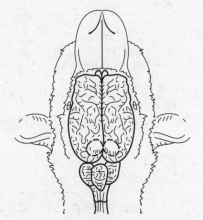

Reptile   **Bird**   **Mammal**

Use the diagrams to answer the question.

1. Which vertebrate has the most complex cerebrum?

_____

© Pearson Education, Inc., publishing as Pearson Prentice Hall.

Chapter 33   Comparing Chordates

Vocabulary Review

Completion   *Use the words below to fill in the blanks with terms from the chapter.*

adaptive radiation	endotherm
ectotherm	notochord

1. All chordates, at some stage of life, have a long, flexible, supporting structure called a(an) _____ that runs just below the nerve cord.

2. An animal whose body temperature is mainly determined by the temperature of its environment is a(an) _____.

3. _____ is the process characterized by rapid growth in the diversity of a group of organisms.

4. An animal that generates its own body heat and controls its own body temperature from within is a(an) _____.

Completion   *Use the words below to fill in the blanks with terms from the chapter.*

alveolus	ventricle
cerebrum	vertebra

5. The structure in the lungs of mammals through which gas exchange takes place is a(an) _____.

6. One segment of the backbone is called a(an) _____.

7. The _____ is the lower chamber of the heart that pumps blood.

8. In most vertebrates, the _____ is responsible for voluntary activities of the body.

© Pearson Education, Inc., publishing as Pearson Prentice Hall.

Chapter 34   Animal Behavior

Summary

34–1 Elements of Behavior

Behavior is the way that an organism reacts to change. The change may be within the body or in the environment. Most behavior takes place when an animal reacts to a **stimulus.** A **response** is a reaction to a stimulus. Animals detect stimuli with their sense organs. **When an animal responds to a stimulus, different body systems interact to produce the resultant behavior.**

Innate behaviors are fully functional the first time they are performed, even though the animal may have had no previous experience with the stimuli to which it responds. Examples of innate behaviors are the suckling of a newborn mammal and the weaving of a spider web.

Learning is the way that animals change their behavior as a result of experience. **Animals learn in four major ways:**

- **Habituation** is the simplest form of learning. In habituation, an animal's response to a stimulus slows or stops when the animal is neither rewarded nor harmed for responding. For example, ragworms will retreat into their burrows if a shadow passes overhead. However, when repeated shadows pass overhead, they will stop retreating to their burrows.
- **Classical conditioning** occurs when a mental connection between a stimulus and an event is made. Ivan Pavlov rang a bell each time he fed his dog. Eventually, he found that the dog would start salivating whenever the bell rang, whether or not food was presented.
- In **operant conditioning,** an animal learns to act in a certain way to get a reward or to avoid punishment. Operant conditioning is known as trial-and-error learning. It begins when a random behavior is rewarded.
- **Insight learning** is the most complex form of learning. In insight learning, an animal applies something already learned to a new situation. Insight learning occurs mostly in humans.

Most behaviors are the result of both innate behavior and learning. An example is **imprinting.** Newborn ducks and geese have an innate urge to follow the first moving object they see. Usually, this object is their parent. They are not born knowing what that object will look like. The newborn must learn from experience which object to follow.

© Pearson Education, Inc., publishing as Pearson Prentice Hall.

34-2 Patterns of Behavior

Animal behaviors may occur in patterns. **Many animals respond to periodic changes in the environment with daily or seasonal cycles of behavior.** Dormancy, migration, and circadian rhythms are examples. **Circadian rhythms** occur in a daily pattern, such as sleeping at night and going to school during the day.

Behaviors can help animals reproduce. **Courtship behavior is part of an overall reproductive strategy that helps many animals identify healthy mates.** Some courtship behaviors include elaborate rituals. Most rituals have specific signals and responses.

Animals exhibit social behavior when they interact with members of their own species. Many animals form societies. A society is a group of related animals of the same species that interact closely and often cooperate with one another. Being a part of an animal society helps improve an individual's evolutionary fitness. Termites form societies. So do zebras, wild dogs, and primates. Animal societies use "strength in numbers" to better hunt, protect territory, guard young, and fight rivals.

Some animal behaviors keep other animals from using limited resources. These resources may be food, water, or shelter. Such behaviors help protect territories. A **territory** is the area lived in and protected by an animal or group of animals.

Territories have resources that an animal needs to survive and reproduce. Competition occurs when two or more animals claim the same territory. During competition, one animal may use aggression to gain control over another. **Aggression** is threatening behavior.

Communication is the passing of information from one animal to another. **Animals communicate in many ways.**

- Animals with good eyesight may communicate with visual signals. These signals may include movement and color.
- Animals with a well-developed sense of smell communicate with chemicals called **pheromones.** The chemicals affect the behavior of other members of the species. For example, some animals use pheromones to mark territory.
- Animals with strong vocal abilities communicate with sound. Birds, toads, crickets, and dolphins use sound to communicate.
- **Language** is the most complex form of communication. Language combines sounds, symbols, and gestures according to sets of rules about word order and meaning. Only humans are known to use language.

© Pearson Education, Inc., publishing as Pearson Prentice Hall.

Stimulus and Response

A stimulus is any signal that carries information and can be detected. A response is a specific reaction to a stimulus.

Use the information in the diagrams to answer the questions.

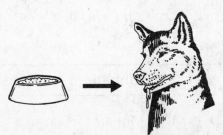

Stimulus: _____ Presence of food _____

Response: _____

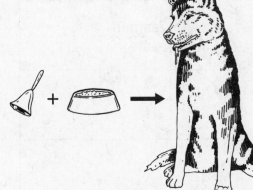

Stimulus: _____

Response: _____

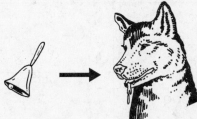

Stimulus: _____

Response: _____

1. Describe the experiment shown in the diagrams.

_____

_____

_____

_____

2. What type of learning is shown in this experiment?

_____

© Pearson Education, Inc., publishing as Pearson Prentice Hall.

Name_____ Class_____ Date _____

Innate and Learned Behaviors

An innate behavior is one that is fully functional the first time an animal uses it, even though the animal has no experience with the stimulus that causes it. These behaviors are inborn. Other behaviors are acquired through experience. These are called learned behaviors.

Identify each behavior as innate *or* learned. *Two examples have been completed for you.*

Behavior	Innate or Learned
spider spinning a web	innate
child riding a bicycle	learned
baby crying	
newborn mammal suckling	
birds conditioned to push a lever	
baby birds recognizing their species' song	
baboons washing sweet potatoes	

Answer the question.

1. What is another example of a learned behavior?

_____

_____

Types of Learned Behaviors

Animals learn behaviors in four primary ways. Most of these ways of learning involve making a connection between a behavior and a reward or punishment.

Use the words below to complete the table.

classical conditioning	insight learning
habituation	operant conditioning

Type of Learning	How It Works	Example
	An animal makes a mental connection between a stimulus and a reward or punishment.	Pavlov's dog learned that the sound of a bell was associated with food, so it salivated at the sound.
	An animal stops responding to a stimulus that brings neither reward nor punishment.	A shore ragworm stops responding if shadows pass over it repeatedly.
	An animal learns through trial and error to behave in a certain way to get a reward or to avoid punishment.	A pigeon learns that if it presses a button, it will receive food.
	An animal applies something it has already learned to a new situation, without a trial-and-error period.	A chimpanzee stacks boxes to reach high-hanging bananas.

Use the table to answer the question. Circle the best answer.

1. Which is the most complicated type of learning?

habituation   insight learning

© Pearson Education, Inc., publishing as Pearson Prentice Hall.

Behavioral Cycles

Many animal behaviors are related to changes in the environment. Environmental cycles, such as the sequence of day and night or the passing of seasons, can lead to cycles in animal behavior.

Use the words below to identify each behavioral cycle.

circadian rhythms	dormancy	migration

Behavior	Description	Example
	Animals periodically move from one place to another and then back again.	Birds fly south for the winter.
	Behavioral cycles that occur in daily patterns	People naturally sleep at night and are awake during the day.
	Animals are active during warm seasons and enter a sleeplike state during cold seasons.	Some reptiles hibernate through the winter.

Use the table to answer the question.

1. Why is dormancy useful to some animals?

_____

_____

2. Why do animals usually migrate?

_____

_____

© Pearson Education, Inc., publishing as Pearson Prentice Hall.

Communication

Bees can communicate the distance and location of food through their dances. In the "waggle dance," a bee runs in a straight line, waggling its abdomen. It then circles back, runs straight again, and circles back the other way. The distance it runs before circling tells other bees how far away the food is. The longer the bee runs and the more it waggles, the farther away the food. The direction of the dance also indicates the location of the food.

The solid arrows show how long the bee's straight path is.

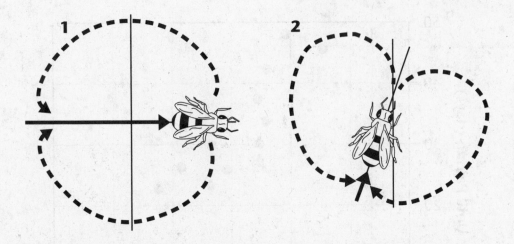

Use the diagrams to answer the question.

1. If a bee wanted to find a food source nearby, which bee would it be most likely to follow?

_____

2. Draw a diagram showing another "waggle dance." The food source for your dance is the same distance away as the food source shown by bee 1. However, the new food source is located in the opposite direction as the source shown by bee 1.

Name_____ Class_____ Date_____

Courtship Behavior

Animals use many behaviors to find and attract mates. Successful courtship behaviors help animals identify healthy mates. For many birds, songs are courtship behaviors. The graph shows the relationship between the number of songs that the males of a particular species of warbler know and the length of time it takes the birds to find a mate.

On the graph, draw a straight line that best fits the data.

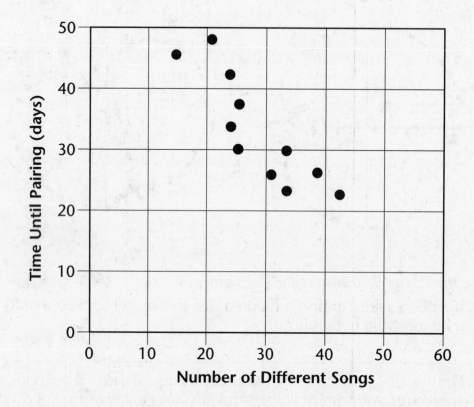

Use the graph to answer the questions.

1. Describe the relationship between the number of songs that a male warbler knows and the time until it pairs with a mate.

_____

_____

2. How could the number of songs that a male warbler knows affect its chances for reproductive success?

_____

_____

© Pearson Education, Inc., publishing as Pearson Prentice Hall.

Chapter 34 Animal Behavior

Vocabulary Review

True or False *If the statement is true, write* true. *If it is false, write* false.

_____ 1. Learning based on early experience, such as geese learning to follow the first moving object they see during a certain time early in their lives, is called migration.

_____ 2. Habituation involves decreasing or stopping a response to a repetitive stimulus that provides neither reward nor harm.

_____ 3. A circadian rhythm is a behavioral cycle that occurs in a daily pattern.

_____ 4. Trial-and-error learning is often called classical conditioning.

_____ 5. A stimulus is any signal that carries information and can be detected.

_____ 6. An animal engages in courtship when it sends out stimuli to attract a member of the opposite sex.

_____ 7. Communication is the passing of information from one organism to another.

_____ 8. Insight learning behaviors are those an animal is born knowing how to exhibit.

_____ 9. A stimulus is a single, specific reaction to a stimulus.

_____ 10. Imprinting is the way an organism reacts to changes in its internal condition or external environment.

© Pearson Education, Inc., publishing as Pearson Prentice Hall.

Chapter 35 Nervous System

Summary

35-1 Human Body Systems

Cells of multicellular organisms are specialized for certain functions. **The levels of organization in a multicellular organism include cells, tissues, organs, and organ systems.**

- A cell is the basic unit of structure and function in living things. **Specialized cells** are suited to perform a particular function.
- Groups of similar cells work together to form tissues. **Epithelial tissue** covers body surfaces. **Connective tissue** supports the body and connects its parts. **Nervous tissue** carries messages throughout the body. **Muscle tissue** allows movement.
- Groups of tissues that work together to perform complex functions are called organs.
- Organs form organ systems.

Organ systems work together to keep conditions in the body stable. This process is called **homeostasis. Homeostasis is the process by which organisms keep internal conditions relatively constant, despite changes in external environments.** Homeostasis may involve feedback inhibition, or negative feedback. For example, the nervous system senses when the body cools and signals the cells to give off more heat.

35-2 The Nervous System

The nervous system controls and coordinates body functions. It responds to internal and external stimuli. Messages move through the nervous system as electrical signals. The signals are called impulses.

Neurons are nerve cells. Each neuron has a cell body, dendrites, and an axon. The **cell body** is the largest part of a typical neuron. It holds the nucleus. Short branches, called **dendrites,** carry impulses toward the cell body. A long fiber, called the **axon,** carries impulses away from the cell body. A **myelin sheath** covers and insulates parts of some axons. A **synapse** is at the end of an axon. One neuron transfers an impulse to another at the synapse. Chemicals called **neurotransmitters** send impulses across the synapse.

There are three types of neurons: sensory neurons, motor neurons, and interneurons. Sensory neurons carry impulses to the spinal cord. Motor neurons carry impulses from the spinal cord. Interneurons link sensory and motor neurons.

© Pearson Education, Inc., publishing as Pearson Prentice Hall.

A resting neuron is one that is not carrying an impulse. When a neuron is resting, the inside of the cell has a net negative charge. The outside of the cell has a net positive charge. This charge difference across the cell membrane is called the **resting potential** of the neuron. **When a resting neuron is stimulated by another neuron or by the environment, an impulse starts.** Positive ions flow into the neuron making the inside of the cell temporarily more positive than the outside of the cell. This reversal of charges across the membrane is the impulse, or **action potential.** Once started, the action potential travels quickly down the neuron's axon. At the end of the axon, impulses can be transmitted to the next cell.

35–3 Divisions of the Nervous System

The nervous system has two major divisions: the central nervous system and the peripheral nervous system.

1) <u>The central nervous system</u> is made up of the brain and spinal cord. It is the control center of the body. **It sends messages, processes information, and analyzes information.** The brain and spinal cord are protected by bone and three layers of connective tissue. Fluid between the layers cushions and protects nerve tissue.

The brain has several regions. The **cerebrum** controls voluntary actions. The **cerebellum** coordinates involuntary actions. The **brain stem** controls basic body functions. The **thalamus** receives impulses from the senses and sends them to the cerebrum. The **hypothalamus** connects the nervous and endocrine systems.

The spinal cord connects the brain with the rest of the body. Some reflexes are processed in the spinal cord. A **reflex** is a quick, automatic response to a stimulus. Sneezing is an example. The path of an impulse during a reflex is called the **reflex arc.**

2) <u>The peripheral nervous system</u> **has two divisions.**
- The **sensory division** sends impulses from sensory neurons to the central nervous system.
- The **motor division** sends impulses from the central nervous system to muscles and glands. The motor division is further divided into somatic and autonomic nervous systems.

The somatic nervous system controls voluntary actions. The autonomic nervous system regulates activities that are automatic. These nerves control functions that are not under conscious control.

© Pearson Education, Inc., publishing as Pearson Prentice Hall.

35–4 The Senses

Sensory receptors are neurons that react to stimuli in the environment. These receptors send impulses to the central nervous system. **There are five types of sensory receptors.** Pain receptors respond to pain. Thermoreceptors respond to temperature. Mechanoreceptors respond to pressure. Chemoreceptors respond to chemicals. Photoreceptors respond to light.

The sensory organ responsible for vision is the eye. Light enters the eye through the pupil. The pupil is a small opening at the front of the eye. Light then moves through the **lens,** which focuses the light on the retina. The retina contains photoreceptors called rods and cones. **Rods** are sensitive to dim light. **Cones** are sensitive to colors.

Ears respond to sound stimuli. Sound vibrations enter the ear and create pressure waves in the fluid-filled cochlea. Sensory receptors in the cochlea send impulses to the brain. Ears also sense balance. Semicircular canals in the ear contain fluid, hair cells, and tiny grains. Movements make the grains bend the hair cells, which send an impulse to the brain.

Chemoreceptors in the nose react to chemicals in the air and send impulses to the brain. **Taste buds** are sense organs that detect taste. Most taste buds are located on a person's tongue. The skin is the largest sense organ. It has receptors that respond to temperature, touch, and pain.

35–5 Drugs and the Nervous System

A **drug** is any substance, other than food, that changes the structure or function of the body. Several types of drugs affect the nervous system.

- Stimulants increase heart rate, blood pressure, and breathing rate.
- Depressants decrease heart rate and breathing rate, lower blood pressure, relax muscles, and relieve tension.
- Opiates act like natural brain chemicals called endorphins. These brain chemicals normally help overcome pain. Opiates are highly addictive.
- Marijuana can cause memory and concentration problems.
- Alcohol is a depressant that slows down the rate at which the central nervous system functions.

Drug abuse can be defined as the intentional misuse of any drug for nonmedical purposes. **Addiction** is an uncontrollable dependence on a drug.

© Pearson Education, Inc., publishing as Pearson Prentice Hall.

Organization of the Human Body

The human body can be organized into a series of levels: *cells, tissues, organs,* and *organ systems.*

In the first column, fill in the correct level of organization. Then, number the levels in order from simplest (1) to most complex (4) in the last column.

Organization of the Human Body			
Level of Organization	**Description**	**Example**	**Order**
	groups of different types of tissue that function together	brain	
	groups of organs that perform closely related functions	nervous system	
	basic units of structure and function in a living thing	neuron	
	groups of cells that perform a particular function	nervous tissue	

Answer the question.

1. All of the organ systems in the human body work together to maintain homeostasis. What is homeostasis?

_____

_____

2. Name one organ system in the human body.

_____

_____

_____

© Pearson Education, Inc., publishing as Pearson Prentice Hall.

The Neuron

Neurons are the basic units of the nervous system. They transmit electrical signals called impulses.

Color the neuron according to the prompts below
- Color the structures that receive signals from the environment or another neuron red.
- Color the structure that carries an impulse away from the cell body orange.
- Color the cell body blue.

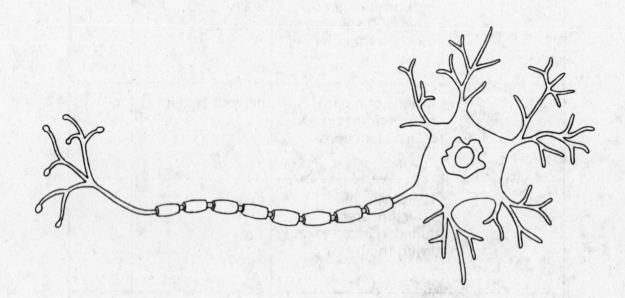

Answer the questions. Circle the correct answer.

1. What is the insulating membrane that surrounds some axons called?

   synapse   myelin sheath

2. What are the structures that carry impulses to the cell body called?

   dendrites   axons

© Pearson Education, Inc., publishing as Pearson Prentice Hall.

Action Potential

A resting neuron has an overall negative charge. Outside the neuron, the environment has a net positive charge. When a neuron is stimulated, positive ions rush into the cell. The area inside the cell becomes temporarily more positive than the outside. This reversal of charges is called a nerve impulse, or *action potential*. As the action potential passes, positive ions flow out of the cell. This restores the net negative charge inside the cell.

Color the action potential in the appropriate diagrams red. One has been done for you.

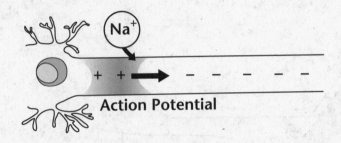

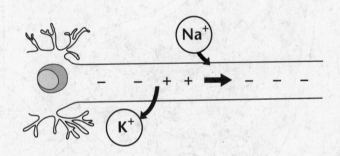

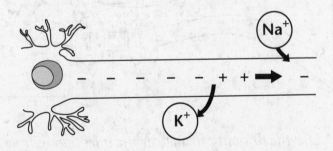

Use the diagram to answer the question. Circle the correct answer.

1. In which direction do potassium ions (K⁺) flow as the action potential passes?

into the cell   out of the cell

© Pearson Education, Inc., publishing as Pearson Prentice Hall.

The Synapse

A neuron transfers an impulse to another cell at a synapse. The signals are transferred by neurotransmitters. Neurotransmitters are chemicals released by the neuron that cross the space between the cells and bind to receptors on the neighboring cell.

Label one neurotransmitter, receptor, and two cell membranes on the diagram. Then, color the neuron transmitting the signal red. Color the cell receiving the signal blue.

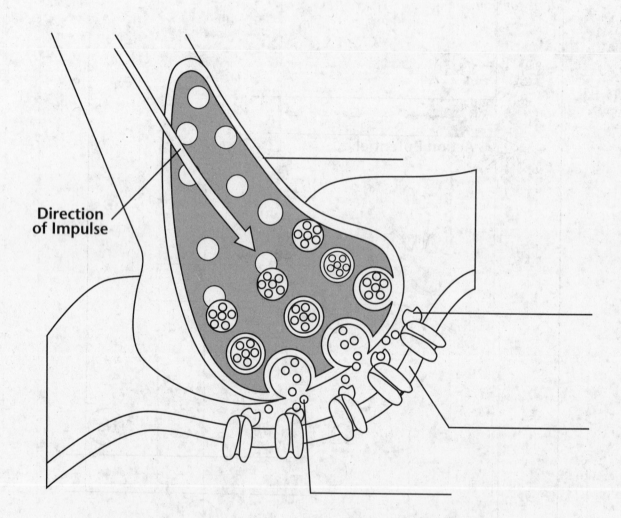

Direction of Impulse

Use the drawing to answer the question. Circle the correct answer.

1. The cell receiving the signal is a neuron. What part of this neuron is pictured above?

    dendrite   cell body

© Pearson Education, Inc., publishing as Pearson Prentice Hall.

The Brain

The brain is a part of the central nervous system. It helps relay messages and processes and analyzes information. Different body functions are controlled by different parts of the brain.

Color different parts of the brain according to the prompts.
- Color the cerebrum brown.
- Color the cerebellum yellow.
- Color the spinal cord green.
- Color the brain stem blue.
- Color the thalamus and hypothalamus red.

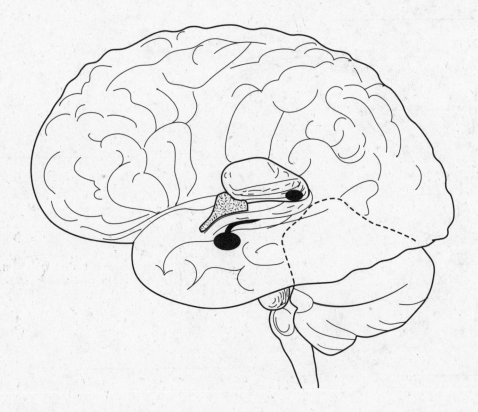

Answer the questions. Circle the correct answer.

1. Which part of the brain controls blood pressure, heart rate, breathing and swallowing?

   brain stem   cerebrum

2. Which part of the brain is the site of intelligence, learning, and judgment?

   thalamus   cerebrum

© Pearson Education, Inc., publishing as Pearson Prentice Hall.

The Eye

The eye is a sense organ that humans use to see. Different parts of the eye perform different functions. For example, the lens focuses light on the retina.

Use the words below to label the diagram.

lens	pupil	vitreous humor
optic nerve	retina	

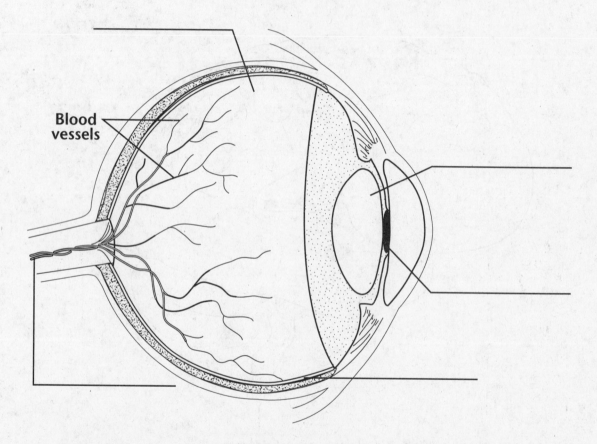

Blood vessels

Answer the question. Circle the correct answer.

1. Rods and cones are two types of cells that can convert light energy into nerve impulses. These cells are located in which structure?

retina   pupil

© Pearson Education, Inc., publishing as Pearson Prentice Hall.

Hearing

The human ear converts vibrations in the air into nerve impulses that can be interpreted by the brain. This process is called hearing.

The following prompts describe different steps in the hearing process. Use the numbers to label the place in the ear in which each step occurs. Some locations may be labeled with more than one step.

1 Vibrations enter the auditory canal.

2 The vibrations cause the eardrum to vibrate.

3 Vibrations from the eardrum are picked up by the hammer, anvil, and stirrup.

4 Vibrations from the stirrup are transmitted to the oval window.

5 Pressure waves are created in the fluid-filled cochlea. Hair cells respond to pressure waves by producing nerve impulses.

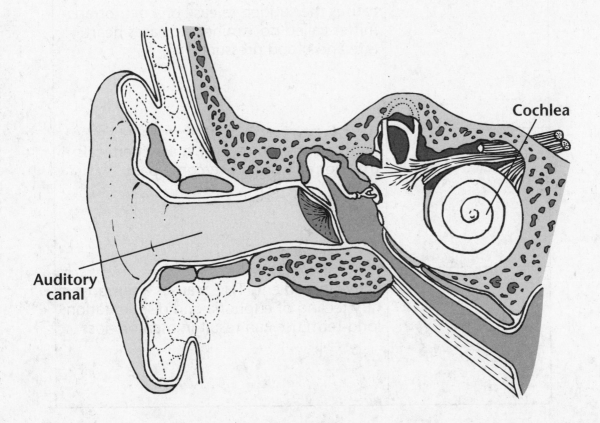

Cochlea

Auditory
canal

Answer the question. Circle the correct answer.

1. Which of the following best describes sound?

light waves in the air   vibrations in the air

© Pearson Education, Inc., publishing as Pearson Prentice Hall.

Drugs

A drug is a substance, other than food, that changes the structure or function of the body.

The following table describes how four different drugs—marijuana, cocaine, opiates, and alcohol—affect the human body. Complete the table by filling in the correct drug. The first one is done for you.

Drug	Effects on the Body
alcohol	slows the rate at which the central nervous system functions; slows reflexes; disrupts coordination; impairs judgment; long-term use harms the liver
	causes the sudden release of a neurotransmitter called dopamine; increases heart rate and blood pressure
	mimics endorphins, which are chemicals that normally help overcome pain
	active ingredient, THC, causes a temporary feeling of euphoria and disorientation; long-term use can result in memory loss

Use the table to answer the questions. Circle the correct answer.

1. Which drug is a depressant?   alcohol   cocaine

2. Which drug is a stimulant?   alcohol   cocaine

© Pearson Education, Inc., publishing as Pearson Prentice Hall.

Chapter 35   Nervous System

Vocabulary Review

Multiple Choice   *In the space provided, write the letter of the answer that best completes each sentence.*

_____ 1. A drug that increases the actions regulated by the nervous system is a
  a. depressant.   **c.** stimulant
  b. dendrite.

_____ 2. The part of a nerve cell that carries impulses toward the cell body is the
  a. axon.   **c.** myelin sheath.
  b. dendrite.

_____ 3. The tissue that covers the surface of the body and lines internal organs is
  a. muscle tissue.   **c.** epithelial tissue.
  b. nervous tissue.

_____ 4. The process by which the product of a system shuts down or limits the operation of the system is
  a. feedback inhibition.   **c.** resting potential.
  b. action potential.

_____ 5. The photoreceptors of the eye that are sensitive to light but do not distinguish color are the
  a. rods.   **c.** pupils.
  b. cones.

_____ 6. Neurons that react to light, sound, or other specific stimuli by sending impulses to other neurons are
  a. neurotransmitters.   **c.** sensory receptors.
  b. meninges.

_____ 7. The part of the brain that is responsible for coordination and balance is the
  a. cerebrum.   **c.** brain stem.
  b. cerebellum.

_____ 8. The control center for the recognition of hunger, thirst, fatigue, and body temperature is the
  a. thalamus.   **c.** cerebrum.
  b. hypothalamus.

_____ 9. Chemicals used by a neuron to transmit messages across a synapse are
  a. cerebrospinal fluid.   **c.** neurotransmitters.
  b. depressants.

Summary

36–1 The Skeletal System

The skeletal system has several jobs. **It supports the body, protects internal organs, allows movement, stores mineral reserves, and provides a site for blood cell formation.** The skeleton is divided into two parts.

- The axial skeleton is made up of the skull, ribs, and spine.
- The appendicular skeleton is made up of all of the bones related to the arms and legs. This includes the bones of the shoulders, hips, hands, and feet.

Bones are living tissue. **Bones are a solid network of cells and protein fibers surrounded by deposits of calcium salts.** The **periosteum** is a layer of connective tissue that surrounds a typical bone. Under the periosteum is a thick layer of compact bone. A network of tubes called **Haversian canals** runs through compact bone. These canals hold blood vessels and nerves. Cavities that hold **bone marrow** are inside the bone. Yellow bone marrow is made up of fat cells. Red bone marrow makes blood cells.

The skeleton of an embryo is made mostly of cartilage. **Cartilage** is a tough but flexible connective tissue. Cartilage is replaced by bone in a process called **ossification.** Ossification starts before birth and continues until adulthood.

A **joint** is a place where one bone attaches to another. Joints allow bones to move without damaging each other. **Depending on its type of movement, a joint is classified as immovable, slightly movable, or freely movable.**

- **Immovable joints** allow no movement. Immovable joints are found in the skull.
- **Slightly movable joints,** such those in the spine, allow a small amount of movement.
- **Freely movable joints** permit movement in one or more directions. Four common freely movable joints are: ball-and-socket joints, hinge joints, pivot joints, and saddle joints.

Ligaments are strips of tough connective tissue that hold bones together in a joint. The bony surfaces of the joint are covered with cartilage. A substance called synovial fluid forms a thin film on the cartilage, making the joint surfaces slippery.

Excessive strain or disease can damage bones and joints.

- Arthritis is a disorder that involves inflammation of the joints.
- Osteoporosis is a condition in which bones weaken. Weak bones are prone to fracture, or breaking.

© Pearson Education, Inc., publishing as Pearson Prentice Hall.

36–2 The Muscular System

Working together with the skeletal system, the muscular system produces movement. **There are three different types of muscle tissue.**

- **Skeletal muscles** most often attach to bones. Skeletal muscles allow voluntary movements such as dancing.
- **Smooth muscles** line blood vessels and the digestive tract. They are not under conscious control. Smooth muscles move food through the digestive tract and control the flow of blood through the circulatory system.
- **Cardiac muscle** is found only in the heart. Cardiac muscle is not under voluntary control.

Skeletal muscle cells are called muscle fibers. Muscle fibers are made up of smaller structures called myofibrils. Each myofibril is made up of even smaller structures called filaments. Filaments can be thick or thin. Thick filaments are made of the protein **myosin.** Thin filaments are made of the protein **actin.** Thick and thin filaments are arranged in units called sarcomeres. When the muscle is relaxed, there are no thin filaments in the middle of the sarcomere.

A muscle contracts when the thin filaments in the muscle fiber slide over the thick filaments. During muscle contraction, knoblike heads of myosin filaments attach to binding sites on actin molecules. Each attachment is called a cross-bridge. ATP then causes the myosin cross-bridge to change shape. This change in shape pulls the actin filament toward the center of the sarcomere. The myosin head detaches and the cycle repeats.

Tendons join muscles to bones. Tendons pull on bones, making them work like levers. Muscles supply the force that moves bones.

Most skeletal muscles work in opposing pairs. When one muscle contracts, the other muscle relaxes. For example, in order to bend the arm at the elbow, the biceps contract and the triceps relax. This creates the force necessary to bend the elbow joint. To extend the arm, the triceps contract and the biceps relax.

Regular exercise is important in maintaining muscle strength and flexibility. Regular exercise also strengthens bones. Strong bones and muscles are less likely to be injured.

© Pearson Education, Inc., publishing as Pearson Prentice Hall.

36–3 The Integumentary System

The integumentary system has several jobs. It covers the body and protects against infection, injury, and ultraviolet radiation. It helps regulate body temperature and removes wastes from the body.

The skin is made up of two main layers.

- The **epidermis** is the outer layer of the skin. The epidermis is composed of two layers. The inner layer of the epidermis is made up of living cells. These cells quickly divide and push older cells up toward the surface of the skin. Eventually, the older cells die. The outside layer of the epidermis is made up of dead cells. It provides a tough, flexible, waterproof outer covering for the body. The epidermis also contains cells that produce melanin. **Melanin** is a dark brown pigment. It helps protect the skin from ultraviolet radiation in sunlight.

- The **dermis** is the inner layer of skin. The dermis contains many different types of structures such as blood vessels, nerve endings, hair follicles, and glands. There are two main types of glands in the dermis: sweat glands and sebaceous glands. Sweat glands produce sweat. Sweat evaporates off of the surface of skin and helps keep the body cool. Sebaceous glands produce sebum. This oily substance helps keep the epidermis flexible and waterproof.

Hair and nails are also parts of the integumentary system. Hair and nails are made mainly of keratin. Hair is made by structures called **hair follicles.** Nails grow from an area called the nail root. Nails protect the tips of the fingers and toes.

© Pearson Education, Inc., publishing as Pearson Prentice Hall.

Structure of a Bone

Most human bones are composed of compact bone and spongy bone. Spongy bone provides strength and support to the bone while limiting mass. Compact bone contains Haversian canals, which contain blood vessels. The bone is covered by a tough layer of tissue called the periosteum.

Color the spongy bone *yellow. Color the* compact bone *red. Then label the* Haversian canals *and* periosteum.

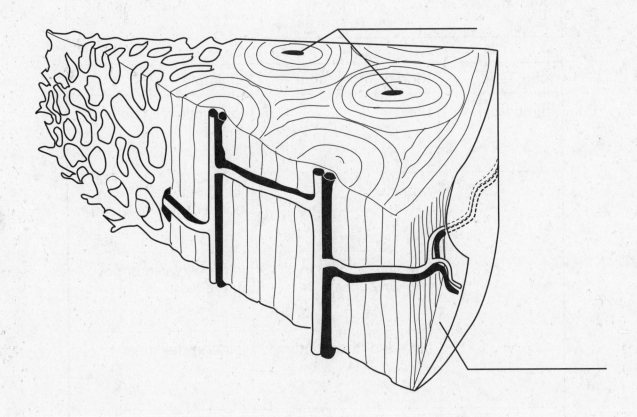

Use the diagram to answer the questions.

1. Where in long bones is spongy bone found? Circle the correct answer.

   in the middle   at the ends

2. What do the Haversian canals contain?

_____

© Pearson Education, Inc., publishing as Pearson Prentice Hall.

Types of Joints

Any place where two bones attach to each other is called a joint. There are three major categories of joints: immovable, slightly movable, and freely movable. The four most common kinds of freely movable joints, named for how they work, are: ball-and-socket joints, hinge joints, pivot joints, and saddle joints.

Use the words below to fill in the table. One row has been completed for you.

| ball-and-socket | pivot | slightly movable |
| hinge | saddle | |

Joint Type	Kind of Movement	Example
immovable	none	joints between bones in the skull
	restricted	joints between the two bones of the lower leg
	one bone sliding in two directions	joints between bones in the wrist
	back-and-forth motion	joints in the knees
	one bone rotating around another	joints in the elbows
	movement in many directions	joints in the shoulders

Use the table to answer the question.

1. Which type of joint allows the greatest range of movement?

_____

© Pearson Education, Inc., publishing as Pearson Prentice Hall.

Types of Muscle Tissue

Use the words below to identify each of the three types of muscle found in the human body.

cardiac muscle	skeletal muscle	smooth muscle

Muscle Type	Structure and Function	Example
	Cells are spindle-shaped with one nucleus and no striation; muscles are usually not under voluntary control.	muscles that move food through the digestive tract
	Cells are striated, with one or two nuclei; muscle is found in only one place in the body; it is generally not under voluntary control.	heart muscle
	Cells are large and striated and have many nuclei; muscles are used for voluntary motion.	muscles attached to bones

Use the table to answer the questions. Circle the correct answer.

1. Which muscles can you consciously control?

   smooth   skeletal

2. Where in the body is cardiac muscle found?

   _____

© Pearson Education, Inc., publishing as Pearson Prentice Hall.

Muscle Contraction

Skeletal muscle fibers are made up of thick and thin filaments arranged in units called sarcomeres. The thick filaments contain the protein myosin, and the thin ones contain the protein actin. When a muscle contracts, cross-bridges form between the myosin and actin fibers. The myosin fibers pull on the actin fibers. This motion, repeated in many sarcomeres, causes a muscle to contract.

Use the words below to label the diagrams.

actin	cross-bridges	myosin	sarcomere

Relaxed Muscle

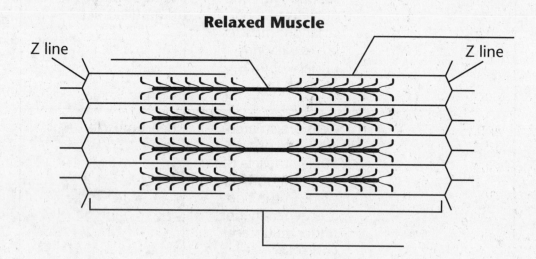

Z line   Z line

Contracted Muscle

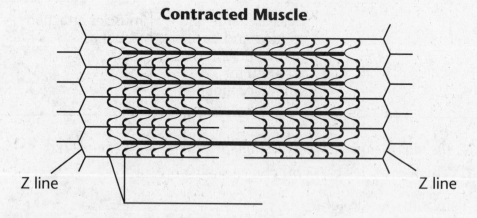

Z line   Z line

Use the diagram to answer the question.

1. Describe how the position of the actin filaments changes during muscle contraction.

_____

_____

© Pearson Education, Inc., publishing as Pearson Prentice Hall.

Opposing Pairs

When you straighten or bend your arm, two muscles work together: the biceps and triceps. The biceps is located on the inside of your upper arm. The triceps is on the outside of your upper arm. When one muscle is contracted, the other muscle is relaxed.

Label whether each muscle is contracted or relaxed.

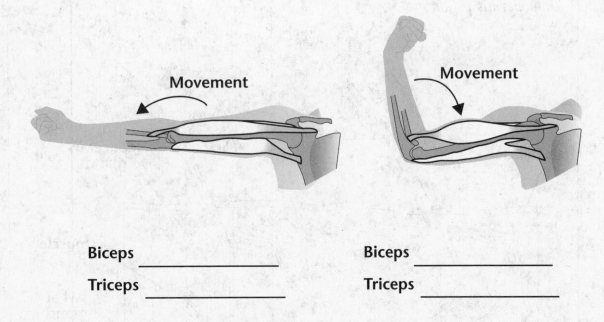

Biceps _____   **Biceps** _____

Triceps _____   **Triceps** _____

Use the diagram to answer the questions.

1. Which muscle contracts when you bend your arm? Circle the correct answer.

   biceps   triceps

2. Which muscle relaxes when you extend your arm? Circle the correct answer.

   biceps   triceps

3. Which muscles are used in the controlled movement of holding a tennis racket?

   _____

© Pearson Education, Inc., publishing as Pearson Prentice Hall.

Structures of the Skin

Human skin has three layers: the epidermis, dermis, and hypodermis. The epidermis is the outer layer. The dermis is the inner
layer that contains blood vessels, nerve endings, muscles, hair
follicles, and other structures. The hypodermis is a layer of fat
and connective tissue.

*Color the epidermis red. Color the dermis orange. Color the
hypodermis yellow.*

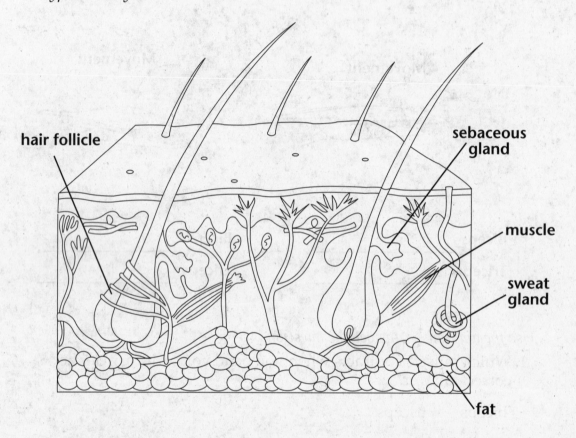

Use the diagram to answer the questions.

1. In which layer are sweat glands found? Circle the
   correct answer.

   dermis   epidermis

2. In which layer are hair follicles found? Circle the correct answer.

   hypodermis   dermis

3. What is the function of the hypodermis?

   _____

© Pearson Education, Inc., publishing as Pearson Prentice Hall.

Chapter 36 Skeletal, Muscular, and Integumentary Systems

Vocabulary Review

Matching *In the space provided, write the letter of the definition that best matches each term.*

_____ **1.** cartilage

_____ **2.** joint

_____ **3.** melanin

_____ **4.** ossification

_____ **5.** tendon

a. place where one bone is attached to another

b. process in which cartilage is replaced with bone

c. dark brown pigment found in skin

d. connective tissue that supports the body and is more flexible than bone

e. tough connective tissue that joins skeletal muscles to bones

Matching *In the space provided, write the letter of the definition that best matches each term.*

_____ **6.** keratin

_____ **7.** epidermis

_____ **8.** actin

_____ **9.** Haversian canal

_____ **10.** ligament

a. outer layer of skin

b. network of tubes in bones that contains blood vessels and nerves

c. protein that makes up most of the thin filaments of muscle fibers

d. connective tissue that holds bones together at a joint

e. tough, fibrous protein made by skin cells

Completion *Fill in the blanks with the correct term. Use the words listed below.*

bone marrow	dermis	myosin

11. The inner layer of skin is called the _____.

12. The protein that makes up the thick filaments in muscle

is called _____.

13. _____ is the soft tissue contained in the cavities of bones.

Chapter 37 Circulatory and Respiratory Systems

Summary

37–1 The Circulatory System

Working with the respiratory system, the circulatory system supplies the body's cells with oxygen and nutrients and removes carbon dioxide and other wastes. **The circulatory system includes the heart, blood vessels, and blood.**

The Heart. The heart is located near the center of the chest. The thick layer of muscle that forms the heart's walls is called the **myocardium.** Contractions of the myocardium pump blood through the body. A contraction begins in a group of cells called the **pacemaker.** The impulse travels through the rest of the heart, causing it to contract.

The heart is divided into right and left halves by the septum. The septum prevents the mixing of oxygen-poor and oxygen-rich blood. Each half of the heart has two chambers. The upper two chambers, or **atria** (singular: atrium), receive blood entering the heart. The lower two chambers, or **ventricles,** pump blood out of the heart. Flaps called **valves** lie between chambers. The valves keep blood from flowing backward in the heart.

Pumping of the heart produces pressure. Blood pressure is the force of the blood on artery walls. Blood pressure moves blood through the body.

The human body has a double-loop circulatory system. Blood moves through two basic pathways.

- In **pulmonary circulation,** oxygen-poor blood flows from the heart to the lungs. In the lungs, carbon dioxide is released from the blood and oxygen is absorbed. This oxygen-rich blood then returns back to the heart.
- In **systemic circulation,** oxygen-rich blood is pumped throughout the body. In the body, oxygen is delivered to body cells and carbon dioxide is picked up by the blood. This oxygen-poor blood returns to the heart.

Blood Vessels. **As blood flows through the circulatory system, it moves through three types of vessels.**

- **Arteries** are large vessels that carry blood away from the heart.
- From arteries, blood flows into **capillaries,** the smallest vessels. In capillaries, materials such as carbon dioxide, oxygen and nutrients are exchanged between the blood and body tissues.
- From the capillaries, blood flows into **veins.** Veins carry blood to the heart. Large veins have valves that keep blood moving forward.

© Pearson Education, Inc., publishing as Pearson Prentice Hall.

Cardiovascular diseases, such as atherosclerosis and high blood pressure, are diseases of the circulatory system. **Atherosclerosis** is a condition in which fatty deposits build up in arteries. Both high blood pressure and atherosclerosis make the heart work harder. Both can lead to heart attack and stroke. You can prevent these diseases by exercising regularly, eating a low-fat diet, controlling your weight, and not smoking.

37–2 Blood and the Lymphatic System

Blood is a type of connective tissue that contains both dissolved substances and specialized cells. Blood regulates body temperature and pH. It protects the body from disease. In addition, blood can form clots to repair damaged blood vessels.

Just over half of blood is a watery fluid called **plasma.** Proteins in plasma help to clot blood and fight infections.

The cellular portion of blood is made up of red blood cells, white blood cells, and platelets.

- **Red blood cells carry oxygen.** A protein called **hemoglobin** in red blood cells binds to oxygen and carries it throughout the body.
- **White blood cells guard against infection, fight parasites, and attack bacteria.** There are many types of white blood cells. White blood cells called lymphocytes make antibodies. Antibodies are proteins that help fight infection.
- **Blood clotting is made possible by plasma proteins and platelets. Platelets** are cell fragments. Platelets cluster around a wound and release proteins called clotting factors, leading to the formation of a clot.

As blood circulates, some fluid called **lymph** leaks from the blood into surrounding tissues. **The lymphatic system collects the fluid that is lost by the blood and returns it back to the circulatory system.** The lymphatic system is a network of lymph vessels, lymph nodes, and organs. Lymph nodes act as filters and produce certain white blood cells that protect body cells. The lymphatic system also helps absorb nutrients and fight infection.

© Pearson Education, Inc., publishing as Pearson Prentice Hall.

37–3 The Respiratory System

The respiratory system allows for the exchange of oxygen and carbon dioxide between the blood, the air, and tissues. The nose, pharynx, larynx, trachea, bronchi, and lungs are organs of the respiratory system.

Air enters the body through the nose (or mouth) and passes to the **pharynx,** a tube in the throat. The air then moves into the **trachea,** or windpipe. The **larynx,** which contains the vocal cords, is at the top of the trachea. From the trachea, air moves into two large tubes in the chest called **bronchi** (singular: bronchus). Each bronchus enters a lung.

Within each lung, the bronchus divides into smaller tubes, called bronchioles. The bronchioles keep subdividing until they end in millions of tiny air sacs called **alveoli** (singular: alveolus). Capillaries surround each alveolus. Oxygen crosses the thin capillary walls from the alveolus into the blood. Carbon dioxide in the blood crosses in the opposite direction into the alveolus.

<u>Breathing</u>. Breathing is the movement of air into and out of the lungs. During inhalation, air is pulled into the lungs, delivering oxygen. During exhalation, air is pushed out of the lungs, removing carbon dioxide.

The **diaphragm** is a muscle at the bottom of the chest cavity. When the diaphragm contracts, the chest cavity gets larger. This forms a partial vacuum in the chest. This draws in air that fills the lungs. When the diaphragm relaxes, the chest cavity gets smaller. Pressure rises inside the chest forcing air back out of the lungs.

Breathing is an involuntary action. Carbon dioxide levels in the blood control breathing rate. When carbon dioxide levels rise, the medulla oblongata in the brain sends impulses to the lungs to take a breath.

<u>Dangers of Smoking</u>. Tobacco smoke contains dangerous substances that harm the respiratory system. **Nicotine** increases heart rate and blood pressure. Carbon monoxide is a toxic gas that blocks the transport of oxygen by blood. Tar contains substances that cause cancer.

Smoking can cause such respiratory diseases as chronic bronchitis, emphysema, and lung cancer. Emphysema is a loss of elasticity in lung tissues. Smoking also can cause heart disease. Passive smoking is inhaling the smoke of others. Passive smoking can harm nonsmokers, especially young children. Quitting smoking can improve a smoker's health. The best way to protect your health is to not begin smoking.

© Pearson Education, Inc., publishing as Pearson Prentice Hall.

The Human Heart

The human heart has four chambers: right atrium, right ventricle, left atrium, and left ventricle. Blood flows from the body into the right atrium. Valves keep blood flowing in only one direction.

Follow the prompts to identify parts of the human heart. The diagram shows the heart as if viewed from the front, so left and right are switched.

- Color the left atrium orange.
- Color the left ventricle red.
- Color the right atrium yellow.
- Color the right ventricle blue.

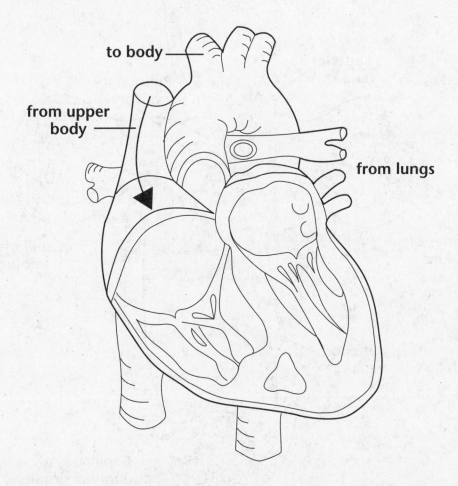

Use the diagram to answer the question.

1. A valve is located between the right atrium and the right ventricle. What is the role of valves in the heart?

_____

_____

© Pearson Education, Inc., publishing as Pearson Prentice Hall.

The Circulatory System

The human circulatory system moves blood through two primary pathways. One connects the heart and lungs, and the other connects the heart and the rest of the body.

Draw arrows to show how blood moves through the circulatory system. One has been drawn for you.

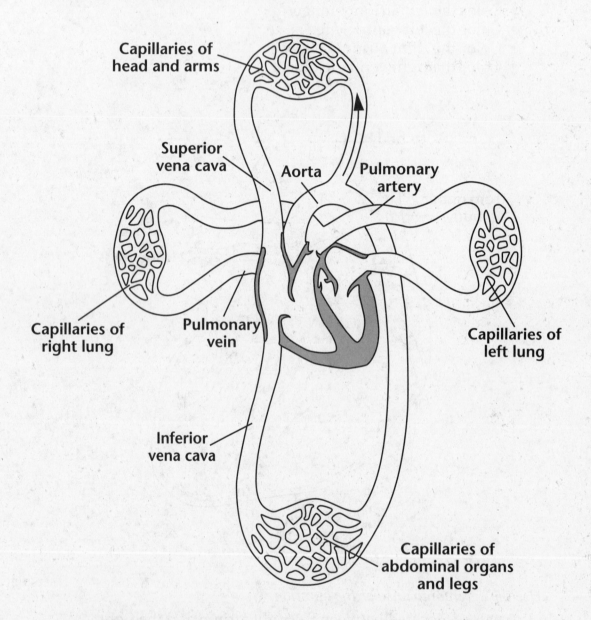

Use the diagram to answer the question.

1. Through which blood vessel does blood return to the heart from the head and arms?

_____

© Pearson Education, Inc., publishing as Pearson Prentice Hall.

Blood Vessels

As blood flows through the body, it passes through three types of blood vessels—arteries, veins, and capillaries.

Complete the table. Fill in the missing information.

Blood Vessels	Structure	Function
arteries	thick walls containing connective tissue, endothelium, and smooth muscle	
	walls containing connective tissue, endothelium, and smooth muscle; large ones also have valves to control the direction of blood flow	carry blood toward the heart
capillaries		bring nutrients and oxygen to cells and remove carbon dioxide and waste

Use the table to answer the questions.

1. Which are the smallest blood vessels? Circle the correct answer.

    capillaries   veins

2. How does exercise help veins function?

_____

_____

© Pearson Education, Inc., publishing as Pearson Prentice Hall.

Blood Clot Formation

When a blood vessel is injured, platelets release proteins that start a series of chemical reactions. These reactions lead to the formation of filaments called fibrin. The fibrin forms a clot that stops the bleeding.

Color the red blood cells *in the diagrams red. Color the* platelets *blue. Color the* fibrin *yellow.*

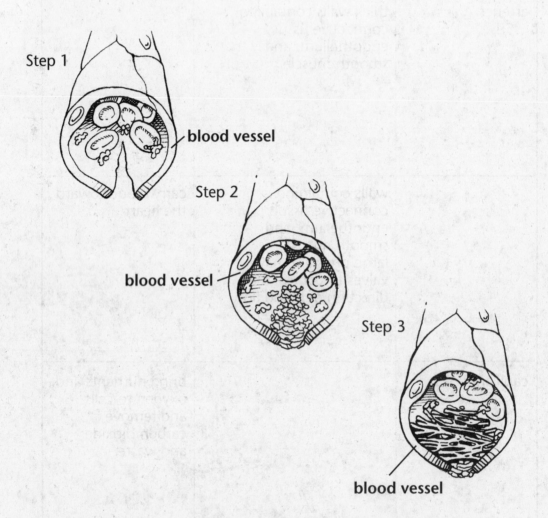

Step 1

blood vessel

Step 2

blood vessel

Step 3

blood vessel

Use the diagrams to answer the questions.

1. In step 2, what is clumped at the site of injury? Circle the correct answer.

   platelets   fibrin

2. Why is it important for blood to form clots?

   _____

© Pearson Education, Inc., publishing as Pearson Prentice Hall.

The Lymphatic System

The lymphatic system collects fluid that leaks out of blood vessels and returns it to the circulatory system.

Color the lymphatic system. Then label the thymus *and* spleen.

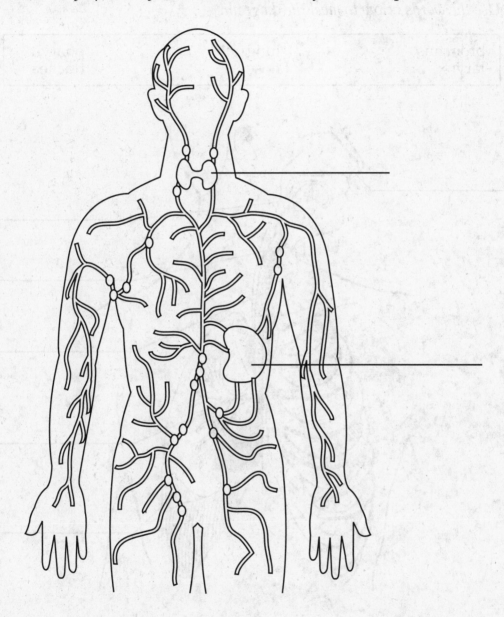

Answer the question.

1. What happens when large numbers of pathogens are trapped in lymph nodes?

_____

© Pearson Education, Inc., publishing as Pearson Prentice Hall.

The Respiratory System

Air enters the body through the mouth and nose. It passes through air passages and fills the lungs. In the lungs, oxygen enters the bloodstream and carbon dioxide leaves the bloodstream.

Use the words below to label the diagram.

bronchus	lung	pharynx
larynx	nose	trachea

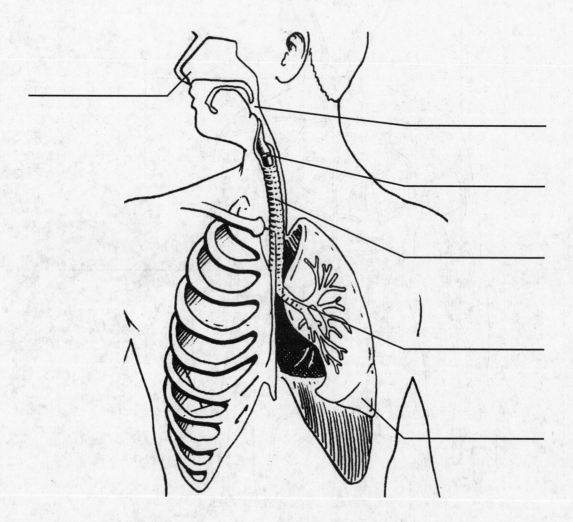

Use the diagram to answer the question. Circle the correct answer.

1. Which structure does air enter after the nose?

     bronchus   pharynx

© Pearson Education, Inc., publishing as Pearson Prentice Hall.

Gas Exchange

In the lungs, gas exchange takes place in millions of tiny air sacs called alveoli. Oxygen diffuses from the alveoli through the capillary walls into the blood. Carbon dioxide diffuses in the opposite direction.

Follow the prompts to identify important parts of the diagram.
- Color the areas containing oxygen-poor blood blue.
- Color the areas containing oxygen-rich blood red.
- Color the areas in which gas exchange takes place purple.

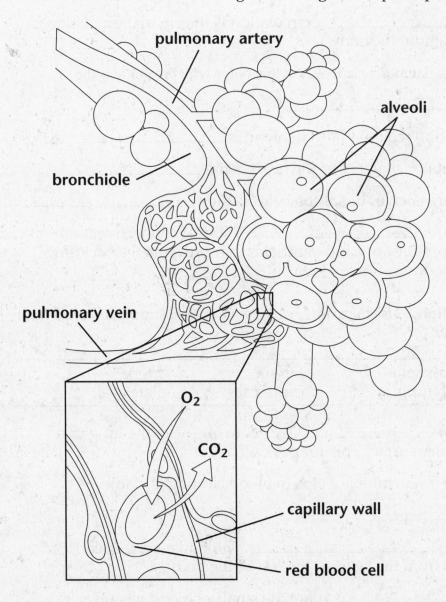

Use the diagram to answer the question. Circle the correct answer.

1. What diffuses from red blood cells into the alveoli?

carbon dioxide   oxygen

© Pearson Education, Inc., publishing as Pearson Prentice Hall.

Chapter 37   Circulatory and Respiratory Systems

Vocabulary Review

Completion   *Use the words below to fill in the blanks with terms from the chapter.*

atrium	systemic	diaphragm
valve	plasma	ventricle

1. _____ circulation is the circulation of blood throughout the body.

2. A large flat muscle in the chest that helps with breathing is the

_____.

3. The straw-colored fluid in blood is _____.

4. The upper chamber of the heart is the _____.

5. The lower chamber of the heart is the _____.

6. A(An) _____ is a flap of connective tissue between the atria and ventricles that prevents the backflow of blood.

Completion   *Use the words below to fill in the blanks with terms from the chapter.*

alveolus	larynx	artery
lymph	capillaries	platelet

6. A(An) _____ is an air sac in the lung that provides surface area for gas exchange.

7. A cell fragment that helps in blood clotting is a(an)

_____.

8. A(An) _____ is a blood vessel that carries blood from the heart to the rest of the body.

9. _____ are the smallest blood vessels.

10. Fluid that is lost by blood and that collects in lymph capillaries

is called _____.

© Pearson Education, Inc., publishing as Pearson Prentice Hall.

Chapter 38   Digestive and Excretory Systems

Summary

38–1 Food and Nutrition

One calorie is equal to the amount of energy needed to raise the temperature of one gram of water by one degree Celcius. The energy in food is measured in dietary Calories (with a capital C). One **Calorie** is equal to 1000 calories. The number of Calories you need each day depends on your age, sex, and activity level.

Nutrients are substances in food that supply the body with energy and raw materials needed for growth, repair, and maintenance. **The nutrients that the body needs are water, carbohydrates, fats, proteins, vitamins, and minerals.**

Every cell in the human body needs water because many of the body's processes take place in water. Water makes up a large part of blood and other body fluids. Sweating removes water in order to cool the body by evaporation. Water must be replaced regularly.

Simple and complex **carbohydrates** are the body's main source of energy. Simple carbohydrates do not have to be digested or broken down. They provide quick energy for the body. Complex carbohydrates must be broken down into simple sugars to be used for energy.

Fats are formed from fatty acids and glycerol. Saturated fats are usually solid at room temperature. Unsaturated fats are usually liquid at room temperature. Fats protect organs and joints. They help make up cell membranes, and insulate the body.

Proteins supply raw materials for growth and repair of the body. Amino acids form proteins. The human body can produce twelve of the twenty amino acids. The other eight must be obtained from food. These amino acids are called essential amino acids.

Vitamins are organic molecules that help regulate body processes. Fat-soluble vitamins can be stored in fatty tissues. Water-soluble vitamins cannot be stored and should be in the foods that a person eats every day. Some diseases result when the body does not receive a sufficient supply of vitamins. Vitamins can have serious effects on a person's health.

Minerals are inorganic nutrients. Your body usually needs minerals in small amounts. Examples of minerals include calcium and iron. The body loses minerals in sweat, urine, and other waste products, so they must be replaced by eating foods.

The new food pyramid—MyPyramid—can help you choose a balanced diet. MyPyramid is designed to help you make smart food choices from every food group, get the most nutrition out of your calories, and emphasize the importance of daily exercise.

© Pearson Education, Inc., publishing as Pearson Prentice Hall.

38–2 The Process of Digestion

The digestive system breaks down food into simpler molecules that can be absorbed and used by cells. The human digestive system is a one-way tube. It includes the mouth, pharynx, esophagus, stomach, small intestine, and large intestine. Other structures—salivary glands, pancreas, and liver—add secretions to the digestive system.

1. Digestion starts in the mouth. Teeth tear and crush food to begin mechanical digestion. Mechanical digestion is the physical breakdown of large chunks of food into smaller pieces. Salivary glands in the mouth secrete saliva, which contains enzymes that break down starches into sugars. This begins the process of chemical digestion. Chemical digestion breaks down large food molecules into smaller food molecules.

2. The swallowed clump of food passes through the pharynx and into the **esophagus.** A flap of skin, the epiglottis, keeps the food from entering the trachea. Muscle contractions, called **peristalsis,** squeeze food through the esophagus to the stomach.

3. Chemical and mechanical digestion take place in the **stomach.** Glands in the stomach lining make hydrochloric acid and the enzyme pepsin. The hydrochloric acid and pepsin start the chemical digestion of protein. Stomach muscles contract to churn and mix the stomach contents. This mechanical digestion forms a liquid mixture.

4. Most chemical digestion and absorption of food occurs in the **small intestine.** Enzymes from the **pancreas** help digest starch, protein, and fat. A liquid called bile from the **liver** dissolves and breaks up fat droplets. Several enzymes help break down carbohydrates and proteins. Tiny fingerlike projections called **villi** (singular: villus) increase the surface area of the small intestine. Cells at the small intestine's surface absorb nutrients.

5. The **large intestine** removes water from the undigested material. The remaining waste passes out of the body.

Peptic ulcers, diarrhea, and constipation are digestive system disorders. Bacteria cause most peptic ulcers. Diarrhea occurs when too little water is removed from waste in the large intestine. Constipation occurs when too much water is removed.

© Pearson Education, Inc., publishing as Pearson Prentice Hall.

38–3 The Excretory System

During metabolism, cells make wastes such as carbon dioxide and urea. Excretion is the process in which the body eliminates wastes. The main organs of excretion are the **kidneys. The kidneys play an important role in maintaining homeostasis. They remove waste products from blood, maintain blood pH, and control the water content of blood.**

Two **kidneys** are located in the lower back. Blood containing wastes enters the kidneys. The kidneys remove urea, excess water, and other substances from the blood. This cleaned blood returns to circulation. The wastes are excreted. The wastes are removed and passed to the ureter.

The basic unit of function in a kidney is the **nephron.** Each nephron is a small self-sufficient processing unit. **As blood enters a nephron, impurities are filtered out and emptied into the collecting duct.** The purified blood exits the nephron through the venule. The processes of filtration and reabsorption take place in the nephrons.

- Filtration removes wastes from the blood. It occurs in a part of the nephron called the glomerulus. The **glomerulus** is enclosed within a structure called **Bowman's capsule.**
- Reabsorption returns some of the filtered materials back to the blood. These materials include nutrients and water.

Fluid that remains in the kidneys is called urine. Urine contains urea, excess salts, and other substances. After some water is removed the urine leaves each kidney through a tube called the **ureter.** The ureters carry urine to the urinary bladder, where urine is stored. Urine leaves the body through a tube called the **urethra.**

The kidney's activity is controlled by hormones and by the composition of blood. Drinking excess water increases the amount of water in the blood. This causes the kidneys to decrease the amount of water they reabsorb and return to the blood. Similarly, salty foods result in excess salt in the blood. To keep the composition of blood the same, the kidneys excrete the excess salt in urine.

A person can live with only one kidney. If both kidneys fail, the person must receive a kidney transplant or undergo dialysis. Dialysis purifies the blood by passing it through a filtering machine.

Nutrients

Carbohydrates, fats, proteins, vitamins, minerals, and water are all nutrients that are important to body functions. Each serves a different function in the body.

Use the words below to complete the table. The first one has been done for you.

carbohydrates	minerals	vitamins
fats	proteins	

Nutrient	Function in Body
water	essential for many body processes; makes up the bulk of blood, lymph, and other fluids; helps with temperature regulation
	main energy source for the body; some help food and wastes move through digestive system
	material for producing membranes and hormones; help the body absorb some vitamins; protect body organs; insulate the body; store energy
	raw materials for growth and repair; used for regulation and transport
	organic molecules that help regulate body processes
	inorganic nutrients used for making bones, teeth, and hemoglobin; essential in small amounts for other body processes

Use the table to answer the question.

1. Which nutrients are needed for growth and repair?

_____

© Pearson Education, Inc., publishing as Pearson Prentice Hall.

MyPyramid

MyPyramid is a guide to healthful eating. It divides food into six groups. It also suggests how many servings from each group make up a healthful diet.

Use what you know as well as the information in MyPyramid to write the letter of the description that best matches the food group.

Description

Food Group

_____ 1. This group contains calcium-rich foods. Calcium is needed for bone density and helps maintain normal blood pressure.

_____ 2. This group provides the best source of protein but also contains fat.

_____ 3. This group contains a wide variety of vegetables and minerals that can reduce the risk of heart disease and cancer.

_____ 4. This group contains a variety of nutrients, including vitamin C.

a. vegetables
b. fruits
c. milk
d. meat and beans

© Pearson Education, Inc., publishing as Pearson Prentice Hall.

The Digestive System

When you eat food, digestion begins in your mouth. Food then travels through the digestive tract. Other organs, such as the liver and salivary glands, produce secretions that help with digestion but are not part of the digestive tract.

Use the words below to label the diagram.

esophagus	mouth	stomach
large intestine	small intestine	

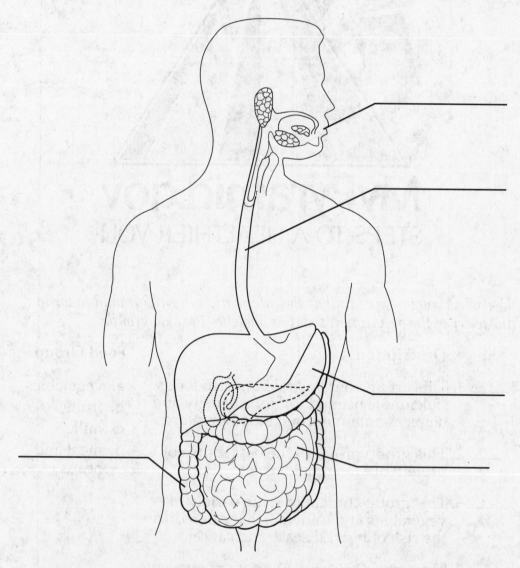

Use the diagram to answer the questions.

1. Through which organ does food pass first? Circle the correct answer.

esophagus   stomach

© Pearson Education, Inc., publishing as Pearson Prentice Hall.

The Small Intestine

The inner surface of the small intestine is covered with circular folds. The folds are covered with fingerlike projections called villi (singular villus). Each villus holds blood and lymph vessels that absorb nutrients and carry them to the body.

Use the words below to label the diagram.

capillaries	lymph vessel	villi

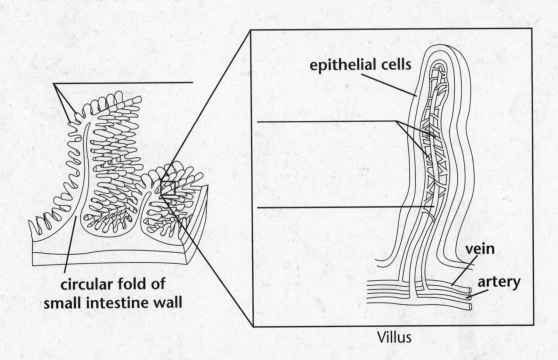

circular fold of
small intestine wall

epithelial cells

vein

artery

Villus

Use the diagram to answer the questions.

1. Where do nutrients enter the bloodstream?

_____

_____

2. How is the surface of the small intestine wall adapted for its function?

_____

_____

_____

© Pearson Education, Inc., publishing as Pearson Prentice Hall.

Structure of the Nephron

Nephrons are structures within the kidneys that filter wastes out of blood. Most of the filtration occurs in the glomerulus, a network of capillaries inside a structure called Bowman's capsule. Some of the material filtered out is reabsorbed into the blood.

Use the words below to label the diagram.

Bowman's capsule	collecting duct	loop of Henle
capillaries	glomerulus	

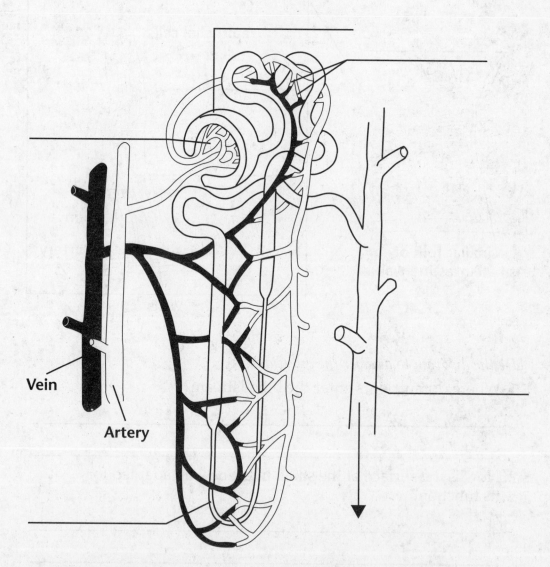

Vein

Artery

Answer the question. Circle the correct answer.

1. Which of the following is reabsorbed into the bloodstream?

water   urine

© Pearson Education, Inc., publishing as Pearson Prentice Hall.

Chapter 38   Digestive and Excretory Systems

Vocabulary Review

Completion   *Use the words below to fill in the blanks with terms from the chapter.*

minerals	kidneys	stomach
small intestine	large intestine	

1. In the body, most chemical digestion takes place in the

   _____.

2. Food from the esophagus empties into a large muscular sac

   called the _____.

3. _____ are inorganic nutrients that the body needs.

4. The primary job of the _____ is to remove
   water from undigested material before it is excreted by
   the body.

5. The _____ are the organs that remove waste
   materials from the blood.

Completion   *Use the words below to fill in the blanks with terms from the chapter.*

filtration	nephrons
urethra	peristalsis

6. The removal of water, urea, salts, and amino acids from the

   blood involves the process of _____.

7. Urine is released from the body through the

   _____.

8. _____ are the small, functional units of
   the kidneys.

9. Food is moved through the esophagus by the process

   of_____.

© Pearson Education, Inc., publishing as Pearson Prentice Hall.

Chapter 39 Endocrine and Reproductive Systems

Summary

39–1 The Endocrine System

A gland is an organ that makes and releases a secretion. **Exocrine glands** release their secretions through ducts directly to the organs that use them. **Endocrine glands** release hormones into the bloodstream. **The endocrine system is made up of endocrine glands.**

Hormones are chemicals made in one part of the body that affect cells elsewhere in the body. Hormones bind to target cells. **Target cells** are specific chemical receptors on cells.

There are two types of hormones: steroid hormones and nonsteroid hormones. Steroid hormones can cross cell membranes of target cells, enter the nucleus, and turn genes on or off. Nonsteroid hormones cannot cross cell membranes. Compounds called secondary messengers carry the messages of nonsteroid hormones inside target cells.

All cells, except for red blood cells, produce hormonelike substances called **prostaglandins.** Prostaglandins usually affect only nearby cells and tissues. They are known as "local hormones."

The endocrine system is controlled by feedback mechanisms that help maintain homeostasis. For example, the level of a hormone in the blood may be the feedback that signals a gland to make more or less of the hormone. Two hormones with opposite effects may work together to maintain homeostasis. This is called complementary hormone action.

39–2 Human Endocrine Glands

There are several endocrine glands scattered throughout the body.
- The **pituitary gland** secretes nine hormones that regulate body functions and control the actions of other endocrine glands.
- Hormones from the **hypothalamus** control the secretions of the pituitary gland.
- Hormones from the **thyroid gland** regulate metabolism.
- Hormones from the thyroid gland and **parathyroid glands** maintain blood calcium levels.
- The **adrenal glands** make hormones that help the body prepare for and deal with stress.
- The **pancreas** is both an exocrine gland and an endocrine gland. Hormones produced in the pancreas help keep levels of glucose in the blood stable.
- **Reproductive glands,** or gonads, make gametes and secrete sex hormones. The female gonads, **ovaries,** produce eggs. The male gonads, **testes,** produce sperm.

© Pearson Education, Inc., publishing as Pearson Prentice Hall.

39–3 The Reproductive System

Hormones released by the ovaries and testes cause puberty. **Puberty** is a period of rapid growth and sexual maturation. It usually starts between the ages of 9 and 15. At the end of puberty, the male and female reproductive organs are fully developed and become fully functional.

- **The main role of the male reproductive system is to make and deliver sperm.** The testes are the main organs of this system. The testes are held in the **scrotum.** In the testes, sperm are made in tiny tubes called **seminiferous tubules.** The mature sperm move through a tube and leave the body through the urethra. The urethra is the tube in the penis that leads to the outside. Contractions eject sperm from the penis in a process called ejaculation.
- **The main roles of the female reproductive system are to make eggs and prepare the female body to nourish an embryo.** The ovaries are the main organs of this system. Each ovary has thousands of follicles. A **follicle** is a cluster of cells that surround an egg. A mature egg moves through the **Fallopian tube** to the **uterus.** The uterus is connected to the outside of the body by the **vagina.**

Beginning in puberty, the female body goes through a series of events that prepares the body to care for a fertilized egg. This is called the **menstrual cycle.** The endocrine system and reproductive system are both involved in the menstrual cycle. **The menstrual cycle has four phases:**

- During the **follicular phase,** an egg matures in its follicle.
- **Ovulation** occurs when the mature egg is released from the ovary. If sperm are present in the Fallopian tube, the egg may be fertilized.
- During the **luteal phase,** the follicle develops into a structure called the **corpus luteum.** If the egg was fertilized, it implants in the lining of the uterus. If the egg was not fertilized, it moves through the uterus without implanting.
- During **menstruation,** the lining of the uterus falls away and leaves the body through the vagina.

Diseases spread during sexual contact are called **sexually transmitted diseases** (STDs). Bacteria and viruses can cause STDs. Chlamydia, syphilis, gonorrhea, and AIDS are STDs. Abstinence is the only sure way to prevent infection from STDs.

39–4 Fertilization and Development

Fertilization is the joining of a sperm and an egg. A fertilized egg is a **zygote.**

- The zygote divides and undergoes repeated mitosis and develops into a hollow ball of cells called a blastocyst. About a week after fertilization, the blastocyst **implants** in the lining of the uterus.
- Cells of the blastocyst start to specialize through **differentiation.** Some cells migrate to form two cell layers. A third layer is produced by a process of cell migration called **gastrulation.** The three layers eventually develop into the different organs of the embryo.
- Gastrulation is followed by **neurulation,** or the development of the nervous system.

As the embryo develops, membranes form to protect and nourish it. One membrane forms the **placenta.** The mother and embryo exchange gases, food, and waste products across the placenta. **It is the embryo's organ of respiration, nourishment, and excretion.**

After eight weeks of development, the embryo is called a **fetus.** By the end of three months, most organs are fully formed. During this time, the umbilical cord forms. The umbilical cord connects the fetus to the placenta.

During the next six months before birth, the organ systems mature. The fetus grows in size and mass.

Childbirth occurs when hormones cause contractions in the mother's uterus. The contractions push the baby out through the vagina.

Growth and development continue throughout childhood. Adolescence begins with puberty and ends with adulthood. Development continues during adulthood. The first signs of aging often appear in the thirties.

© Pearson Education, Inc., publishing as Pearson Prentice Hall.

Steroid Hormones

Steroid hormones can cross cell membranes easily. Once inside the cell, the hormone binds to a receptor, forming a hormone-receptor complex. The hormone-receptor complex initiates mRNA transcription. This leads to protein synthesis.

Draw arrows to show the sequence of steps in steroid hormone function.

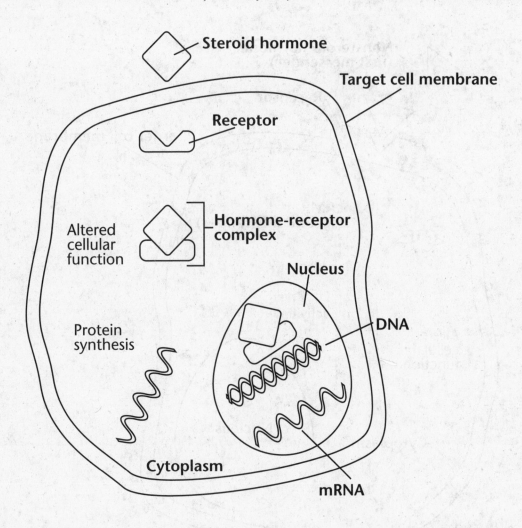

Use the diagram to answer the questions. Circle the correct answers.

1. To what does the hormone-receptor complex bind?

cytoplasm   DNA

2. What are steroid hormones?

lipids   nucleic acids

© Pearson Education, Inc., publishing as Pearson Prentice Hall.

Nonsteroid Hormones

Nonsteroid hormones bind to receptors on cell membranes. The binding activates an enzyme on the inner surface of the cell membrane. This enzyme activates secondary messengers that carry the message of the hormone inside the cell.

Draw arrows to show the sequence of steps in nonsteroid hormone function.

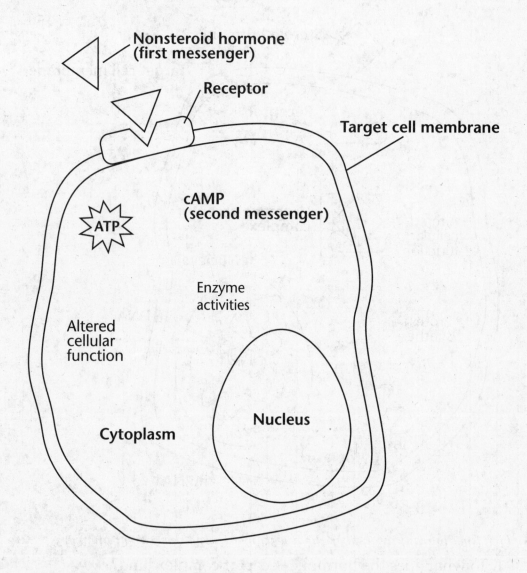

Use the diagram to answer the questions. Circle the correct answer.

1. Which kind of hormone generally cannot cross cell membranes?

steroid   nonsteroid

2. Which of the following is found inside the cell?

first messenger   second messenger

© Pearson Education, Inc., publishing as Pearson Prentice Hall.

Feedback Inhibition

Feedback inhibition occurs when high levels of a substance inhibit the process that produces the substance. This is similar to the way that a thermostat regulates the temperature in a house. The diagram below shows how feedback inhibition works in a thermostat.

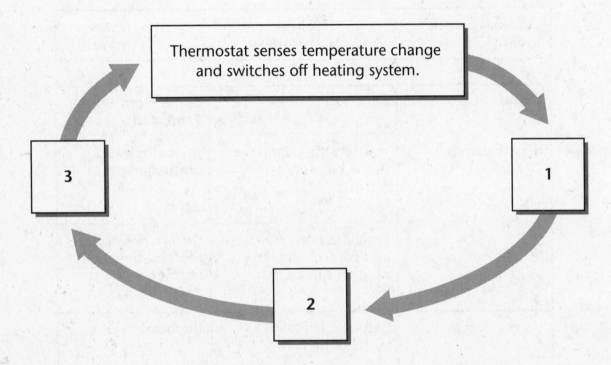

Number the descriptions below to identify the parts of the feedback inhibition process.

_____ Thermostat senses temperature change and switches on heating system.

_____ Room temperature increases.

_____ Room temperature decreases.

Answer the question.

1. Why is feedback inhibition important to the human endocrine system?

_____

_____

Endocrine Gland Functions

The table shows some important endocrine glands in the human body and their functions.

Use the words below to complete the table. The first one has been completed for you.

adrenal glands ovaries	pancreas pituitary	testes thyroid

Gland	Function	Some Hormones Produced
hypothalamus	controls the secretions of the pituitary gland	thyroid-releasing hormone
	regulates body functions and controls actions of other glands	growth hormone, thyroid-stimulating hormone
	regulates the body's metabolism	thyroxine
	helps the body prepare for and deal with stress	corticosteroids, epinephrine, norepinephrine
	maintains the level of glucose in the blood	insulin, glucagon
	produce eggs and female sex hormones	estrogen, progesterone
	produce sperm and male sex hormones	testosterone

© Pearson Education, Inc., publishing as Pearson Prentice Hall.

The Male Reproductive System

Sperm are produced in the testes and mature in the epididymis. To leave the body, they travel through the vas deferens and the urethra. Glands, including the seminal vesicles, produce seminal fluid that nourishes and protects the sperm.

Use the words below to label the diagram.

epididymis	seminal vesicle	urethra
testis	vas deferens	

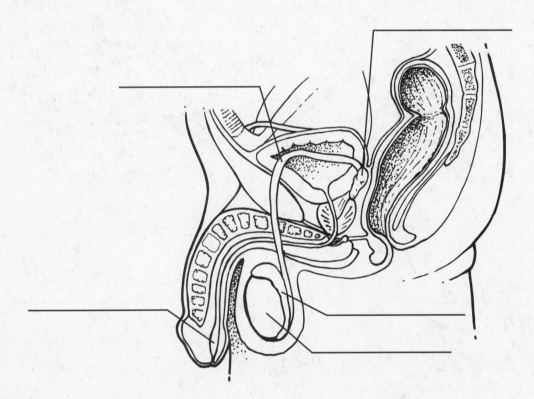

Use the diagram to answer the questions. Circle the correct answer.

1. Through what structure does the urethra pass?

testis   penis

2. Through which structure do sperm pass?

seminal vesicle   vas deferens

© Pearson Education, Inc., publishing as Pearson Prentice Hall.

The Female Reproductive System

Eggs are produced in the ovaries. They travel through the Fallopian tubes to the uterus. The vagina is a canal that leads from the uterus to the outside of the body.

Follow the prompts to identify important structures in the female reproductive system.

- Color the ovaries blue.
- Color the Fallopian tubes yellow.
- Color the uterus red.
- Color the vagina orange.

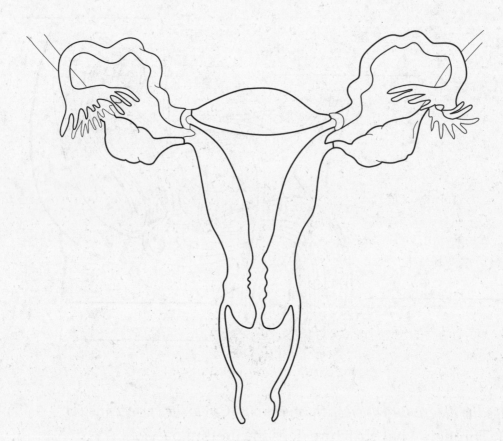

Use the diagram to answer the question. Circle the correct answer.

1. Which structure allows a baby to pass out of the body during birth?

ovary   vagina

© Pearson Education, Inc., publishing as Pearson Prentice Hall.

Fertilization and Development

Use the words below to identify important events and structures in early human development. The first one has been completed for you.

amniotic sac	implantation	placenta
gastrulation	neurulation	umbilical cord

Event or Structure	What It Is
fertilization	the process of a sperm joining an egg
	early stage in which the blastocyst attaches to the wall of the uterus
	process that results in the formation of three cell layers
	development of the nervous system
	fluid-filled structure that cushions and protects the embryo
	embryo's organ of respiration, nourishment, and excretion
	structure that connects the fetus to the placenta

Use the table to answer the question. Circle the correct answer.

1. Which step occurs shortly after gastrulation?

implantation   neurulation

© Pearson Education, Inc., publishing as Pearson Prentice Hall.

Name_____ Class_____ Date _____

Vocabulary Review

Matching *In the space provided, write the letter of the definition that best matches each term.*

_____ **1.** endocrine

_____ **2.** exocrine

_____ **3.** gastrulation

_____ **4.** hormone

_____ **5.** implantation

_____ **6.** menstruation

a. type of gland that releases its chemicals directly into the bloodstream

b. chemical made in one part of the body that travels through the bloodstream and affects the activities of cells in other parts of the body

c. attachment of the blastocyst to the uterine wall

d. type of gland that releases its chemicals through ducts

e. discharge of uterine tissue and blood through the vagina

f. the process of cell migration that produces a third layer of cells in the blastocyst

Matching *In the space provided, write the letter of the definition that best matches each term.*

_____ **7.** ovary

_____ **8.** placenta

_____ **9.** puberty

_____ **10.** vas deferens

_____ **11.** zygote

a. period of rapid growth and sexual maturation

b. a fertilized egg

c. organ for respiration, nourishment, and excretion

d. female reproductive gland that produces eggs and sex hormones

e. the tube that carries sperm from the epididymis to the urethra

© Pearson Education, Inc., publishing as Pearson Prentice Hall.

Chapter 40   The Immune System and Disease

Summary

40–1 Infectious Disease

A **disease** is any change, other than an injury, that disrupts normal body functions. **Some diseases are produced by agents, such as bacteria, viruses, and fungi. Others are caused by materials in the environment, such as cigarette smoke. Still others, such as hemophilia, are inherited.**

Before the 1800s, scientists did not know that microorganisms caused infectious diseases. Disease-causing microorganisms are called **pathogens.** The idea that infectious diseases are caused by pathogens was introduced by Louis Pasteur and Robert Koch. This idea is called the **germ theory of disease.** Koch also developed a series of rules called **Koch's postulates.** These rules help scientists identify which organism causes a specific disease.

Viruses, bacteria, protists, worms, and fungi all can be pathogens. Some pathogens cause disease by destroying cells. Some release toxins into the body. Other pathogens disrupt body functions. Infectious diseases can be spread in several ways.

- **Some infectious diseases are spread from one person to another through coughing, sneezing, or physical contact.** Most are spread through indirect contact, such as when pathogens are carried through the air. These pathogens can be inhaled, or they can be picked up from surfaces.
- **Other infectious diseases are spread through contaminated water or food.**
- **Still others are spread by infected animals.** Animals that carry pathogens from person to person are called **vectors.**

Antibiotics are drugs that kill bacteria without harming the host's cells. Antiviral drugs fight some viral diseases. Rest, a balanced diet, and fluids also help treat disease.

40–2 The Immune System

The function of the immune system is to fight infection through the production of cells that inactivate foreign substances or cells. This system makes cells that recognize, attack, destroy, and "remember" each type of pathogen that enters the body. This process is called **immunity.**

The immune system has nonspecific defenses to stop pathogens from entering the body. These defenses include physical and chemical barriers.

© Pearson Education, Inc., publishing as Pearson Prentice Hall.

- **First line of defense.** The function of the first line of defense is to keep pathogens out of the body. This role is carried out by skin, mucus, sweat, and tears. **Your body's most important nonspecific defense is the skin.** It forms a barrier that few pathogens can get through. Mucus, saliva, and tears trap pathogens and contain an enzyme that kills bacteria.

- **Second line of defense.** When pathogens do enter the body, other nonspecific defenses go to work. **The inflammatory response is a nonspecific defense reaction to tissue damage caused by injury or infection.** Blood vessels near the wound expand. White blood cells enter the tissues to fight infection. A **fever,** or higher than normal body temperature, can slow pathogen growth. Fever is a chemical response to pathogens.

If a pathogen gets past the nonspecific defenses, specific defenses go to work. This is called the **immune response.** There are two types of immune response.

- In **humoral immunity,** white blood cells, called B cells, make antibodies that attack pathogens in the blood. **Antibodies** are proteins that recognize and bind to specific antigens.

- In **cell-mediated immunity,** white blood cells, called T cells, find and destroy abnormal or infected cells. When a pathogen is destroyed, memory cells are formed. These cells respond if the same pathogen enters the body again.

You can acquire immunity without having a disease. **Vaccination** is the injection of a weakened or mild form of a pathogen to cause immunity. Immunity that results from vaccines is called **active immunity.** Active immunity appears after exposure to an antigen. **Passive immunity** forms when antibodies are introduced into the body. Passive immunity lasts only as long as the antibodies stay in the body.

40–3 Immune System Disorders

Sometimes, disorders occur in the immune system itself. The most common disorder is **allergies.** Allergies occur when antigens enter the body and bind to mast cells. Mast cells are immune cells found throughout the body. The mast cells become activated, and release chemicals called **histamines.** Histamines increase the flow of blood and fluids to the area. This causes allergy symptoms.

When the immune system makes a mistake and attacks the body's own cells, an autoimmune disease results. Autoimmune diseases include Type I diabetes, rheumatoid arthritis, and multiple sclerosis.

© Pearson Education, Inc., publishing as Pearson Prentice Hall.

Immunodeficiency diseases occur when the immune response breaks down. AIDS is one example of an immunodeficiency disease. AIDS is caused by HIV (human immunodeficiency virus). HIV attaches to receptors on helper T cells. Once inside the cells, HIV copies itself and kills the infected cells. HIV gradually kills off all the helper T cells. As a result, the immune system can no longer fight infections.

AIDS can be transmitted from mother to child during pregnancy, childbirth, and breast-feeding. It can also be transmitted from one person to another through shared needles, contact with infected blood, and sexual intercourse. **The only no-risk behavior with respect to HIV and AIDS is abstinence.**

40–4 The Environment and Your Health

Anything that increases the chance of disease or injury is a **risk factor. Environmental factors that can affect your health include air and water quality, poisonous wastes in landfills, and exposure to solar radiation.**

Bioterrorism is a new health threat. Bioterrorism is the intentional use of biological agents, such as viruses, to disable or kill people.

Cancer is a life-threatening disease in which cells multiply uncontrollably and destroy healthy tissue. Cancer may cause a tumor, a mass of cells that grows out of control. Some tumors are not cancerous.

All forms of cancer result from harmful mutations. Mutations may be inherited. Viruses, chemicals, and radiation can also cause mutations. Sunlight and radon gas are sources of potentially harmful radiation. Radon gas is found in rocks and can leak into buildings. **Carcinogens** are chemicals that cause cancer. Some carcinogens are produced in nature. Others are made by humans. For example, tobacco smoke contains carcinogens. Cigarette smoking is responsible for nearly half of the cancers that occur in the United States.

You can choose behaviors that help keep your immune system functioning properly. **Some healthful behaviors include:**
- **eating a healthful diet**
- **getting plenty of exercise and rest**
- **abstaining from harmful activities**
- **having regular checkups**

© Pearson Education, Inc., publishing as Pearson Prentice Hall.

Nonspecific Defenses

Nonspecific defenses are immune responses that do not distinguish between one pathogen and another.

Use the words below to complete the table. The first one has been done for you.

cilia	inflammatory response	skin
fever	interferon	

Nonspecific Defense	Role
mucus	traps pathogens in the nose and throat
	increases body temperature to slow the growth of pathogens
	inhibits the synthesis of viral proteins and helps block viral replication
	push pathogens away from the lungs
	provides a barrier that prevents pathogens from entering the body
	produces white blood cells to fight infection

Use the table to answer the question. Circle the correct answer.

1. Which nonspecific defense, considered part of the first line of defense, helps keep pathogens out of the body?

skin   fever

© Pearson Education, Inc., publishing as Pearson Prentice Hall.

Humoral Immunity

When an antigen first enters the body, some B cells recognize the antigen. They grow and divide rapidly, producing plasma cells and memory B cells. The plasma cells produce antibodies against the antigen. The memory B cells remain able to produce those antibodies. The next time that antigen enters the body, the body's reaction is much faster.

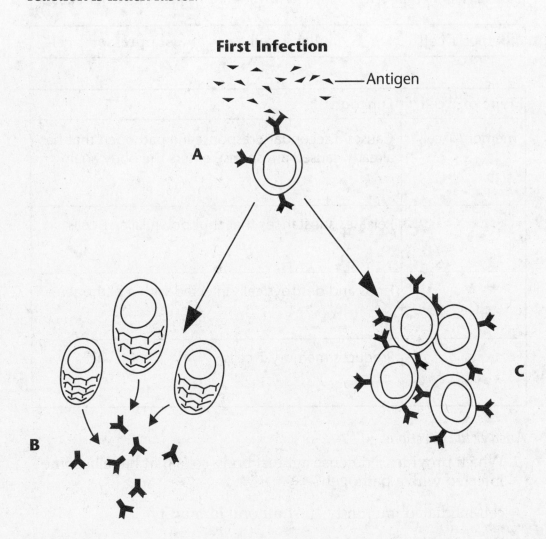

First Infection

Antigen

A

B

C

Identify each step shown in the diagram. Write A, B, or C to match the descriptions with the diagram above.

_____ Antigen binds to B cell.

_____ Some B cells develop into memory B cells.

_____ Some B cells develop into plasma cells. Plasma cells produce antibodies that are released into the bloodstream.

© Pearson Education, Inc., publishing as Pearson Prentice Hall.

Cell-Mediated Immunity

When a body cell becomes infected with a pathogen, cell-mediated immunity occurs. Different types of T cells are involved in cell-mediated immunity. These include killer T cells, helper T cells, suppressor T cells, and memory T cells.

The table describes the function of four different types of T cells. Use the words below to complete the table. The first one has been done for you.

| helper T cell | killer T cell | suppressor T cell |

Type of T cell	Function
memory T cell	Causes a secondary response if a pathogen that has already caused a response enters the body again
	Releases substances that shut down killer T cells
	Finds and destroys cells infected with a pathogen
	Produces memory T cells

Answer the questions.

1. Which provides a defense against body cells that have become infected with a pathogen?

   cell-mediated immunity   humoral immunity

2. Why might patients that receive organ transplants need to take medicines that suppress the cell-mediated immune response?

   _____

   _____

   _____

© Pearson Education, Inc., publishing as Pearson Prentice Hall.

Environmental Health Factors

Factors in your environment, such as air quality, water quality, wastes, and solar radiation, can affect your health.

Use the words below to complete the table. The first one has been completed for you.

carbon monoxide	ozone	radiation	water contaminants

Environmental Factor	Source	Effect on Health
particulates	dust mites, pollen, mold, dander, lead, asbestos	trigger allergic reactions; lead can poison the liver, kidneys, and nervous system; asbestos can cause lung cancer
	automobile exhaust, cigarette smoke, heaters	prevents hemoglobin from carrying oxygen
	vehicle exhaust and factory emissions	can aggravate respiratory conditions
	untreated sewage, chemicals	can cause digestive diseases, hepatitis, cholera; interfere with organ and tissue development; chemicals can cause cancer
	sunlight, X-rays, nuclear radiation, radon	can cause cancer

Answer the question. Circle the correct answer.

1. What is the term for a chemical compound that can cause cancer?

carcinogen   tumor

© Pearson Education, Inc., publishing as Pearson Prentice Hall.

Chapter 40   The Immune System and Disease

Vocabulary Review

Matching   *In the space provided, write the letter of the definition that best matches each term.*

_____ **1.** antibiotic

_____ **2.** antibody

_____ **3.** asthma

_____ **4.** disease

_____ **5.** histamine

a. chronic respiratory disease in which air passageways in the lungs are reduced in size

b. compound that kills bacteria without harming the cells of the animal host

c. change other than injury that disrupts normal body functions

d. protein that recognizes and binds to antigens

e. chemical that increases the flow of blood and fluids to the surrounding area

Matching   *In the space provided, write the letter of the definition that best matches each term.*

_____ **6.** inflammatory

_____ **7.** interferon

_____ **8.** pathogen

_____ **9.** tumor

_____ **10.** vector

a. mass of growing tissue that is a result of uncontrolled cell division

b. disease-causing agent

c. type of response that is a nonspecific defense reaction to tissue damage caused by injury or infection

d. protein that helps cells resist viral infections

e. animal that carries disease-causing organisms from person to person

© Pearson Education, Inc., publishing as Pearson Prentice Hall.